Practical Programming
for
Strength Training

2ⁿᵈ Edition

Practical Programming for Strength Training

Mark Rippetoe & Lon Kilgore

with Stef Bradford

Revised 2nd edition
Copyright © 2010 by the Aasgaard Company
Second edition 2009
First edition 2006

Copy Editor – Carrie Klumpar
Indexing & Proof – Mary Conover

ISBN 978-0-9825227-0-7

Printed in the United States of America

The Aasgaard Company
3118 Buchanan, Wichita Falls, TX 76308, USA
www.aasgaardco.com

Contents

"Does history record any case in which the majority was right?"

—Robert Heinlein

"The Iron never lies to you ... The Iron will always kick you the real deal. The Iron is the great reference point, the all-knowing perspective giver. Always there like a beacon in the pitch black. I have found the Iron to be my greatest friend. It never freaks out on me, never runs. Friends may come and go. But two hundred pounds is always two hundred pounds."

—Henry Rollins

1 – Introduction

"The most erroneous stories are those we think we know best –
and therefore never scrutinize or question."

– Stephen Jay Gould

The ability to effectively design, organize, and implement training programs is an absolute requirement for success in all areas of exercise: performance, coaching, physical education, and rehabilitation. Volumes have been written on programming aerobic exercise for a variety of populations. They are usually written by academics with practical experience and publishing history in long, slow distance training. Guidelines exist for programming aerobic exercise for virtually any population, little of it based on more than mere conjecture and opinion. The literature in the scientific, medical, and exercise journals on this topic is abundant, even though its quality may be suspect.

On the anaerobic side of the street, where weight training resides, the situation is much different. While there is a great deal of material available for consumption by the general public, its quality is equally suspect. The supposed "gold standard" for exercise prescription recommendations, the American College of Sports Medicine (ACSM) *Guidelines for Exercise Testing and Prescription*, provides only a cursory description of a method for programming weight training. Frequently, the "experts" on whom the public relies for guidance come from one of two camps: 1) individuals with practical experience and little or no specific education and training, or 2) individuals with degrees (usually not in the area of anaerobic physiology) who have very little practical experience with weight training. The end result is that the typical coach, gym member, or athlete trying to maximize performance is very poorly served by inappropriate instruction in weight training and inadequate program design.

Professionals – both practitioners and academics – in weight training seem to avoid addressing this issue, likely for a variety of reasons. With little or no available information providing strong evidence in favor of a particular approach to programming, a practitioner can never actually be "wrong" in programming for a client, athlete, patient, or student as long as the program stays reasonably close to the ACSM's nebulous position. And if it is close, he cannot be legally challenged in terms of professional liability. Even if he obtains less than optimal results for his trainee, according to the conventional wisdom he is being "technically correct" in his approach. As a result, there is really no initiative to rock the boat within either the industry or academia – to find out what really works, what actually doesn't, and therefore to potentially be held to more rigorous standards of practice.

Practitioners without education are not truly "professionals," in the sense that one prepares oneself academically as a professional before practicing as such. But it is not only the practitioners who have failed to address the shortage of informed guidance on weight training programming; it is also the academics. Many well-meaning professors have taken it upon themselves to write texts on how to train with weights and how to program weight training. With very few exceptions, there is something missing in these individuals' professional preparation: practical experience. How many of these exercise science teachers have experience on the platform? How many of them have worked in a varsity weight room as athletes or coaches? How many have coached actual weightlifters or powerlifters? How many have trained bodybuilders? How many have operated commercial gyms, serving clients with a wide range of age, ability, and motivation? A true strength and conditioning professional must be versed in all areas of practice and competition, through experience and education. To ignore either the contributions of experienced practitioners or the underpinning theoretical concepts of any professional specialization is to actively choose to be a less competent professional.

Many books have been written by practitioners, but they typically lack a sound scientific basis. For each of these, there is at least one book written by a Ph.D. lacking the usefulness that only experience can provide. The gap between theory and practice is a large problem within the strength and conditioning profession, one that has yet to be adequately addressed by either academicians or coaches.

The training of academics is a problem. How many universities have masters and doctoral programs specifically aimed at the extension of knowledge surrounding weight training and its role in health and human performance? They can be counted on one hand. The paucity of institutions where the physiology, mechanics, and psychology of weight training is a focus at the graduate level means that academics operating as "experts" in the field were not trained by experts in the field. This is a problem. Quite frequently you can find expert field practitioners who have trained themselves through reading and on-site applied research who possess a much better command of the application of research into weight training than many academic "experts."

There is a trickle-down effect here. Academics at universities train our coaches, trainers, and teachers. Poorly trained professors produce poorly trained practitioners. This is an area of tremendous concern, especially in athletics. The strength coach will likely spend more individual time with an athlete than any other coach during the athlete's career. Would we send an inexperienced, untrained, unmentored, person out to run a season of practices for a football or volleyball team? Obviously not. Just because someone has run a marathon or played Division I football does not mean that they are capable of coaching the sport. Playing and coaching are two different skills. The same applies to weight training: just because an individual exercised with weights while they played a sport does not mean that they are qualified to coach strength for that or any other sport. It takes training, mentorship, and education – either formal or practical. Disregarding the value of proven, certifiable knowledge and practical ability and gambling an athlete's or team's physical readiness on the effectiveness of the good-ol'-boy system of hiring strength and conditioning staff is not wise. Further, this system of hiring limits the potential for professionalism and public recognition in the career field.

The lack of preparatory courses in the average physical education or kinesiology degree program is a problem for other reasons as well. Data from 2004 U.S. exercise participation statistics indicates that 21% of the population trains with weights two or more times per week. The lack of educated and experienced professionals in the classroom, weight room, and fitness club means that there may be 63,000,000 Americans training with weights who were not taught to do so correctly. Additional data from the Sporting Goods Manufacturing Association shows that weight training is consistently in the top three recreational exercise activities in the United States, which further underscores the importance of providing quality instruction specific to teaching and programming weight training to physical educators, coaches, and personal trainers. This void in professional preparation prevents a huge number of trainees from making the progress that they expect and are capable of. Professional education programs should begin to address this overlooked area of instruction.

Educating Practitioners

The root of the problem can be found in the lack of a sense of identity within physical education: who are physical educators, and what do they do? An academic exercise department at a large Division I school will generate teachers, clinicians, coaches, athletic trainers, fitness trainers, gym managers, sports administrators, recreation workers, cardiac rehabilitation specialists, exercise rehabilitation specialists, exercise physiologists, biomechanists, and sports psychologists. Programs are typically general in nature, producing generally trained students intended to occupy specific occupational and professional jobs. The names of the university departments that offer what are considered traditional "physical education" degrees are generic, nondescript names that the public does not recognize as being related to physical education. This lack of recognition actually starts on college campuses themselves; other academic program faculty will refer to kinesiology, exercise science, or any other permutation of the name simply as "the PE department."

It is a common practice among graduate PE programs to prepare students as "generalists," meaning that the curriculum is constructed to produce faculty who are supposed to be able to teach exercise psychology, biomechanics, motor control, PE pedagogy, exercise anatomy, and exercise physiology. Generalists working in small college and university PE programs reduce the cost of operation; since they feel capable of teaching a variety of courses, there is no need to hire trained experts in the specialties, and the program remains viable. But by the very nature of his preparation, a generalist is not in a position to be an expert in any field.

It would behoove "physical education" departments to clearly define a mission, a philosophy, and a specific professional employment preparation track, and staff it with experts in that specialty. A program that is intended to produce public school physical educators, as they are currently prepared, cannot at the same time produce top-flight cardiac rehabilitation specialists. By the same token, a clinical program intended to produce an athletic trainer, a cardiac rehabilitation specialist, or an exercise rehabilitation practitioner, as they are currently prepared, cannot at the same time produce a strength coach. A rethinking of modern physical education is warranted. Without change, trained professionals capable of contributing to the *profession* of sport and exercise will be a rarity. Graduates capable of occupying low level *jobs* subservient to some other professional managerial group, one that is actually less qualified to supervise and program exercise, will be the rule.

There are more than 300 different certifications available to exercise professionals, with nearly as many businesses and organizations offering them. California alone has nearly 40 organizations offering some type of credential. This is an unregulated industry, and as such there are "professional certifications" that can be obtained by writing a check to a company, receiving some course material in an envelope in the mail, taking a test at home or online, and then receiving your certification in the mail in a second envelope. Suddenly you have become a certified training professional with letters after your name. Others offer an evening or Saturday workshop that upon completion renders you a "certified professional." These certifications benefit no one except the business offering the certification. They certainly cannot develop – or even measure – the skills and knowledge required of a competent strength professional. An untrained person with no previous education or mentored experiences cannot develop the necessary knowledge and skills to become an effective practitioner by quickly reading a study guide before a test or by spending an afternoon with a certification instructor. An "education" is required, formal or otherwise, as is time in the trenches working with trained, knowledgeable professionals. Only after gaining a satisfactory working theoretical knowledge and a set of practical skills should someone sit for a rigorous certification examination offered by a professional organization with a professional membership.

Periodization in Print

The scientific literature related to weight training is frequently limited in scope and applicability. The individuals conducting the research are not trained to ask the right questions, and they frequently have no concept of how the research they do in the lab actually applies in the field. For example, a common problem is that findings derived from a specific population – untrained college-age males, for example – are frequently considered to be generalizable to all populations, including trained athletes. But where can an academic researcher gain access to a trained population of athletes to experiment upon? Specifically, where can you find a large experienced group of athletes to participate in experimental programs that potentially might not provide an increase in performance, or worse, a performance loss? You don't. Their coaches will not allow it. We will see later why this problem is sufficiently serious that it invalidates much of the research that has been done. Experienced coaches and trainers are frequently amused by the writings of the scientific "experts" who dogmatically propose and defend all-encompassing theories of training that have little relevance to the real world, or who claim that rehabilitation-based exercise programs are applicable for improving the performance of healthy athletes.

Specific to the task of programming weight training, consider the concept of periodization and its supporting research. Periodization has been called one of the "core principles" in the preparation of athletes for competition. It is a very simple idea: the athlete trains very hard for a "period" of a time and then trains less hard for a "period." One would expect a core principle such as this to be heavily supported in the scientific literature, since a joint consensus statement from the ACSM and the United States Olympic Committee states that the primary reason athletes are overtrained is that coaches fail to periodize. The fact is that Western research regarding periodization is sparse. There are far more reviews and interpretations of how to use periodization than there is data to support its use. A search on the Medline and SportDiscus academic search engines reveals only a dozen or so reports that can be characterized as controlled experimental studies of periodization. In fact, one of the "hallmark" texts on periodization, written in a very scientific tone, provides 12 pages of more than 120 references to support the author's concepts of periodization. While this may appear impressively thorough, none of the research cited in that text actually came from experiments in periodization. The most definitive case for periodization comes from Hans Selye's 1936 original synthesis of the General Adaptation Syndrome, a statement of hypothesis regarding human adaptation to stress.

Why is it that the evidence supporting periodization is not present? Why is it that there has not been a concerted effort on the part of the major exercise professional organizations to encourage their scientific members to systematically investigate periodization, both as a concept in itself and in its many proposed variant applications? One possible explanation is that exercise performance enhancement research is not an area identified by the U.S. Department of Health and Human Services (the parent organization of the National Institutes of Health and the Centers for Disease Control and Prevention) as relevant to their mission to improve and safeguard America's health. The implicit duty of the Department of Health and Human Services (HHS) is to determine how much physical activity is needed to stave off disease, not improve a maximum bench press or advance athletic performance. This means that the major scientific research funding pool in the U.S. has no interest in determining the most effective means of improving fitness.

This has trickle-down effects that are far reaching with respect to research into fitness and sports performance. The most apparent result of HHS's position is that virtually all research into sports and fitness is confined to small-scale studies. Conducted with only a handful of research subjects, these projects are limited in scope and duration, and therefore plagued by an inability to exclude confounding external and unidentified internal variables.

Physiological systems are among the most complicated things studied by science, and inherent in the vast majority of biological research is a large degree of uncertainty. Many relevant (and irrelevant) variables have overlapping effects; many more variables may be as yet unidentified in the systems in question. The awareness of this tempers the conclusions of responsible investigators, and plays an important role in the resulting quality of the research that actually gets done. When the effects of one training protocol versus another are compared, even in the most stringently controlled setting, any conclusions must be taken with a rather large grain of salt.

Large-scale research into human performance – the kind that is actually required to draw valid conclusions in the context of human adaptation – is expensive and underfunded, and therefore many projects that could answer valuable basic questions are never conducted. The small-scale research that represents the norm in the exercise sciences can at best move us along the continuum of understanding from pure conjecture to the point where we can form intelligent hypotheses. But all too often, with no larger, better designed, more reliable studies out there, the findings of small-scale research in exercise are both inappropriately extrapolated to apply to larger populations, and at the same time given the standing of theory or even law. This is the case with respect to periodization.

So the dearth of valid periodization literature is the product of a lack of funding to support it, as well as the infeasibility of doing the required research into complex physiological systems whose many variables are hard to control or even identify. What is present in the existing literature on periodization is of limited utility, as it is almost always done over short experimental periods on small groups representing inappropriate populations.

The quality of the literature notwithstanding, the history of periodization is quite interesting. The communist-bloc countries' sports scientists applied a form of periodization to a variety of training models used in the development of Olympic athletes in the 1940s, 50s, 60s, and 70s. If you compare their models of periodization with the reviews and opinion pieces in Western sports science literature, you'll see that the ideas and content presented in Western literature are essentially adapted from old Soviet literature.

Bud Charniga (fig. 1-1) did a great service to American sports scientists when he translated a series of Soviet documents into English in the 1980s. However, the information presented in those works must be applied cautiously. Communist-bloc sports science literature is very loosely annotated. It is not necessarily bad science, but it is reported in a form that does not lend itself to the independent verification of results. There is no accurate, reliable way to evaluate their conclusions or methods, since they often summarize their findings without providing any substantiating data; it is as though they were writing it for their own purposes and were unconcerned with the subsequent verification of their work.

Figure 1-1. Bud Charniga, translator of Russian weightlifting literature into English, snatching 358 lbs. at a 1976 competition in Kansas City.

And sometimes the literature to which they refer is not accessible. The bottom line is that the works of Leonid Matveyev, Yuri Verkhoshansky, Alexey Medvedev and other communist-bloc writers have been adopted as truth without independent confirmation of their theories and practices. And their practices are often applied to all populations without regard to their original intended uses and intended target populations.

Periodization and the American Kid. Periodization fits well with a worldview characterized by a high degree of planning, an attempt to quantify everything, and the need to control it all. (This may be why academics in the American education system like it so well too). Communist societies suffered the consequences of this manic desire to apply order to systems that cannot be easily ordered, systems composed of too many variables to handily control. As a weightlifting regimen, this kind of Soviet-type periodization program works when it has sufficient numbers of available athletes, enough that it can simply replace the ones who can't function within the training paradigm dictated by the coach's particular periodization model.

It doesn't work as well with smaller talent pools and in situations less tolerant of artificially imposed order, as in the culture of American youth.

When evaluating Communist bloc sport science data, we must also consider which data may have been acquired while the subject athletes were taking part in "better lifting through chemistry" experiments. Training models appropriate for chemically enhanced athletes are not applicable to frequently tested drug-free athletes.

Communist-bloc countries had (and still have) large-scale sports performance selection processes intended to direct young athletes into the most appropriate sport, based on specific criteria. Once there, athletes achieve and stay in the program or fail to achieve and are sent home. The result is a pyramidal selection structure that eliminates less competent athletes, leaving only those who have the best chance for international success. In the United States and most Western countries, some sports have a developmental pipeline. Football does. Basketball does. In fact, most nationally recognized high school sports that have a counterpart at the collegiate and professional levels have selection pipelines comparable in scale to those seen at the zenith of the Soviet bloc's sporting success. High school sport in the United States is the base of our selection pyramid. However, high school students in the United States represent a different population than students of the same age in the old Soviet Union. U.S. kids play sports to get in shape, while kids in Soviet-type systems get in shape to play sports. In the former bloc countries, sport was one of the few ways to rise above the constraints of the economic system, and this was a very powerful motivator. This difference is fundamental and significant, creating two distinct populations of athletes that reflect two distinct cultures generating two different levels of motivation for success. Soviet models of periodization were developed for and apply best to only one of these groups.

The U.S. high school student of today does not have the level of general physical preparation (GPP) and movement skills developed by the programs inherent in communist systems, programs in which children learned how to move effectively and began developing base fitness at age 6, long before they entered sport-specific training. Elementary school PE programs in the United States are underemphasized and understaffed and ignore GPP as a formal part of what abbreviated curriculum might exist. Effective physical education is best done in small groups with adequate time. While the educational literature supports this concept, the actual norm is one instructor, sixty students, and 45 minutes of class time. "Roll out the ball" physical education is the mode in which the teacher (whose own training may not be in physical education at all) operates in the context of overcrowded classrooms, poor administrative support, and inadequate equipment. And now that physical labor (farm chores, household responsibilities, etc.) has been largely removed from the daily life of a child, an incoming high school freshman "athlete" is a huge challenge. He typically has no fitness base, few movement skills, and presents the coach with a daunting task, in that he must be prepared to participate in possibly combative high school sports in as little as two weeks from the day the coach first lays eyes on him. Periodization cannot be applied to incoming freshmen who are going to play fall sports. Even in the presence of the desire to use it, there is no time.

But if the schedule permits and there happens to be sufficient time prior to the playing season, the coach must use the most effective means available to make the athlete as strong as possible as quickly as possible. These methods are examined in detail in subsequent chapters.

Periodization's American Heritage. Periodization is practiced widely in track and field and is used by a majority of NFL and virtually all NCAA strength and conditioning programs. The concept of periodization is logical. Some very avant garde thinkers and practitioners, such as Carl Miller in 1974 (weightlifting), John Garhammer in 1979 (track and field), and Mike Stone in 1981 (all sports) turned on the light for those who followed. The idea that the practice of a sport itself was sufficient conditioning for the sport became inadequate for preparing high-level athletes many years ago. The early models of periodization used with advanced strength and conditioning techniques have been absolutely essential to sport development in the United States. Dr. Stone followed his early work with a few experiments further examining the effects of periodization. But by and large, research on periodization has been extremely limited in volume. What has been produced is narrow in scope and has limited broader application.

Even in the absence of science to support its use, periodization has worked in the field, and 30+ years of Western athletic success has earned it a place in the elite coach's arsenal of training tools. But what is the correct model of periodization for an athlete or team, and how does a coach learn its actual application? In most university physical education programs, periodization is a small footnote somewhere in the curriculum, if presented at all. PE courses are intended to prepare physical educators and coaches to teach general physical fitness and some commonly practiced sports skills. Very few courses, if any, are available that teach exercise programming beyond ACSM guidelines, which were developed to enhance health and wellness, not to optimize sports performance. Even the best texts on periodization do not teach the reader how to program training plans. Rather they present lots of line graphs and bar charts, lots of data tables, physiology, and biomechanics, but little useable material for either coach or athlete.

So the questions remain: How do you design an effective program for your athletes, students, or clients? When is it appropriate to periodize that program? What follows in this text is a logical approach to understanding the concepts of programming, including periodization, and examples of how it is used. We have made every attempt to incorporate the relevant science into a practical approach to programming barbell exercise. It is derived from our academic training, decades of combined experience in the weight room, participation in more than 300 competitive events in powerlifting and weightlifting, experience in coaching hundreds of elementary, middle school, high school, collegiate, amateur, and professional athletes toward their goals, and from working with thousands of average people who just want to be stronger.

Cooking Up Training Programs for the Gym

This is not a typical programming "cookbook." There are many weight training books for sale, some at rather exorbitant prices, that lay out a program in current use by a winning sports team or an individual of some note (athlete, actor, model, etc.). These are "cookbooks": they propose to provide recipes for training success. Follow the recipes, they promise, and you will be as good as the Spurs and as ripped as Vin Diesel.

Actual cookbooks are usually written by skilled chefs who design the dishes with their trained staff, test them privately, and then cook them publicly – in restaurants or on TV shows – using their skills and experience, specific tools, fully equipped kitchens, and just the right high-quality ingredients. Many people have attempted to cook gourmet food from cookbooks and had results that were less than satisfactory. Why did the recipe fail? After reading a recipe, do you magically develop the skills of a chef? Did you use the right tools? There is a big difference between a good Solingen steel French knife and a Veg-O-Matic. And the ingredients might not be quite the same; when the recipe called for shiitake mushrooms, did you use a can of stems and pieces? When the recipe called for Maui onions, did you use onion salt?

If a coach decides to use a weight training cookbook, the following are required: 1) the coach must be trained and think the same way as the original coach (the chef who wrote the recipe), 2) the training equipment (cooking tools) used in the program must be available, and most importantly, 3) the athletes to be trained (ingredients) must be exactly like the athletes who trained with the original program, the one that actually might have worked. Failure to meet these requirements will result in a less-than-ideal performance (an inedible mess). Following someone else's specific program is usually a recipe for failure.

Reading the training cookbooks and seeing how other people solve the programming puzzle is part of the education process, but coaches and athletes must understand why successful programs are put together the way they are so they can develop their own programs specific to their circumstances. Copying and cannibalizing successful programs without understanding why they were successful is never a good idea. An understanding of the realities and practicalities of progressive training and periodization is.

A Theoretical Approach. In this book, the terms "novice," "intermediate," "advanced," and "elite" describe the trainee with respect to the time it takes for recovery from a homeostatic disruption induced by training. We do not use these terms as descriptors of a trainee's strength or absolute athletic ability. These terms may in fact be applied differently to athletes in different sports, but our use of the terms here is specific to the model illustrated in figure 1-2.

10

Because a novice lifts weights that are light relative to his genetic potential for strength and power development, the rate of recovery following training should be rapid. Essentially, this trainee can recover from a single training session in a period of 24 to 72 hours. The novice can train "heavy" on Monday and be ready to go "heavy" again on Wednesday. These trainees are quite far away from their genetic potential, and therefore lack the strength and the neural efficiency to generate a stress heavy enough to impede rapid recovery. For them, "heavy" is not really heavy. At the same time that strength and power are improving, recovery ability is improving too. Recovery processes are as trainable as any other physical parameter, and this is an extremely significant factor in training progress. But it is important to remember that recovery processes can always be exceeded by the injudicious application of training stress. Recovery must occur before progress can be made.

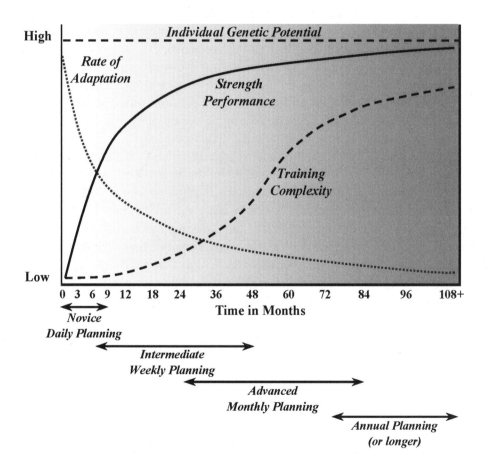

Figure 1-2. The generalized relationship between performance improvement and training complexity relative to time. Note that the rate of adaptation to training slows over a training career.

Simply put, a **novice**, as we use the term here, is a trainee for whom the stress applied during a single workout and the recovery from that single stress is sufficient to cause an adaptation by the next workout. The end of the novice phase is marked by a performance plateau, typically occurring sometime between the third and ninth month of training, with variations due to individual differences. Programming for the novice is essentially the linear progression model that is described in the ACSM manual and defined specifically for weight training in our book *Starting Strength: Basic Barbell Training* (Aasgaard, 2007). It is important to understand here that the novice is adapted to inactivity (as it relates to weight training) and therefore can make progress even with training programs that are not specific to the task involved. For example, doing high-volume hypertrophy work would also increase a novice's absolute strength for a one-repetition lift. A previously sedentary beginner can even improve his 1RM (one-repetition maximum) squat by riding a bike. This would not be the case with intermediate or advanced trainees, where progress in strength, power, or mass is absolutely linked to appropriate application of specific training programs.

Novices accomplish two things with every workout: they "test" their strength, and the test loads the body to become stronger in the next workout. The act of moving 10 more pounds for the prescribed sets and reps both confirms that the previous workout was a success at improving the novice's strength and causes his body to adapt and become stronger for the next workout.

As the lifter begins to handle training loads closer to his genetic potential, his recovery ability is also affected differently by the stress. Recovery requires a longer period of time – a period encompassing multiple workouts (efficiently managed using a weekly schedule). This is because the athlete has developed the ability to apply stress to the system that requires a longer period of time for recovery. For an **intermediate** trainee, the stress required for a disruption of homeostasis exceeds the capacity for recovery within that period of time (say, within the week). To allow for both sufficient stress and sufficient recovery, then, the training load must be varied over the week. This variation can take several forms, but the critical factor is the distribution, which allows enough stress to be applied in a pattern that facilitates recovery. The key to successful training in this stage of development is to balance these two important and opposing phenomena. Simple weekly periodization of training loads facilitates recovery following one or more heavier training bouts within a single week.

Intermediate trainees benefit from exposure to more exercises than novices. These athletes are developing their skills with new movement patterns, and as this happens they are developing their ability to *acquire* new skills. It is during this period that trainees actually become athletes, choosing a sport and making decisions that affect the rest of their competitive careers. These decisions are more effectively made if they are based on a broad exposure to a wide variety of training and competition options.

The end of the intermediate phase of training is marked by a performance plateau following a series of progressively more difficult weekly training organizations. This can occur in as little as two years or in as many as four or more, depending on individual tolerances and adherence to year-round progressive training. It is likely that 75% or more of all trainees will not require programming complexity beyond the intermediate level (remember, the amount of weight lifted or years of training do not classify a trainee). Virtually all sports-specific weight training can be accomplished with this model. Athletes in non-weightlifting sports will not train progressively in the weight room all year; they will focus much of their training on their primary competitive sport. This effectively extends the duration of this stage in the trainee's development to the extent that even very accomplished athletes may never exhaust the benefits of intermediate-level weight training programming.

Advanced trainees in the barbell sports work relatively close to their genetic potentials. The work tolerance of the advanced trainee is quite high, given that the ability of an athlete to recover from training is itself trainable. However, the training loads that the advanced athlete must handle in order to produce an adaptation are also quite high, since the adaptation that brought the athlete to the advanced stage has already occurred. This level of training volume and intensity is very taxing and requires longer periods of recovery than do intermediate training loads. Both the loading and the recovery parameters must be applied in more complex and variable ways and over longer periods of time. When combined, the loading and recovery periods required for successful progress range in duration from a month to several months. For example, we may apply a single week of very heavy training to induce adaptation. That week of training may require three or more weeks of work at lighter loadings for complete recovery and improvement to occur. The average slope of the improvement curve here is very shallow (fig. 1-3), closely approaching maximum genetic potential at a very slow rate, and rather large amounts of training effort will be expended for rather small degrees of improvement. For this reason too, the number of exercises advanced trainees use is typically lower than for intermediates; they do not require exposure to new movement patterns and stress types, since they have already specialized and adapted to those that are specific to their sport. Complex manipulation of training parameters is appropriate for use with these trainees. The majority of trainees will never attain the level of development that makes advanced periodization necessary, since most trainees voluntarily terminate their competitive careers before the advanced stage is reached.

The **elite** athlete is in a special subset of the advanced category. Elite athletes are the genetically gifted few who also happen to be motivated to achieve success despite the enormous physical and social costs. They have stayed in their sport by virtue of their success and have dedicated themselves to training at this level because their training investment has been returned. An advanced lifter is one who has progressed beyond the intermediate; an elite lifter is one who performs at an elite level within the standards of the sport. (By this definition, the "elite" designation could actually be applied to an intermediate lifter performing at the national/international level. There occasionally exist a few athletes so talented and genetically endowed that this situation occurs.)

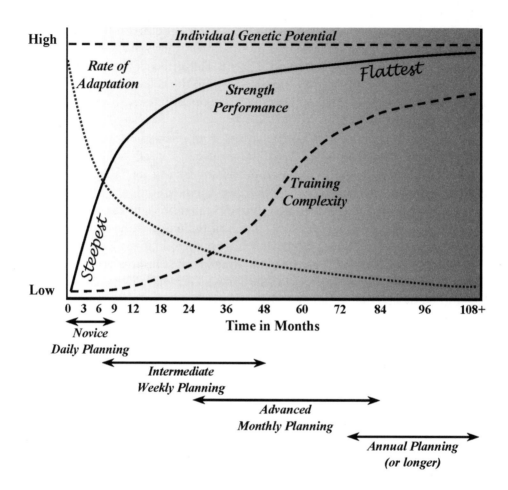

Figure 1-3. The rate of strength gain in trainees over a training career. Note the slope of improvement towards genetic potential is slower in an intermediate than that of a novice trainee. The slope further flattens as a trainee reaches the elite level of training progression. Although the rate slows, strength can be gained for one to two decades with continuous, progressive, and planned training.

Previous training has brought the elite athlete very close to genetic potential, and additional progress requires much greater program complexity to scratch out any small improvements that might still remain unrealized. These athletes must be exposed to training programs that are very complex – highly variable in terms of stress, although probably simple in terms of exercise selection – forcing the already adapted athlete closer to the ultimate level of performance. At this point the program may be considered in terms of several months, a year, or even an Olympic quadrennium. Any approach to the training of an athlete of this caliber is a highly individualized matter and is beyond the scope of this text. We propose that far less than 1% of all trainees regardless of training history will ever reach this level.

Unlike beginners or intermediates, advanced and elite trainees need large amounts of intense work to disrupt homeostasis and force adaptation. This means that the stress required for progress will creep nearer and nearer to the maximal tolerable workload that the body can perform and recover from. An elite athlete who is doing ten sets of squats and making progress may not make any progress with nine sets and may "overtrain" by doing eleven. The window for progress is extremely small.

If workload is not increased, then neither performance nor comprehensive recovery processes will improve, since no disruption of homeostasis is forcing them to do so. The manner in which increases in training load are applied is determined by the level of training advancement. The ability of a novice to adapt to training differs enough from that of the intermediate and advanced trainee that similar training organizations will fail to produce results for both. Each level of training advancement requires its own specific approach.

Periodization is a useful tool in achieving training goals, but like any tool it must fit the job it is being used for. By understanding the theoretical basis and proper application of the models of programming, anyone who coaches weight training can become better equipped to improve the fitness and performance of those entrusted to their guidance.

"Sometimes exercise can be painful, but it's worth it in the end."

—The Grim Adventures of Billy and Mandy

2 – Training and Overtraining

When considering the need for specific programming approaches for trainees of different levels of advancement (novice, intermediate, or advanced), one must clearly understand the processes working to affect physical readiness. The coach and athlete need to have a firm grasp of how training affects the basic anatomy, physiology, and physics of human movement. An effective coach must be able to use that information to teach athletes. All such human responses to training can be considered within the context of a single overarching theory, the General Adaptation Syndrome, proposed by Hans Selye on July 4, 1936, in his paper titled "A Syndrome Produced by Diverse Nocuous Agents" in the journal *Nature*. The basic premise of this theory states that the body goes through a specific set of responses (short-term) and adaptations (longer-term) after being exposed to an external stressor. In our context, the external stressor is lifting weights.

General Adaptation Syndrome

Selye considered exercise to be a "nocuous" or poisonous stressor capable of causing death if the loading was too large or applied too frequently. His theory was the result of observations of animals under stress and optical microscope examinations of stressed cells. He was working without any knowledge of the basic details of human metabolism and the mechanism of skeletal muscle contraction, which were not yet understood when his paper was published. Despite the comparatively sparse information on which he based his observations, his ideas were at the time, and remain, quite sound. Now, scientific data allows us to better interpret and apply Selye's theory. Our understanding of the acute phase response and the stress protein response, both possessing very identifiable time courses, along with modern insights into post-stress cellular events, has added weight to Selye's prescient concepts.

Selye's premise is that repeated sub-lethal exposures to a stressor lead to a tolerance of subsequent exposures to the same stressor (thus lending support to the concept of specificity – that a training stress needs to be relevant to the performance being trained for to elicit an applicable adaptation). The theory holds that the body will go through three stages, the first two contributing to survival and the third representing the failure of the body to withstand or adapt to the stressor.

Stage 1 - Alarm or Shock. The Alarm phase is the immediate response to the onset of stress, in which a multitude of events occur. Selye noted that a major characteristic of stage 1 was a rapid loss of "muscular tone" lasting up to approximately 48 hours. We now know that other occurrences during this stage are inflammation, the acute phase response, and the stress protein response, processes which enable adaptation at the cellular level. One of the major results of these latter responses is a general suppression of basic cellular processes in order to stabilize cellular structure and metabolism until the withdrawal of the stressor. This is a survival process, and one that can also serve as a marker of an effective exercise stimulus. Mild musculoskeletal discomfort may accompany this stage, indicating the disruption of homeostasis and the possible micro-ruptures of muscle cell membranes, events that are thought to stimulate structural and functional changes in the muscle after training. A trainee may not perceive soreness or pain in this stage; he is more likely to describe the sensation as "stiffness," feeling "flat," or having "heavy legs." Regardless of the subjective perception, a transient reduction in performance accompanies this stage, although it may be imperceptible within the constraints of a barbell's typical 2.5-lb incremental loading system. Performance decreases will be more discernible in technique- and power-based exercises and less noticeable in absolute strength exercises.

Selye did not foresee his theory being central to exercise programming for healthy individuals. If he had, this first stage might have been described with more variation in duration dependent on an individual's work capacity. With novice trainees, disruption of homeostasis occurs with smaller loads than those used by advanced trainees, since training has not yet developed either strength or work tolerance. As the level of advancement increases (from novice to intermediate to advanced), so does the magnitude and/or duration of stress needed to induce stage 1.

Stage 2 - Adaptation or Resistance. In stage 2, the body responds to the training load through the modification of gene activity, increased production of the relevant hormones, and the accumulation of structural and metabolic proteins. In essence, the body is attempting to ensure survival by equipping itself to withstand a repeated exposure to the stress. In the context of exercise, fitness and performance increase when this occurs. Selye generalized that the Adaptation stage typically begins at about two days post-stress and that if the same stressor is reapplied periodically, complete adaptation could occur within four weeks or less.

We now believe that adaptation occurs on a sliding scale that varies with an individual's existing level of work tolerance and proximity to their genetic potential. Someone far away from genetic potential (the novice) will adapt quickly, within 24 to 72 hours; a stressor large enough to disrupt such an individual's homeostasis is not really a gigantic physical insult, and it can be easily recovered from within that time frame under even sub-optimal conditions. On the other end of the spectrum, the advanced trainee might require one to three months, and possibly longer, to adapt to a training stress sufficiently large and cumulative that it exceeds his highly developed work tolerance enough to disrupt homeostasis and permit further adaptation.

Stage 3 - Exhaustion. If the stress on the body is too great, either in magnitude, duration, or frequency, the body will be unable to adequately adapt and exhaustion will occur. Selye proposed that an overwhelming stress of one to three months in duration could cause death. This is an interesting observation if we consider maximal exercise to be an overwhelming stress. In practice this concern is most applicable to intermediates and advanced trainees, and probably means that an extended period of excessively relentless maximal work should be avoided. The bottom line is that no one wants to be in stage 3, which we call "overtraining."

The application of Selye's theory to exercise training is presented graphically in figure 2-1. Progressive training within the context of the General Adaptation Syndrome requires that an increase in training load be applied as soon as it is apparent that recovery has occurred. Continued use of the initial, already-adapted-to load will not induce any disruption of homeostasis and therefore cannot lead to further progress. Using the same training load after adaptation to it has occurred represents ineffective (if not typical) coaching and training if performance or fitness improvement is the goal.

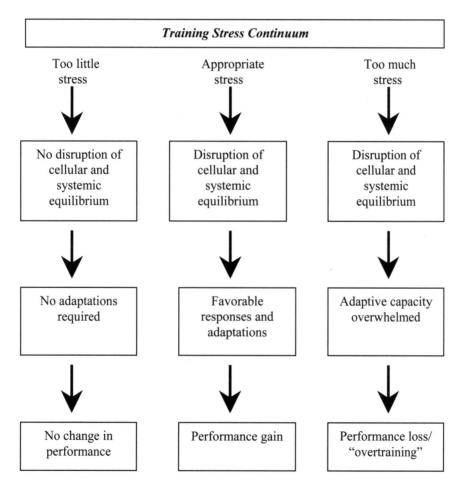

Figure 2-1. Within the parameters of Selye's theory, there are three possible outcome pathways following a training stress: no progress, progress, or loss of progress, depending on the appropriateness of the stress applied.

The Single-Factor Model of Training

If a single episode of weight training can disrupt homeostasis in the novice, a predictable set of outcomes can be detailed based on the degree of disruption. This model is presented in figure 2-1. We can examine this concept in both simple and broad terms as it affects a single factor: an individual's ability to lift a maximal weight, as measured by his one- (or two-, or five-) repetition maximum.

In the novice, a single training session will disrupt biological equilibrium locally within the muscle and systemically within the body. The result of this is a transient and very slight depression of performance. It is only slight because novice performance levels are already low and typically inconsistent, and small losses are hard to measure at this level. This depression occurs immediately after the training session and represents stage 1 of Selye's theory. In the hours and days after the training session, performance abilities will recover to normal and then performance ability will exceed the pre-stress level. This is **supercompensation**. At this point the trainee has successfully completed Selye's second stage and has adapted to the initial workload (fig. 2-2, line A).

It is important to understand that the trainee is not getting stronger *during* the workout. He is getting stronger during the recovery period *after* the workout. The next logical step is to increase the workload in the next workout – i.e., to employ simple progressive overload. Applying the same workload again produces no progress, since this stress has already been adapted to, but merely reinforces the existing level of fitness. At this point, a small increase in exercise load will once again take the trainee through Selye's stages 1 and 2 to repeat the overload/adaptation cycle at a slightly higher level. When the overload increment is the same for each successive increase, the training program is referred to as a *linear progression*.

This organization of training can continue for many months, until the trainee's progress plateaus. At this point it is likely that it will require a series of two or three training sessions specifically arranged to have a cumulative effect, plus a longer work/recovery cycle of perhaps a week's duration, to adequately take the trainee through Selye's first two stages. This represents the response of the intermediate trainee (fig. 2-2, line B). The intermediate period of a trainee's career, depending on the purpose of training, can be quite long, possibly years.

As the body gets better at producing force against a load, it is also getting better at recovering from that stress. As both performance competence and recovery ability increase with progressive training over time, eventually it will take weeks to adequately disrupt homeostasis to stimulate adaptation, and then another length of time for recovery and supercompensation. The advanced trainee may require even up to a month's time to progress through stage 1 and stage 2 (fig. 2-2, line C).

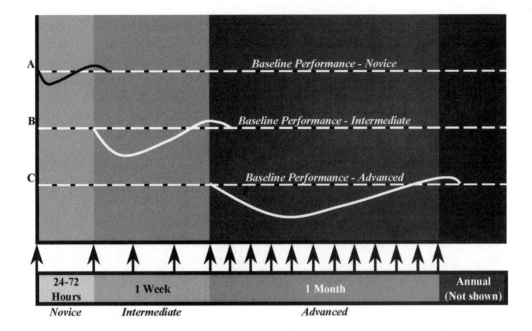

Figure 2-2. The intended result of a training stimulus is to induce supercompensation in the form of performance competence above baseline. As the trainee progresses from novice to advanced, a longer training and recovery cycle is required to induce supercompensation increases. In fact, the duration of the supercompensation cycle is one way to classify the level of training advancement. In the novice, a single training stimulus results in supercompensation in 24 to 72 hours (A), just in time for the next training session. For the intermediate trainee, multiple training sessions in a week are required to induce supercompensation (B). For the advanced trainee, the cumulative effects of weeks of training are needed to induce supercompensation in a month's time or longer (C). Arrows represent workout sessions.

The Two-Factor Model of Training

The two-factor model derives from and elaborates on the single-factor model, in that it considers the *reasons* for the performance response typical of training, not just the performance response itself. Two-factor models of training responses and adaptations are not new. Vladimir Zatsiorsky proposed such a model in his years at the Central Institute for Physical Culture in Moscow and reiterated it in his text *The Science and Practice of Strength Training* (1995). In his model, "fitness" and "fatigue" are the factors that affect "preparedness." Although the details of his theory are not well defined, the basic concept is sound.

If we consider performance competence the result of "metabolic and structural fatigue" and "comprehensive recovery processes," we can better understand the rationale for using different programming models for specific levels of trainee advancement. "Metabolic and structural fatigue" can be defined as the localized intramuscular and synaptic perturbations that are associated with the slightly reduced performance capacity in Selye's stage 1. Such fatigue is short-lived, an acute variable. "Comprehensive recovery processes" are the collective repair status of the various organ systems and processes affected by the training bout: endocrine and immune systems, chronic inflammatory processes, and protein synthetic responses. Fatigue and recovery together contribute to adaptation and progress, with supercompensation considered complete adaptation to the workload used in the training session or series of sessions – stage 2 of Selye's theory (fig. 2-3). For optimal fitness and performance gains, the effects of metabolic and structural fatigue must abate before the effects of comprehensive recovery processes diminish.

The more advanced an athlete becomes, the greater the importance and usefulness of the two-factor model and its approach to balancing the two opposing forces of constructive human adaptation, in that: 1) the workload must be sufficient to disrupt biological equilibrium enough to necessitate an adaptation, and 2) recovery must be sufficient to enable the adaptation to occur while avoiding overtraining (figs. 2-4 through 2-7). The athlete walks a knife's edge here. For the novice, it is very dull and wide, not really much of an edge at all, and rather easy to negotiate. The edge for the intermediate trainee is sharper, requiring a more complex approach. For the advanced trainee, it is razor sharp, and balancing on it without damage requires careful manipulation of all the programming variables.

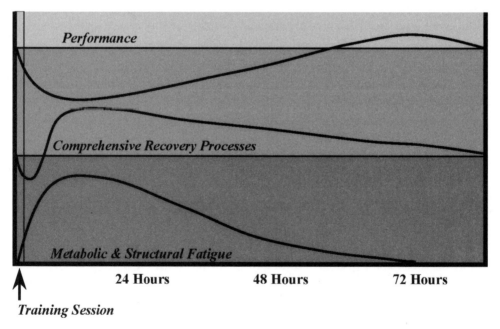

Figure 2-3. The two-factor model of the human responses and adaptations to a single bout of training. During and immediately after training, there is a suppression of comprehensive recovery processes (Selye's stage 1). Shortly after training ceases there is a general increase in recovery process activity (Selye's stage 2). An important observation here is that the increase in fatigue that results from training has a short-lived negative effect on performance. This deficit is not made up until recovery processes near completion.

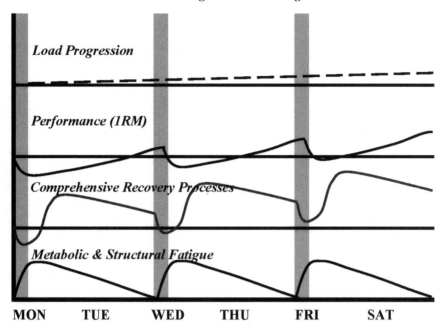

Figure 2-4. Two factors affecting both performance and tolerable workload in the beginner are 1) metabolic and structural fatigue and 2) comprehensive recovery processes. There is an inverse relationship of fatigue to performance: as fatigue increases, performance decreases. The relationship of recovery to performance is direct: as recovery increases performance increases. Gray bars represent workout sessions.

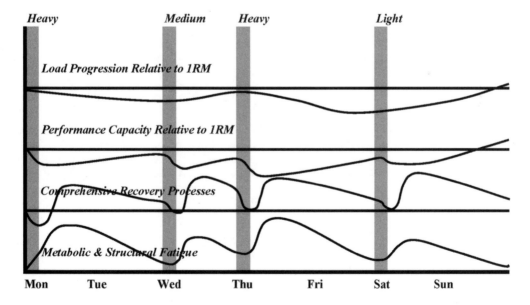

Figure 2-5. The two-factor model of an intermediate trainee's responses and adaptations to a series of training stresses over a week's duration. While similar to the single-workout cycle of the novice, note that fatigue does not entirely dissipate between each training session, nor do recovery processes catch up until the conclusion of the week. This defines the difference between the novice and the intermediate trainee. The workout load presented here is a heavy-medium-heavy-light organization that would repeat the following week.

23

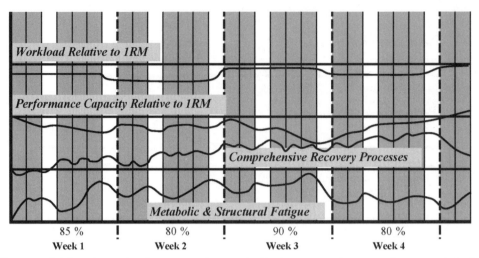

Figure 2-6. The advanced trainee responds to periodized programming over a longer period of time than either the novice or the intermediate trainee. Gray bars are days of training. White bars are days off. Percentages are loads relative to 1RM.

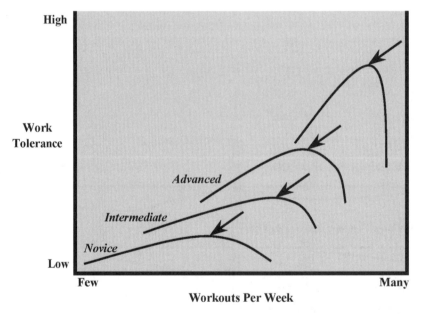

Figure 2-7. The relationship between workload and work tolerance. Regardless of training classification there is a ceiling of work tolerance (designated by arrows) that once breached decays into "overtraining" and an inevitable loss of work tolerance and performance capacity. Note that 1) work tolerance increases significantly throughout the training career, and increased tolerance is due to a progressive increase in workload, and 2) a descent into overtraining and the manifestation of performance decrements will occur more rapidly and precipitously as the training career advances (note the sharper drop-off for more advanced trainees after the work tolerance peak is reached). Although overtraining can be a problem at every stage, prevention is critical at the advanced and elite stages, as the rate of performance decay is very rapid once work tolerance is exceeded. Conversely, the diagnosis of overtraining may be a problem at the novice and intermediate stages, as the reduction in performance capacity occurs at a much slower rate after work tolerance is exceeded, and easily could be missed or misinterpreted.

Understanding Overtraining

Key to understanding progress in any athletic endeavor is the concept of **overload**. Overload represents the magnitude of work required to disrupt biological equilibrium and induce an adaptation. For progress to occur, the physiological system must be perturbed, and in weight training the perturbation is heavier weight or more volume (or, for an intermediate or advanced trainee, less rest between sets) than the athlete is adapted to. The overload is applied to the system through training, with the specific work that disrupts equilibrium referred to as an **overload event**. For novice trainees, each workout constitutes an overload event. For intermediate and advanced athletes, the heavier elements in a week or more of training might constitute the overload events.

But without recovery from an overload event, the overload does not contribute to progress. Overload without adequate recovery just induces overtraining. The term **microcycle**, traditionally defined as a week of training, is better thought of as the period of time required for both the overload event and the recovery from that overload event. This period will vary with the level of training advancement of the trainee. For a novice, a microcycle is the period of time between two workouts. The more advanced a trainee becomes, the longer the microcycle becomes, until the term loses its usefulness for elite athletes, who might require a period of time for this process that would more traditionally be described as a **mesocycle**. For us then, these terms lack the concise nature required for utility.

Overtraining is the bane of any program. When the demands of training outstrip the ability of the body to adapt, the trainee is at risk of not only ceasing to progress but actually regressing. To put it in the terms we have been using, the overtrained athlete has entered into Selye's stage 3. Understood within the single-factor model of training, an imbalance between training volume or intensity and recovery has occurred, such that the trainee will not recover from the stress and supercompensation cannot occur. Performance will remain depressed from the initial overload and will suffer further decline with continued loading. Or, in the two-factor model, overtraining can be understood as the failure of comprehensive recovery processes to overcome metabolic and structural fatigue. The effects of fatigue are so pronounced that recovery processes, which may be either unaffected or diminished, are nevertheless overwhelmed, leading to persistent and potentially escalating fatigue. The end result is the inability to train and to perform at the previous level.

There are three possible effects of exercise stress: 1) fatigue, 2) overreaching, and 3) overtraining. Each of these is associated with a reduction in performance ability, but only one is a training problem.

Fatigue. Fatigue is usually defined physiologically as a reduction of the force-production capacity of a muscle. It could be described as simple and transient "tiredness" resulting from physical effort – a necessary component of training and the one that results from the stress necessary to enter Selye's stage 1. In the novice it is expected that fatigue will abate within 24 to 72 hours. In the intermediate lifter fatigue may not dissipate completely until the completion of the training week. And in the advanced trainee complete recovery to supercompensation may not occur for a month or more. For the intermediate and advanced trainee it is not expected nor desired that each workout begin free from fatigue. If an intermediate, advanced, or elite trainee is persistently fatigue-free, the loading scheme is not rigorous enough to induce homeostatic disruption and adaptation. In fact, if an athlete is chronically fatigue-free, he is by definition still a novice.

Overreaching. Overreaching has been described as the cumulative effects of a series of workouts, characterized by a short-term decrease in performance, feelings of fatigue, depressed mood, pain, sleep disturbances, and other miscellaneous effects that require up to two weeks to recover from. Certain hormonal changes such as a short-term reduction in testosterone and increase in cortisol occur at this level of perturbation, and in fact these are among the factors that produce the positive systemic effects of barbell training. A significant problem with this definition is that it differs from that of overtraining only in that "overreaching" can be recovered from with approximately two weeks of reduced work or rest – a rather arbitrary distinction – whereas recovery from overtraining takes longer.

In addition, this definition of overreaching does not consider the level of training advancement of the individual and the recovery abilities associated with that level, a problem typical of the conventional exercise science literature. The novice trainee will not experience so-called overreaching on a properly constructed novice program, since recovery to supercompensation occurs within the 24- to 72-hour period. It is important to understand that the novice trainee will not overreach unless far more than the recommended load is used, because the hallmark of novice status is the ability to recover quickly from the incremental increase in workload used to produce gradual, steady progress. Even when a late-stage novice plateaus within a simple progression regimen, a single additional short-term reduction in training load is adequate to restore homeostasis. The intermediate trainee can recover from a stage 2-level homeostatic disruption in the time allotted for a weekly training period, since intermediate-level trainees characteristically respond to short-term cumulative training loads. The advanced trainee, after a long cumulative disruption of homeostasis, might require four or more weeks to recover and supercompensate, more than the two weeks allowed for by the definition. The utility of the term "overreaching" is therefore questionable.

Moreover, the concept of overreaching defined as a negative effect misses the point. Overreaching simply represents the target stress necessary to disrupt homeostasis, intentionally breaching the maximal workload the trainee has adapted to in order to induce supercompensation. It is more relevant, practical, and understandable to discard the term and simply use the term "overload," since it describes both the load and the stimulus for inducing adaptation in all trainees, regardless of advancement level. Every fitness or performance enhancement training program should include periods of overload, as is required by any practical application of Selye's theory; these periods should be understood as adaptive, not detrimental; and they should be appropriate to the trainee's level of advancement if they are to produce the desired effects. Judging this level of effort can be difficult and requires vigilant monitoring, since a rapid descent into overtraining can occur if loading is too severe or recovery is inadequate.

Overtraining. Overtraining is the cumulative result of relentless high-volume or high-intensity training, or both, without adequate recovery, that results in the exhaustion of the body's ability to compensate for training stress and adapt to it. The primary diagnostic indicator is a reduction in performance capacity that doesn't improve with an amount of rest that would normally result in recovery. Although the accepted (American College of Sports Medicine and U.S. Olympic Committee) definition of overtraining holds that recovery from it requires no less than two weeks, overtraining is obviously relative to the advancement level of the trainee, and there are actually no hard and fast rules governing its onset or its abatement. Even the heinous abuse of a novice with an overwhelming workload, one that induces a loss of performance ability, would resolve fairly quickly. Although the time frame would be compressed, the symptoms observed by the coach would be those of overtraining. Although overtraining in the novice can occur, it may not be easily diagnosed because the magnitude of the loss of performance might be difficult to perceive, due both to a lack of training history for comparison and the low level of performance overall (as represented in fig. 2-7). Once again, as with overreaching, the overtrained intermediate fits the commonly accepted ACSM/USOC definition: an overtrained intermediate will not be able to recover in less than two weeks. In the advanced trainee, however, recovery is never planned to be complete for a minimum of four weeks anyway, and for the elite trainee, it may be considerably longer than that. The existing definition is inadequate for these trainees. It is also easier to diagnose overtraining in advanced and elite trainees, since the performance reduction is quite noticeable against the background of an extensive training history.

A working definition of overtraining that applies to all levels of training advancement requires a better way to quantify recovery time in each stage. **Overtraining occurs specifically when performance does not recover within one reduced-load training cycle.** The duration of that cycle will vary according to the athlete's level of advancement. For example, if a novice training every 48 hours has a workout that is markedly off due to excessive load in the previous workout, this will be apparent during warm-up. His range of motion will be decreased due to the soreness, and his bar speed will be noticeably slower and more labored as the weight increases through the sets. The coach should then stop the workout, having determined the problem (in the last workout he did five extra work sets while another trainee was being coached in the other room, for example) and send him home with orders to rest until the next workout 48 hours later. He comes back in for his next workout, and warm-ups reveal that he is fine now, recovered and capable of the sets he should have done the previous workout. He was overtrained, and now he is recovered. This is possible because he is a novice, and this recovery time frame is consistent with a novice's ability to recover, both from normal overload and from overtraining, since the mechanism is the same.

If an advanced trainee on a four-week cycle of loading declines below expected performance levels during a cycle, either the athlete has come into the cycle overtrained or the current cycle has exhausted recovery capacity. In such a case, as much as four more weeks of reduced training load might be required to facilitate recovery. For both the novice and the advanced trainee, a repeated and dramatically reduced load cycle of equal duration should immediately follow the diagnosis of overtraining in order to reestablish homeostasis. Elite lifters using very long training cycles cannot afford the time required to deal with a programming error that might take months to notice, and even longer to correct.

Overtraining is yet another example of the profound differences between novice and advanced athletes, in that the more advanced an athlete becomes, the more costly overtraining becomes. A novice might be inconvenienced by a missed training session or goal, but that inconvenience lasts for a couple of days, and is of no consequence to anything other than the next workout. Intermediate athletes have committed to their training to the point of selecting a sport, and are in the process of becoming competitors. An advanced athlete is by definition always training for a competition, has invested many thousands of hours, many thousands of dollars, and many gallons of sweat in his training up to this point, and has much to lose as a result. Elite athletes may have titles, sponsorship money, endorsements, and post-competitive careers riding on their performance at the next competition. As careers advance, so does the price of failure, even if it is temporary.

Is consideration of overtraining important? According to the USOC/ACSM "Consensus Statement on Overtraining," 10 to 20% of all athletes are suffering from overtraining on any given day. If this is true, it is a problem. How many coaches can afford to have 20% of their team performing below par on game day? Having a significant number of athletes overtrained at any given time has important ramifications for team success, as well as for the careers of the individual athletes. The culprit here is a lack of the appropriate application of the principles of exercise programming to the training of athletes.

Diagnostic signs of overtraining in non-novices are severe, when finally apparent: obviously compromised performance, disrupted sleep, increased chronic pain, abnormal mood swings, elevated heart rate, change in appetite, and other physical and mental abnormalities. (In fact, these are the same physical symptoms characteristic of severe depression, a clinical problem also arising from the accumulation of unabated stress.) However, not all trainees will display the same symptoms even if they become overtrained on the same program. Once again, the coach's eye is essential in determining changes in the performance and well-being of the trainee. Once overtraining is diagnosed, it is imperative to take remedial action, as longer periods of overtraining require longer periods of recovery. It quite possibly can take as much as twice as long to get a trainee out of overtraining as it took to produce the condition. Horror stories about severe overtraining abound, with examples of athletes losing entire training years. No effort must be spared in recognizing and treating this very serious situation.

Factors Affecting Recovery

The topic of overtraining is usually treated in a fairly narrow sense, with only the ratio of work to recovery discussed. These are the two controlling factors in disrupting homeostasis and forcing adaptation, but, ultimately, recovery is multifactorial and is affected by much more than just time off between workouts. The importance of attention to detail during rest and recovery is essential in avoiding overtraining. Unless the coach and trainee both understand and actively attempt to facilitate optimal recovery, no method of training can produce optimal results or be effective in preventing overtraining.

Aside from the work/rest ratio, several factors affect or contribute to recovery, the most important being adequate sleep, hydration, and proper intake of protein, energy, and micronutrients. Each of these factors is under the direct control of the trainee (but not the coach). A good coach will explain why these things are important for progress, attempt to reinforce their importance on a regular basis, and then realize that better athletes will treat this responsibility as they should, and that average athletes will not. The best training program in the entire universe will be a dismal failure if athletes fail to hold up their end of the deal. The success of any program is ultimately the trainee's responsibility.

Sleep. It should be intuitive, but trainees and coaches alike often overlook the importance of sleep during periods of increased physical demand and stress. While rather limited in scope, the scientific literature on this topic does support the following observations:

1) Lack of adequate sleep during recovery leads to a decrease in competitive ability, reduced determination, and lack of tolerance for intensity in training.

2) Lack of adequate sleep negatively affects mood state, leads to a greater level of perceived fatigue, promotes depression, and can induce mild confusion.

3) Lack of adequate sleep can reduce the capacity of the physiological mechanisms that enable adaptation to the stress of training.

A number of physiological changes occur during sleep. Among them, hormonal secretion is perhaps the most important for recovery from physical exertion. An increase in anabolic (muscle-building) hormone concentrations and a decrease in catabolic (muscle-wasting) hormone concentrations and activity take place during the sleep cycle. Levels of the anabolic hormone testosterone begin to rise upon falling asleep, peak at about the time of first REM, and remain at that level until awakening. This means that sleeping shorter durations limits the recovery contributions possible from testosterone. Another anabolic hormone, somatotropin, or human growth hormone, also has a characteristic secretion pattern during sleep. Shortly after deep sleep begins, growth hormone concentrations begin to rise, leading to a sustained peak lasting 1.5 to 3.5 hours. A major function of growth hormone is the mitigation of the negative effects of the catabolic hormone cortisol. A disruption or shortening of the sleep period will reduce the beneficial effects of these important anabolic hormones.

How much sleep is required? The U.S. military believes that four hours of continuous sleep per night allows for survival and the maintenance of basic combat function. Your mom tells you that eight hours a night is needed to be healthy and happy. The average American adult gets somewhere between six and seven hours per night. So what is right? Military combat is a rather specialized situation, and during non-combat times the Army advises more sleep. The "average" sedentary person is not significantly stressing the body's recuperative capacity. But Mom knows. An average of eight hours of sleep, especially during very rigorous training, will aid in recovery. After all, the purpose of sleep is to induce a state of recovery in the body. The longer the period of sleep, the better the quality of recovery.

The number of hours of sleep is not necessarily the same thing as the number of hours spent in bed. Very few people go to sleep when their head hits the pillow. A trainee going to bed at 11:00 and getting up at 7:00 may not be getting eight hours of sleep. It is more realistic to add extra time to account for any delay in actually falling asleep, ensuring that eight hours is obtained.

Hydration. Water is essential for recovery from strenuous exercise. After all, nearly every biochemical process occurring in the human body takes place in water. Dehydration causes loss of performance, and when it is severe it can be catastrophic. But how much water do we need to drink to support recovery and avoid overtraining?

Everybody's physician, dietician, nutritionist, trainer, coach, and friend "know" that it is "absolutely necessary" to drink "8 × 8": eight 8-ounce glasses of water per day. This equals half a gallon, or about 1.9 liters, of water a day. Note that standard beverage cans or bottles are 12 ounces or 20 ounces, and that a 16-ounce cup is usually a sold as a "small" drink at a restaurant, so the requirement is not necessarily eight commonly available "drinks."

But do we really need to drink this much water? The 8 × 8 recommendation is not actually based on any scientific evidence obtained through research, but on a subjective viewpoint stated in a 1974 nutritional text that was seized upon by the clinical professions and has slowly entrenched itself in both clinical dogma and conventional wisdom. Most fluid intake values found in the research data indicate that between 1.2 and 1.6 liters per day, less than the 1.9 liters of the 8 × 8 prescription, is sufficient for maintaining hydration status in healthy humans who exercise mildly. These recommendations must of course account for different environmental conditions – the hydration status of a person in Florida in June will be different than that of a person in Manitoba in October – so in reality there can be no absolutes with respect to fluid intake. It is also hard to imagine that the human body has spontaneously lost the ability to self-regulate hydration status since the bottled-water industry developed; after all, very few human societies developed a penchant for sipping water all day from a convenient container carried in the hand or the backpack. So self-selected fluid intake in response to thirst probably represents an appropriate method for maintaining health and function under most circumstances. But does it represent an intake that can support recovery from intense training?

An increased metabolic rate increases the requirement for water. Increasing storage of energy substrates (such as ATP, CP, and glycogen) in the muscle increases the need for intracellular water. So how much fluid is needed beyond the 1.2 to 1.6 liters per day that reportedly supports a healthy mildly active life? Larger, more active individuals require more water intake to support their greater quantity of metabolically active tissue, the increased caloric cost of incrementally larger workloads, and their less-efficient heat dissipation characteristics. One size does not fit all in terms of hydration. A good rule of thumb might be one liter for every 1000 calories expended. A 5000-calorie per day expenditure would require five liters (or 1.3 gallons) of fluid. This volume of fluid may seem quite high, but considering the needs of an extremely active athlete training several hours per day, it is a reasonable recommendation, and in fact might still be inadequate for a warm training environment. This requires that attention be paid to fluid intake, since 5+ liters per day is a lot of water to drink. Excessive water consumption is extremely dangerous, but the intake of toxic levels of water requires a conscious effort far above any effort to assuage thirst under any circumstances, and it cannot be done accidentally.

One last consideration is which fluids count toward hydration. Many popular health practitioners and advocates will boldly state that only water and a few other "natural" beverages count toward hydration. They discount anything with caffeine or alcohol or even sugar as a viable rehydrating beverage. The statement has actually been made that "You wouldn't wash your car with a diet soft drink – why would you use it for hydration?" Such an attitude demonstrates a misunderstanding of the mechanism by which water is absorbed from the gut: anything that contains water, even food high in water, counts toward water consumption. Water itself is the best rehydrating fluid since it can be taken up faster than commonly consumed commercial beverages (if that is actually a practical consideration in normal hydration situations), but every fluid consumed contributes. The water content of a 20-ounce diet cola counts toward hydration even though it contains caffeine and artificial sweeteners. A 20-ounce regular cola full of high-fructose corn syrup also counts even though it contains caffeine and sugar. Alcoholic beverages have been quite effective hydrating agents at various points in human history. Beer and wine, in more primitive times, were major rehydrating fluids necessary for survival, since they were safer than the available untreated water supply, as was the grog – rum mixed with water – of the British Navy in the eighteenth century. We are not proposing that soft drinks, beer, and wine should be staple components of the training diet, but honesty compels the consideration of the realities of the American lifestyle and how it may affect recovery. Aside from the question of their other benefits or detriments, moderate consumption of these beverages does in fact contribute to hydration.

Protein. How much protein do athletes really need? Recently, a growing pool of research has surfaced regarding the protein needs of strength-trained athletes. The United States Recommended Daily Allowance (RDA) values call for a protein intake of 0.8 +/- 0.35 g/kg/day (grams per kilogram of bodyweight per day) for males and females fifteen years and older. The RDA is based on the needs of the average population, and the average American is sedentary. Is it logical to expect the nutritional requirements of a sedentary individual to be the same as the requirements of anyone undergoing a program of systematically increasing physical stress and adaptation? It has been well documented that any type of exercise increases the rate of metabolism in the muscle and also accelerates the rate of muscle protein degradation and turnover. Research shows that resistance exercise stimulates muscle protein synthesis that lasts well past the end of the exercise bout.

Protein synthesis, the process by which new muscle is built, requires a dietary protein source. The primary way muscles recover from stress and improve in fitness is for muscle protein synthesis to occur faster than the muscle protein breakdown that is the inevitable result of exercise. If protein synthesis is to exceed protein degradation, anabolism, or constructive processes, must exceed negative catabolic processes. If nutrients needed for protein synthesis (to maintain or repair damaged tissue) are not sufficiently available from dietary sources, the body will take them from its own protein stores – its existing muscle mass. In essence, the body will rob Peter to pay Paul in order to maintain function. By ensuring adequate dietary protein intake, the trainee provides the body with the building blocks necessary for new protein synthesis.

So, how much protein is needed to support training? The literature includes a broad range of recommendations that go as high as 2.5 g/kg/day. Some coaches and trainees don't like to do arithmetic, or aren't comfortable converting pounds to kilograms. An easy way to ensure enough dietary protein, and the tried-and-true method used by the weightlifting and strength training communities for many years, is simply to eat one gram of protein per *pound* of bodyweight per day: a 200-pound athlete should try to get about 200 grams of protein per day, from various dietary sources. This works out to 2.2 g/kg/day, a value that, while in excess of the consensus recommendation of between 1.2 and 1.8 g/kg/day, remains below the highest recommended value in the literature of 2.5 g/kg/day, and will ensure a target high enough that missing it a little will still be sufficient for full recovery. This calculation disregards considerations of lean body mass and therefore assumes an already "normal" body composition; individuals with a higher bodyfat percentage should take this into account when planning protein intakes.

It is important to note that there is absolutely no evidence to support the notion that "excessive" amounts of protein are harmful to normal kidneys with unimpaired excretory function, despite the ill-informed advice of some health-care professionals. In fact, in people without active kidney disease there are no unsafe levels of protein consumption in the context of dietary intake.

Protein supplementation is useful in that it can help an athlete get a sufficient protein intake, making up the difference between that found in the diet and the recommended level. And a protein drink, being convenient to make and consume, is useful for post-workout recovery. Despite the marketing efforts of many manufacturers, there is very little difference in the net effect of the quality or purity of the protein supplement – in the grand scheme of things, the most expensive whey protein has no significant advantage over ground beef in terms of the body's ability to use the amino acids it contains for protein synthesis.

Energy Intake. Since calories are expended during exercise, mostly derived from the body's ready reserves of stored carbohydrate and fat, an obvious requirement for recovery after exercise is an increased need for energy to replace that consumed during training. There are two reasons exercise creates a need for calories: 1) exercise of all types, volumes, and intensities expends some fraction of the body's energy stores, and these must be replaced before another bout of activity, and 2) exercise of sufficient load disrupts homeostasis and muscle structural integrity, producing a requirement for both protein and fat/carbohydrate calories to facilitate repair and recovery.

The source of the energy – carbohydrate or fat – is not terribly important as long as is sufficient in caloric content and a protein source accompanies it. Fat requires a longer time for breakdown and utilization than carbohydrate, but the body's metabolic rate is elevated for many hours after exercise and having a very energy-rich substrate (fat has more energy by weight than carbohydrate) slowly metabolized over a number of hours rather than a mass of carbohydrate digesting for an hour or so after eating may be beneficial. In fact, it has been clearly demonstrated that the primary fuel source used in the 18 hours following exhaustive exercise is, in fact, fat. Given adequate caloric intake and adequate protein, the composition of the diet must also consider the requirements of vitamin intake, essential fatty acids, and fiber, as well as the glycemic index of the balance of the food and the resulting insulin effects of the meal. The quality of the diet should be as high as the resources of the trainee permit.

It is important that the total caloric content of the diet be at least equal to, but preferably greater than, the total caloric expenditure of the training day. Matching intake to expenditure will maintain fitness and strength but will not support maximal fitness gain. As a practical matter, caloric surplus is needed to drive progress, regardless of the precision with which we are able to calculate energy expenditure and intake. If we simply pay back the energy used during exercise and daily activities, we are not providing the extra energy required to drive homeostatic recovery and adaptation through muscle mass increase. To get stronger and more fit, the conventional literature advises the consumption of around 200 to 400 calories more energy than we expend. It has been the experience of the authors that a more reasonable intake to ensure recovery and strength gains would be 500 to 1000 calories per day. If a gain in muscular bodyweight is the primary goal, a surplus of at least 1000 calories per day, and perhaps much more for some people who are inefficient metabolizers, will be needed.

Vitamins and Minerals. Frequently, it is stated that the average American diet provides all the vitamins and minerals necessary for a healthy life, and that statement is almost always considered to extend to hard-training men and women. Virtually no one is ever tested for vitamin and mineral levels unless they display deficiency disease symptoms. Therefore, few individuals, sedentary or athletic, ever know for sure whether they have all the required vitamins and minerals present in sufficient quantities.

Severe vitamin and mineral deficiencies are not common in the United States, but they do occur. Mild deficiencies are much more common – the majority of American females are consistently iron and calcium deficient to a small but significant degree, for instance. Calcium has a tremendous variety of functions in nervous and muscular physiology, growth, and performance and a deficiency can limit recovery from training. Iron has a crucial role in oxygen transport and metabolic function. A mild iron deficiency can have significant negative effects on the body's ability to recover after exercise.

Vitamins and minerals act as mediators of biochemical reactions in the body. Referred to as "micronutrients," they are needed in relatively small amounts and occur naturally in foods in varying concentrations. To obtain all the vitamins and minerals required for life – and certainly for training – we must consume a variety of foods. The average American kid does not. If parents were aware of the basic need to provide young athletes with a diet of high quality and variety, this would not be an issue. But we are a culture of convenience and habit, and it is common that people consume a very limited selection of foods and food types, often those that are processed to increase the convenience of storage and preparation. Such processing typically reduces the vitamin and mineral content of food to the extent that the quality of the diet – even though sufficient in calories and maybe even protein – is quite low.

The result is that while the typical athlete's diet may not be so woefully inadequate that deficiency symptoms are present, it may contain less than optimal amounts of essential vitamins and minerals, nutrients needed to assist in recovery from rigorous training. Recent research on normal sedentary populations has concluded that vitamin supplementation has no effect on longevity; we are not concerned here with longevity, but rather performance. After all, if it is logical that an athlete in hard training needs increased calories, water, and protein, then a higher vitamin/mineral intake would also be required. Given the diverse regional, ethnic, cultural, and economic tastes and habits within the U.S. population, and without specific and costly laboratory testing, there is no easy way for the coach or athlete to assess the vitamins and minerals present in any given diet. Thankfully, this is not necessary: nutritional supplementation to ensure that these important micronutrients are present for training and recovery is safe, effective, simple, and economical.

The best way is to start simple and cheap. An inexpensive generic vitamin and mineral supplement containing all the commonly supplemented vitamins and minerals is readily available at grocery stores or on the Internet. More money will get you a better, purer, more readily absorbable product. Bill Starr in his famous book *The Strongest Shall Survive* advocated the use of the "shovel method": just take a lot, and the body will excrete what it doesn't use. Since vitamin toxicity is excruciatingly rare, especially among hard-training athletes, this is good advice.

Fatty acids. Another set of compounds that affect recovery are essential fatty acids (EFAs). Although a bias against dietary fat remains currently in vogue in some circles, fats are essential nutrients as well as efficient sources of energy. While there are no essential carbohydrates, there are some essential fatty acids – the body can synthesize many of the lipids it needs from dietary fat sources, but it cannot make omega-3 and omega-6 fatty acids. These two types of lipids play an important role in the maintenance of the body's structural integrity, are crucial to immune function and visual acuity, and are involved in the production of eicosanoids, the precursors of the prostaglandins which regulate the inflammatory process. Of the two, omega-3 fatty acids are the most important to recovery: they support anabolic processes and assist in the management of post-exercise inflammation and pain. They are also less likely to be present in adequate amounts in the diet. Omega-6 fatty acids may actually contribute to inflammatory processes if they are present in the wrong proportions.

Deficiencies in EFAs are fairly common in the United States, since fish, the primary source of omega-3 fats, has never traditionally been an important component of most American diets. Chronic profound deficiencies result in growth retardation, dry skin, diarrhea, slow wound healing, increased rates of infection, and anemia. Sub-clinical deficiencies would likely not produce symptoms that could be easily diagnosed by observation. Acute clinical deficiencies quickly develop in individuals with very low-fat diets, with symptoms evident in two to three weeks.

Only a few grams of omega-3-rich oils are required. This can be done with about one generous serving of fatty fish, such as salmon, per day. Many people find that taking an omega-3 fish oil supplement is helpful, since hard training benefits from higher dietary levels of EFAs. Cod liver oil too is an inexpensive source of EFAs, and is also very high in vitamins A and D.

How Hard and How Much

Periodization. Possibly having encountered Selye's theory and realizing that it had direct applications to the training of athletes, Soviet exercise physiologists proposed several methods of training that capitalized on the body's ability to adapt to increasing workloads. The roots of this method, called **periodization**, are often attributed to Leonid Matveyev in the Soviet Union in the 1960s (advanced versions of Soviet-style periodization can be traced further back to Hungary in the 1940s and 50s). Periodization was brought to the attention of the U.S. weightlifting community in the 1970s by Carl Miller and molded into a hypothetical model for weight training for sports performance by Mike Stone in 1981. Since then, periodization has become one of the primary tools of successful training program design, regardless of the sport.

The objective of all training for performance improvement should be to take the body through Selye's stages 1 and 2 of the stress model, providing enough training stress to induce adaptation without reaching Stage 3, exhaustion. Correctly designed programs achieve positive results by controlling the degree of stress placed on the body through the manipulation of the volume and intensity of training. It is therefore important to have a method of quantifying volume and intensity.

Volume is the total amount of weight lifted in a workout or group of workouts:

$$repetitions \times weight = volume$$

The following table shows an example of volume calculations for a squat workout:

Squat	Warm-up	Warm-up	Warm-up	Work set	Work set	Work set
Weight (lbs)	45	95	135	185	185	185
Repetitions	5	5	5	5	5	5
Volume per set (lbs)	225	475	675	925	925	925
Total volume (lbs)						4150
Work set volume (lbs)						2775

For this one exercise, warm-up reps included, the trainee lifted a volume of 4150 pounds. This calculation is repeated for every exercise included in the workout session. In that way the total volume of stress applied can be quantified. It may be more useful to consider only work set volume, since it is the work sets and not the warm-ups that are disrupting homeostasis and bringing about stage 1. As shown in the table, this significantly reduces calculated volume. If a trainee does an inordinately large number of warm-up sets, it might be appropriate to consider their effect on training volume.

Intensity is the amount of weight lifted, or the average amount of weight lifted in a workout or group of workouts, in relation to the trainee's 1RM ("one-rep max," or the maximum weight that the trainee can lift for a single repetition):

volume / repetitions = average weight used

average weight used / 1RM × 100 = % intensity

For the example in the table above, the average weight used is 4150 pounds/30 reps, or 138.33 pounds per rep. If the trainee's 1RM is 225, the intensity is 138.33/225 × 100 = 61%. It is easy to see how an excessive warm-up can affect the average weight of all the reps, and the average intensity, making it desirable to use only work sets in the intensity calculation. For only the work sets in this example, the intensity is 82%.

Let us reiterate: Intensity is considered as a percentage of 1RM. An intensity of 80% of 1RM is greater than an intensity of 50% of 1RM. While this is a simple concept, there are many different ideas about "intensity" in the scientific, medical, and popular literature. Intensity is sometimes equated with the level of power production in a given exercise. Things as abstract as the amount of mental focus given to a repetition ("Let's really focus on this next rep and get your intensity up!") or the individual's subjective perception of their effort during the exercise (the Borg Rating of Perceived Exertion scale, for example) have been proposed as definitions. Another proposed description is related to fatigue: if it fatigues the muscle, the exercise was intense. All these concepts have been elaborated upon in the literature, but without exception they are not practical for the strength training professional because they are not quantifiable, a characteristic that both scientists and practitioners regard as pivotal. Intensity, as defined with respect % of 1RM may be somewhat simplistic, but is the most practical and useful method, especially for coaches and trainers who program for large groups and need a way to objectively assess work and improvement.

The simple calculation of a range of intensities of an exercise weight relative to 1RM:

Squat 1RM (lbs)	225
95% = 225 x 0.95	214
90% = 225 x 0.90	203
85% = 225 x 0.85	191
80% = 225 x 0.80	180
75% = 225 x 0.75	169
70% = 225 x 0.70	158

Traditionally, the manner in which periodization controls volume and intensity – and therefore the degree of stress placed on the body – is by dividing training into periods whose lengths and load characteristics vary according to the level of the trainee.

Interpretation of the literature on overtraining must be done with an awareness of the fact that much of it is based on aerobic training. The overtraining that can be induced by anaerobic training such as weightlifting has different characteristics than that induced by the quite different stimulus of aerobic work – referred to by lifters as long slow distance work, or LSD. The different ways in which volume and intensity are defined between the two disciplines have a bearing on the analysis of overtraining. Modern competitive road cyclists, for example, may spend hours each day on the bike, generating a huge volume of training. When they want to work harder, they add miles, hours, or training days, accumulating what have been termed "junk miles." They also tend to ride at a sustainable percentage of their VO_2 max, and if this is used as a measure of road cycling intensity every training session typically averages out to be similar to the one before it. It is important to note that VO_2 max occurs at about 30 to 40% of a muscle's maximal strength of contraction. So, intensity (measured as a percentage of absolute strength) is not usually a major training factor in the average self-coached American competitive cyclist's training program. But because volume is essentially the overloaded training variable, road cyclists generally suffer from volume-induced overtraining.

Because weight training programs manipulate both volume and intensity of training, trainees can experience either volume-induced or intensity-induced overtraining. Extremes in programming styles are represented by the "go-heavy-or-go-home" approach, which may precipitate intensity-induced overtraining, and the "train-to-failure" approach on the other hand, which may produce volume-induced overtraining. More common is overtraining that has elements of both types, since most programs manipulate both variables. Understanding the rate of recovery from both types is important. In well-trained weightlifters, intensity-induced overtraining – a function of the nervous system and its interface with the muscular system – seems easier to recover from than its volume-induced counterpart, which affects primarily the contractile components and metabolic systems of the muscle cells. When peaking for a strength or power event, intensity continues to be included in the program, at greatly reduced volume, up to very near the event. When peaking for an endurance event, both the volume and intensity of weight training should be curtailed several weeks in advance, since longer period required for volume recovery will directly affect the competition.

The basic cure for overtraining is the combination of time and reduced workload. The time spent dealing with overtraining costs the coach and athlete valuable progress: reduced workloads do not produce improvement, or even maintenance; a complete layoff results in detraining to some inevitable extent. Since the costs of overtraining are high, prevention is the best approach. Correctly designed training programs appropriate for the athlete and the sport are the key.

Although properly executed simple progression can produce rapid progress without overtraining in the early stages, for more advanced trainees, more complex programming – periodization – is necessary.

"How can I possibly put a new idea into your heads,
if I do not first remove your delusions?"

–Doctor Pinero in "Life-Line"
by *Robert A. Heinlein* (1939)

3 - Understanding Training Goals

Starting at Square One

Planning a program of weight training requires a clearly defined set of goals for the athlete. Once the goals are established, training must be relatively specific, meaning that exercises and programming should pertain specifically to the sport. Training without planning is not much of a program, and if progress occurs it will be in spite of the program rather than because of it.

The average trainee has some type of fitness goal in mind when beginning an exercise program. The competitive athlete certainly does. Despite the fact that most individuals know what they want out of a program, the academic community is less clear about what fitness actually is. Physical fitness is poorly defined in the literature, and the published and conventionally accepted approaches to gaining it are misdirected in many, many instances. A useful definition of physical fitness should center on the "physical" and describe physical readiness in terms of function, as does the following one, proposed in a 2006 article by Kilgore and Rippetoe in the *Journal of Exercise Physiology Online* [9(1):1-10]:

> Possession of adequate levels of strength, endurance, and mobility to provide for successful participation in occupational effort, recreational pursuits, familial obligation, and that is consistent with a functional phenotypic expression of the human genotype.

After all, human survival in a human environment depends on being able to perform a variety of physical tasks at a moment's notice. We can divide the broad spectrum of abilities required to conquer the average person's life tasks into three basic categories: strength, endurance, and mobility. Lifting weights can help develop each of these three areas of fitness to varying degrees, depending on the emphasis of the program, but the usual focus with lifting is on strength and its related characteristics, power and mass.

Coaches and trainees, either consciously or unconsciously, tend to bias their weight training toward strength, power, or mass. Each is defined by specific physical, physiological, and functional characteristics, so training for each requires different strategies and program organization. Any training program needs to reflect the specific needs of the particular training objective it was designed to achieve, since excellence in each requires specific focus on its unique characteristics.

Poor programming choices will significantly affect the development of the desired performance characteristics. In the barbell sports, this can be illustrated by comparing the training objectives of a weightlifter (a competitor in the sport of Olympic weightlifting) and a powerlifter. The weightlifter hopes to achieve a great deal of explosive power in order to successfully perform the snatch and the clean and jerk with big weights which requires great speed. The powerlifter hopes to gain absolute strength in order to squat, bench press, and deadlift big weights. The difference between these goals may not seem apparent, since both lifters need to move heavy weights and thus ultimately depend on strength. But the speed with which the bar moves and the distance it travels, the factors that determine power, are the distinguishing characteristics. As it turns out, the development of power is – or at least should be – the primary goal of training for most athletes in the weight room. To clarify the difference between strength and power we need to understand a few more terms.

> The modern fitness industry's concept of "toning" muscles is specious—it might sound cool, but it lacks any tangible and definable meaning. The term "muscle tone," or *tonus,* describes an electrophysiological phenomenon, a measure of ionic flow across muscle cell membranes. It can be thought of as the muscle's readiness to do anaerobic work. The more "fit" the muscle, the more electrophysiological activity it exhibits at rest. Lack of exercise leads to poor tone, aerobic exercise improves tone a little bit, low-intensity weight training improves tone more, and high-intensity training improves tone the fastest. As a test, go poke the traps or quads of an elite weightlifter at rest, if she'll let you. They'll be hard as rock. The same muscles of an elite road cyclist at rest will be firm, but not hard. Then compare both athletes' muscle tone to that of a sedentary person. The results will be quite enlightening. Most exercise programs that claim to improve muscle tone are actually lower-intensity hypertrophy programs and are only moderately effective for improving muscle tone. If "tone" is the goal, strength is the method.

Power and Its Components

Strength. Strength is a measurement of the ability of a muscle to exert force against external resistance. In its broadest interpretation, strength is the ability to move a weight irrespective of the amount of time it takes, as with a heavy deadlift moving slowly to lockout. The benefits of improving strength for athletes in anaerobic sports are obvious, since force production is such an important aspect of these activities. Less obvious are the benefits of increasing strength in aerobic athletes, but it has been well documented that strength increases improve endurance performance by prolonging the time it takes before muscles fatigue.

Measures of strength are often associated with slow movements or no movement at all. Powerlifters move heavy weights relatively slowly. In so doing, they display a great deal of strength. Consider as an example a lineman trying to move an opposing player after the initial contact (the opposing player is the weight). Upon contact, the movement might stop completely, resulting in isometric muscle action. As the opposing force is overcome, movement speed increases from zero but remains slow relative to the explosion off the line. Overcoming the resistance that the opposing player provides takes superior strength – the ability to hold position isometrically while better mechanical position is obtained, and the ability to produce more force concentrically once it is. Strength improvement should be a goal for all trainees because it always contributes to performance.

Speed. The amount of time it takes an object, or one's own body, to move a given distance is an important component of the vast majority of sports. Speed is critical to the correct performance of many barbell exercises, specifically the Olympic lifts and their variants; bar speed in a snatch is a critical analytical marker for coaching the lift. An object's speed is determined by measuring the distance traveled and dividing it by the time it took for that movement to occur; it is thus the rate of change of the object's position in space. (The object's *velocity* is the rate of change of its position in a given direction, a technical distinction of little importance to this discussion. For our purposes here the terms are used interchangeably.) Beating an opposing player to the ball requires speed. Strength contributes to speed by enabling the body to overcome inertia and initiate *acceleration*, the rate at which speed increases. Once movement is initiated, strength is required for the continuing rapid transfer of force that maintains the velocity of the object against its tendency to slow down.

Power. The production of power is the key to most sports. It is the amount of work performed per unit of time. Work is the force applied to an object and the consequent distance it is moved by that force; an easily understood unit of work is the foot-pound, the energy needed to move a 1-pound load a distance of 1 foot. Therefore a unit of power would be 1 foot-pound per second – the rate at which the work of moving the object is performed. Power is understood best as the ability to exert force rapidly, or as strength applied quickly. If a large muscular force is generated that moves a heavy weight very quickly, power production is high; the highest peak power outputs ever recorded in all of athletics have been produced during the second-pull phase of the snatch. It can be considered as the rate of *force* production, usually measured using a force plate.

     On the other hand, if an athlete in training climbs ten flights of stairs faster today than he did last week, he has moved the mass of his body the distance of ten flights of stairs more quickly. Or if an athlete finishes the task of doing three rounds of 30 pull-ups and running 400 meters faster than she did it last month, the mass of her body has moved faster over a shorter period of time. These are examples of rate of *work* production, and could be improved by merely resting less between the components of the work without increasing the rate of the force production of the movements themselves. In other words, the density of the cumulative efforts increases – an increase in frequency without an increase in the amplitude of the individual component efforts. Improvements in rate of force production and rate of work production require different metabolic adaptations, which may or may not overlap. For our purposes here power is the ability to generate high levels of force rapidly. The successful lineman comes off the line very fast, accelerating his bodyweight quickly enough to meet his opponent, completely stop the opposing forward momentum, and start the process of pushing him out of position. The effects of his power – the momentum created by his speed and the mass of his body moving at that speed, and his subsequent ability to quickly generate force against his opponent – determines more about his performance during the play than any other aspect of his movement.

Some aspects of work, and therefore power, are difficult to measure. If we consider only the power developed against the bar, the calculation is simple, but incomplete. The athlete and the bar form a system, both components of which move. Work done by the muscles against the skeletal components of the system – the maintaining of isometric back extension during a deadlift, for example – is difficult to measure. But the force expended during the effort to maintain a rigid spine for improved force transfer efficiency is in fact a quantity, and must therefore be a part of the development of the power of the movement. Force is being applied to a part of the system that cannot be quantified by measuring its movement. It is usually unnecessary to be this precise, but an understanding of the system as a whole is important for an appreciation of the importance of good technique and its dependence on strength.

This is of extreme importance to every athlete and coach: **the ability to generate power directly affects performance in all sports.** Training programs that increase power output should be used for all athletes, from novice to elite, from tennis players to shot putters. It was noted in the 1980s that even elite Soviet weightlifters could improve their performance by increasing their power development. All other things being equal, the more powerful athlete will always beat the less powerful athlete.

The development of power requires careful program design based on the requirements of the specific sport, a careful assessment of the strengths and weaknesses of the athlete, and an understanding of the effects of various exercises on power production. The simple act of increasing strength for the novice lifter will increase his power, since power depends on strength and strength improves rapidly for a novice. For example, an increase in the deadlift will immediately decrease sprint times for an inexperienced kid much more productively than time spent working on sprint mechanics. For the more advanced trainee, training for power requires the use of exercises in which heavy loads are moved quickly, such as the Olympic lifts – the snatch and the clean and jerk and their derivatives – which cannot be done slowly. For a competitive lifter, sprint training combined with heavy squats will increase sprint velocity and strength, but not necessarily power output. Performing power snatches at 50% of 1RM and then doing snatch-grip deadlifts might very well leave peak power production – as measured by an increase in 1RM snatch – unaffected. An attempt must be made to improve the ability to accelerate increasingly heavy loads if peak power production is to be improved.

The results of two different training methods on power output can be evaluated with a simple set of calculations. Take the example of a very strong offensive lineman who trains with traditional powerlifting exercises:

Bodyweight = 140 kg (308 lb)
Deadlift personal best (1RM) = 300 kg (660 lb)
Distance from floor to lockout = 0.65 meters
Time from floor to lockout = 4.0 seconds

To calculate his power output in the deadlift, first calculate the work performed (force × gravitational constant × distance):

Work = 300 kg × 9.8 m/s² × 0.65 m = 1911 Newton meters (N m)

Next, calculate total power generated (work/time):

Power = 1911 N m / 4.0 seconds = 477.75 watts

This can be expressed in a form that allows for the comparison of two individuals, by calculating watts per kilogram, or relative power output (power/bodyweight):

Relative power = 477.75 watts / 140 kg = 3.41 watts/kg

This measurement of relative power is now scaled for the mass of the athlete.

Next, use the same formulas to calculate the power generated by an offensive lineman who trains specifically for power development by using the power clean (from floor to shoulder):

Bodyweight = 140 kg (308 lb)
Power clean personal best (1RM) = 150 kg (330 lb)
Distance from floor to lockout = 1.27 meters
Time from floor to lockout = 0.6 seconds

Work performed (force × gravitational constant × distance):

Work = 150 kg × 9.8 m/s² × 1.27 m = 1866.9 N m

Total power generated (work/time):

Power = 1866.9 N m / 0.6 seconds = 3111.5 watts

Relative power output (power/bodyweight):

Relative power = 3111.5 watts / 140 kg = 22.2 watts/kg

The main difference between the two is the time it takes to move the load. The work done in the two lifts is essentially the same: 1911 N-m for the deadlift and 1867 N-m for the power clean. The power clean is faster, so much faster that it generates more than six times the power despite the fact that it is only half the weight and moves twice the distance of the deadlift. (See fig. 3-1.) This calculation clearly demonstrates that Olympic-style weight training is "high-power" whereas traditional – and obviously misnamed – powerlifting-style training is "low-power" (but "high-strength"). This doesn't mean that absolute strength training should be avoided by power athletes; in fact, force production is inherent in the production of high levels of power, and strength is actually a neglected component in the training of many American Olympic weightlifters these days. It does mean, though, that the Olympic lifts and their derivatives should be included in any program designed to increase an athlete's power output, because if power is improved during training, the ability to generate power on the field improves too. Both strength and power training have important places in a comprehensive program for athletes.

Figure 3-1. A comparison of the deadlift and the power clean. The deadlift (A) moves a heavy weight over a short distance slowly, while the power clean (B) moves a lighter weight over a longer distance quickly. Much greater power is produced during the power clean.

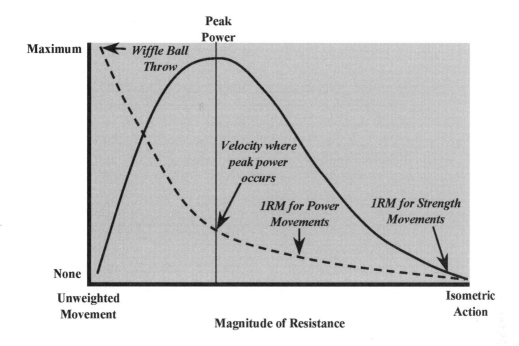

Figure 3-2. Velocity-power graph. The dashed line represents velocity, and the solid line represents power output. Peak power occurs at approximately 30% of maximal isometric force and 30% of maximal movement velocity. This would equate to 50 to 80% of 1RM, depending on the exercise. Strength movements above are those that are limited by strength, such as the squat, press, deadlift or similar exercises. Power movements are those limited by power output such as the snatch, jerk, clean or other similar exercises.

Mass. Muscle size is normally associated with strength. We've all seen people who just *look* strong. They have an imposing muscular appearance. And there is truth in this perception: absolute strength increases as a muscle's cross-sectional area gets bigger. It is an inevitable consequence of weight training that muscles will get larger, and this is why most people do it. This growth happens whether the intent of the training is strength, power, or mass. But by specifically using high-volume lower-intensity training, one can maximize muscle-mass gains. Bodybuilders know that performing five sets of twelve reps of an isolation-type exercise with minimal rest between sets is optimal for producing muscle hypertrophy in the muscle group trained in the exercise. Bodybuilding workouts are organized so that all the muscle groups are trained, although since they are trained separately their coordinated performance remains untrained.

Mass, not strength or power production, is the primary training goal for bodybuilders. Frequently though, coaches and trainers of actual athletes place them all on hypertrophy-type training under the assumption that all hypertrophy is the same and that big muscles – no matter how they are produced – are always equally strong and powerful. This is not the case. The hypertrophy resulting from bodybuilding training is physiologically and functionally different from the hypertrophy resulting from maximal-strength or power training. High-rep, low-intensity training of isolated muscle groups results in hypertrophy of those isolated muscle groups, but strength and power training that relies on multi-joint barbell exercises provides a functional advantage over bodybuilding-type training: more strength and more power, and a body that functions as a coordinated system.

Training for hypertrophy is an important consideration for athletes involved in sports that favor size. Football, for example, is a different game today than it was many years ago, before the advent and necessity of 300-pound linemen and 245-pound defensive ends. Most heavy-implement throwers and strongman competitors are bigger athletes as well. It's simple: size is commonly associated with strength athletes because, in general, stronger is bigger. Bigger is also useful in team sports involving contact, like rugby and basketball, and even those traditionally played under endurance conditions, like soccer, because heavier players are harder to push around than lighter ones.

But bigger muscles also mean more efficient leverage around important joints. Knees, elbows, hips, and shoulders work better when the muscles that operate them are larger, since the angle at which the muscles cross the joint is more mechanically efficient for the joint's third-class lever system: the steeper the angle of attack that the tendon has on the bone, the more efficient the pull. Big quads thus work better than small quads, both because they are stronger in terms of cross-sectional area and because at least a portion of the muscle mass is positioned to extend the knee more efficiently.

When training for mass, specialization is less effective than generalization. The endocrine system responds in a dose-dependent manner to stress. Large-scale, multi-joint (sometimes called "structural") exercises are more effective in producing an anabolic hormonal stimulus than small-scale, single-joint, isolation-type exercises, even when using the same intensities and repetition schemes. In the context of non-chemically enhanced training, exercises such as the squat and the bench press are more effective in producing hypertrophy for athletes who train the body in a systemic, coordinated manner than for those who use isolation-type exercises such as leg extensions or the pec deck.

The Next Step

The conventional wisdom holds that all strength and power training for sports should be done in a manner that mimics the metabolic demands of the sport as closely as possible, requiring specificity with respect to the energy systems used (ATP/CP vs. glycolytic vs. oxidative; see chapter 4), the muscle groups primarily involved in the sport, and the requirements for force generation, speed of movement, range of motion, and frequency of contraction. But as with all other training program considerations, this must be tempered with an understanding of the level of training advancement of the athlete as well as an understanding of the contribution of strength to the sport in question. For example, the marathon or any other long-distance endurance event would probably not greatly benefit in terms of performance from the type of training an Olympic weightlifter would do. Endurance athletes require adaptations in oxidative metabolic capacity to improve performance, an adaptation that weight training at high intensity and low volume develops only peripherally. But higher repetitions and lower-intensity weight training do not develop oxidative capacity anyway. Endurance athletes benefit from the increased strength provided by a typical novice program because the vast majority of endurance athletes are novices with respect to strength development, and increased strength decreases the percentage of the endurance athlete's absolute strength required to sustain the repeated submaximal efforts which accumulate into an endurance performance. An advanced sprinter, however, who operates entirely in anaerobic metabolism during performance, and who needs a great deal of explosion and power, would directly benefit from high-intensity strength and power training. Every coach should be familiar with the metabolic demands of his sport: the longest and shortest effort; the intensity of these efforts; the recovery time between them; the normal duration of the event, and the typical length of its rest periods. He should also be familiar with the beneficial effects of a simple increase in strength, because the absence of sufficient strength limits the development of all other athletic parameters.

So the concept of specificity of training has its limitations. While training should be relevant to the goal at hand in terms of selecting exercises that develop the muscles used in the sport, it is neither necessary nor desirable to exactly mimic either a sport skill or the exact metabolic demands in the weight room. Strength is a very generally acquired and utilized characteristic, developed through *training*. Strength is developed by exercises that use lots of joints and lots of muscles moving lots of weight over a long range of motion. Fundamental strength exercises like the squat, the press, the deadlift, and the bench press, along with power exercises like the clean and the snatch, always form the basis of any strength and conditioning program that is actually useful to an athlete, irrespective of the level of training advancement. This is true precisely because these exercises are quite non-specific – they develop useful strength and power that can be applied in any athletic context. Sports *practice* involves motor patterns and metabolic pathways that apply the general strength of the athlete in ways extremely specific to the activity. In an attempt to be sport-specific with strength and power training, it is quite possible to be so specific with respect to both the movement pattern selected and the anticipated metabolic pathway that the ability to induce strength and power gains is compromised; high-rep training may seem more applicable to a sport that requires sustained effort, but it is an inferior way to develop strength, and strength may be the limiting factor in the ability to sustain an effort. Specificity in programming must be considered in terms of the optimal way in which the most fundamental athletic attribute – strength – is acquired, and the needs of the athlete relative to his level of training advancement.

Metabolic specificity refers to the degree of similarity between the energy substrates used to power the sports performance and that used to power the training activity, and is a more important consideration for intermediate and advanced athletes who have already developed their basic strength. For example, a shot put lasts a little longer than one second, is powered by ATP stored in the muscle (more on this later), and never even remotely approaches muscle fatigue. It depends entirely on the ability to generate force rapidly in a coordinated manner consistent with the technique the athlete has practiced. A training activity specific to the shot put would be one that also utilizes stored ATP at a rate consistent with that of the shot put and that generates force rapidly, even if in a movement pattern that does not at all resemble the shot put. An Olympic weightlifting-type exercise done for very few repetitions at high effort would fit this description. Something like long- or middle-distance running, powered by carbohydrate or fat metabolism and lacking a rapid force-production component, would not. If metabolically similar exercises are utilized to prepare for a sport activity, the transfer of the training adaptation to performance improvement will be larger than if non-similar exercises are used. This should be intuitive to anyone experienced in sports preparation.

The degree of specificity, however, exists on a sliding scale. Compare, for example, push-ups for many, many repetitions, bodybuilding-style bench presses with lighter weights at 12 to 15 reps, and bench presses with heavy weights at 3 reps. For our shot putter, the push-ups, which may take 45 to 60 seconds, are less specific metabolically than the bodybuilding bench press, which in turn is less specific than the heavy bench press. Work-to-rest ratios must also be considered within this metabolic context. An obvious example is a football play, which may involve 6 seconds of intense activity followed by 45 seconds of very low-intensity activity and recovery. Training in the weight room or on the track with similar periods of exercise and rest will better prepare the athlete for the demands of on-the-field performance, while longer durations of rest during barbell workouts may assist in better development of maximal strength, also useful on the field. The coach must use his judgment in order to select the best work-rest ratio to augment the performance of his athletes, often on an individual basis.

Motor specificity refers to the degree of similarity in movement pattern between a sport activity and a training activity. If we consider three superficially similar exercises for the shot put – the press, the incline press, and the bench press – we might visually select the incline press as the most specific, since it most closely mimics the angle of primary effort and release of the shot. Many trainers and athletes regard the incline press as an important exercise, but the press and the bench press develop both the horizontal and vertical ability to generate force, and overlap the area trained by the incline. And the press is the only one of the three with an important characteristic for the throw – the use of the whole body all the way to the ground as an active component of the exercise. All three are useful, and the coach must decide which to emphasize for the needs of each athlete.

Consider another example: a cyclist and the squat. A cyclist's knee is never flexed beyond 90 degrees, so if specificity is considered only in terms of knee flexion, the conclusion would be that squatting above parallel is specific to cycling performance, and that full squats are not. This, in fact, is what many coaches and trainers believe and advise their athletes to do, in more sports than cycling. This is misguided. The problem here is a misunderstanding of the exercise and its relationship to the sport skill: a partial squat does not produce a strong hamstring contraction. Any cyclist who does partial squats is not developing balanced strength around the knee and is neglecting the muscles used in the hip-extension aspect of a properly executed pedaling cycle. In cycling jargon, the trainee will be developing only the ability to "pedal in squares," the mark of a beginner and of mechanical inefficiency, when she should be developing the ability to pedal in circles, the mark of a skillful, strong rider. So although the partial squat may superficially look more specific, in anatomical action and in the quality of muscular function and development the more generalized full squat is more applicable to the activity. The addition of leg curls to the program is not the answer; correct analysis of the squat is.

In a novice, the need for specificity in training is low, since the trainee is far away from his genetic potential for performance. A novice is untrained, and may be accustomed to little or no activity. For a trainee at this stage, any type of training that improves fitness will improve performance. In contrast, an elite athlete must be trained with a high degree of specificity. This trainee is very close to genetic potential in fitness, conditioning, and strength, and is at the elite levels of the sport. *Practice* that contributes directly to maintaining expertise in the sport activity is required but is insufficient in and of itself (fig. 3-3). It is very important to understand that absolute specificity – doing only the sport activity – is not adequate for the vast majority of the athletic population. For everybody except a tiny fraction of the genetically gifted (who quite unfortunately come to represent the norm to the general public), performance *skill* is developed by repeatedly *practicing* the sport activity, but higher-level expression of that skill requires the improvement of other physical parameters that are best affected by *training*. Training should never reach 100% specificity, as this does not allow for varying the nature of training stress in order to continually drive adaptation.

In the clean and jerk, for example, simple performance of the exercise will at some point fail to drive adaptation. Once maximal technical performance has been well established, repetition of the maximum will fail to satisfactorily disrupt homeostasis. This is because at maximal weights, several factors contribute to the lack of progress – technique, psychological factors, power, and strength. Of these, the easiest to affect with other exercises is strength. For this reason, less specific exercises that allow for overloads are necessary even in elite trainees who require the highest level of training specificity. General strength exercises such as the squat, heavy pulls of various types, presses, and overhead support work provide overload, yet are sufficiently specific to the force production requirements of the clean and jerk to be applicable. The additional strength obtained by increasing the squat and the deadlift thus applies to the execution of the clean and jerk.

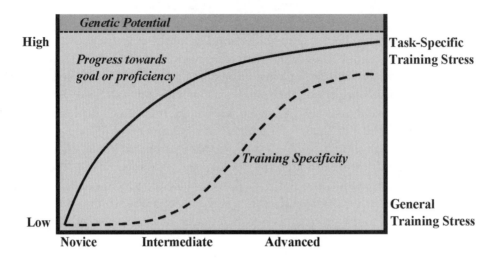

Figure 3-3. Specificity of training as a function of proximity to goal performance in a task. As a trainee comes closer to achieving a performance goal near his genetic potential, the training stimulus must more closely mimic the physical nature of the performance goal. Whereas a novice can make substantial progress with generalized training, an elite trainee must use more specific methods, although absolute specificity is not productive.

"An approximate answer to the right question is worth a great deal more than a precise answer to the wrong question."

— *John Tukey*

4 – The Physiology of Adaptation

Muscular Contraction: The Foundation of Movement

To understand how to train the body for improved performance, you must understand how the performing body actually works. Muscle is the basic physiologic unit of movement. The structure of muscle dictates its function, and training is intended to bring about changes in both structure and function. A familiarity with basic physiologic principles related to muscle and to its training for peak performance is essential for effective program design.

Muscle Structure. The largest structural unit of the muscular system is the muscle itself, which attaches to the skeleton at a minimum of two points by connective tissues called tendons. Individual muscles are separated from each other by a thin sheet of another type of connective tissue called *fascia*. An individual muscle is an organized mass of thousands and thousands of individual muscle cells, also called **muscle fibers**. These cells are arranged in bundles, and separated from other bundles by more connective tissue. The muscle cells that make up the bundles contain hundreds of *myofibrils*, organelles which contain the contractile components. These structures are organized into repeating basic contractile units, the sarcomeres. Sarcomeres are composed of protein strands that interact with each other to produce shortening, or contraction. Muscle cells also contain organelles required for normal metabolic function: cell membranes, cytoplasm (called *sarcoplasm* in muscle cells), nuclei, mitochondria, ribosomes, endoplasmic reticulum, etc., all of which are important contributors to muscle function and all of which also adapt to training.

The myofibrils within a muscle cell have a characteristic striated appearance due to the structural arrangement of each sarcomere. The major contractile proteins, actin and myosin, are aligned in an overlapping thin filament/thick filament pattern (fig. 4-1). There are several other proteins associated with the thin filament, actin. Two of these proteins, troponin and tropomyosin, are major parts of the regulatory mechanism of muscle contraction.

There are several types of muscle fibers. These different types are often generally referred to as "fast-twitch" and "slow-twitch" muscle fibers (fig. 4-2), but this classification scheme does not indicate the actual breadth of difference between the types. A better system of categorizing fiber types is by their primary method of fueling metabolic activity. Table 4-1 illustrates the continuum of fiber types, with a range of anatomic and metabolic properties. These properties dictate how a muscle composed of varying percentages of the different fibers performs and responds to training. Weight training can dramatically change muscle architecture and metabolism, thereby altering function.

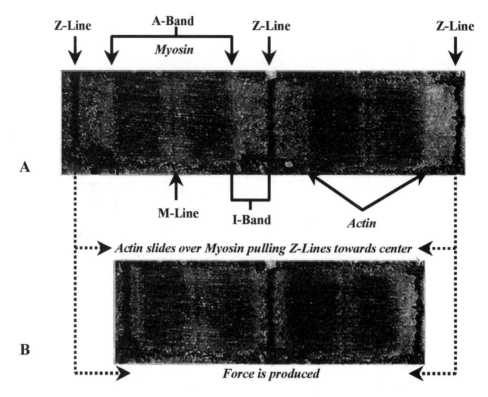

Z-Line   **A-Band**   **Z-Line**   **Z-Line**
Myosin

A

M-Line   **I-Band**   **Actin**

Actin slides over Myosin pulling Z-Lines towards center

B

Force is produced

Figure 4-1. Sarcomeric structure (A). Note the orientation of the contractile elements, actin and myosin. Huxley's sliding filament theory holds that expenditure of ATP will cause actin and myosin to transiently interact with each other in a shortening action that pulls the z-lines at each end of the sarcomere together (B).

Figure 4-2. Type I, sometimes called "slow-twitch" muscle fibers (A, stained black) are chemically, structurally, and functionally distinct from the two categories of type II or "fast-twitch" fibers: fast oxidative fibers (B, stained dark gray) and large, fast glycolytic fibers (C, stained light gray).

Muscle Function. The muscle is composed of several functional units, the largest being the entire muscle itself. When a muscle contracts, it pulls the bones attached at either end toward each other, resulting in movement around the joint between them. Improving this large-scale ability to move is the ultimate goal, and the smaller-scale components of muscle tissue are the elements that must actually adapt to training.

Actin and myosin, proteins of the myofibril (usually referred to as "contractile proteins"), are two of the major players in muscle contraction. When actin and myosin bind to each other, there is a shape change in the myosin molecule that pulls the ends of the myofibrils – and the cells that they are inside of – toward the centerline.

Characteristic	Type I	Type IIA	Type IIB
Contraction speed	Slow	Fast	Very fast
Fiber diameter	Small	Intermediate	Large
Size of motor neuron	Small	Large	Very large
Resistance to fatigue	High	Intermediate	Low
Activity used for	Aerobic	Long anaerobic	Short anaerobic
Force/Power Capacity	Low	High	Very high
Mitochondrial density	High	High	Low
Capillary density	High	Intermediate	Low
Aerobic capacity	High	Intermediate	Low
Anaerobic capacity	Low	Intermediate	High
Major fuel source	Triglycerides	CP, Glycogen	CP, Glycogen

Table 4-1. Muscle fiber types and their properties. While there are other fiber-type classifications in common use, this one applies best to the discussion of adaptation for strength and power.

When adequate numbers of these units interact, enough force is generated to cause the entire muscle to move, producing large-scale movement around a joint. The energy needed to induce the configurational change in myosin comes from adenosine triphosphate (ATP), the high-energy product of a variety of metabolic pathways.

The amount of force a muscle can potentially exert is generally considered to be proportional to its cross-sectional area. This means simply that the bigger the muscle, the more force it can generate. All other factors being equal, the only way to make a stronger muscle is to make a larger muscle, one that contains more contractile protein. But all other factors are seldom equal, and there are several that contribute to effective muscle function. One factor directly related to muscular function is the availability of ATP and the efficiency of the mechanisms by which ATP is utilized and regenerated within the muscle. Low concentrations of ATP or a poor ability to synthesize or utilize it will diminish muscular function, and training induces an increased ability to store and synthesize ATP.

As previously mentioned, there are several types of muscle fibers, each with a characteristic set of metabolic properties that relate to ATP generation and utilization. Type I fibers are described as *slow oxidative*, meaning that they rely primarily on aerobic or oxidative (oxygen-requiring) metabolism and its associated pathways. These fibers are smaller, are capable of generating less force, and have less potential for enlargement than other fiber types. But they are extremely fatigue resistant since they preferentially rely on enzymes that enable the use of an essentially inexhaustible energy substrate: fatty acids. The enzymes that break down fatty acids are dependent on the presence of oxygen for their function; they are thus referred to as oxidative, or aerobic, enzymes.

Type II fibers depend to a greater extent on energy production from carbohydrates than do Type I and display a higher glycolytic activity. Type IIb fibers are termed *fast glycolytic*, meaning that they primarily use the process of glycolysis, by which glucose is broken down to yield ATP, a process that does not require the addition of oxygen. Type IIa fibers are intermediate between Type I and Type IIb.   Their function can be skewed toward either purpose, depending on the training stimulus. Type IIa and IIb are much larger than type I fibers, have higher enlargement potential, metabolize ATP more rapidly, and are less fatigue-resistant. But weight training can change how all of these muscle fiber types behave.

Energy Metabolism: Powering the Muscle

Energy Sources. Muscle contraction, and in fact all intracellular activity, is powered by ATP. It is the very stuff of life. Our bodies produce ATP from the breakdown of food. Everything we eat – carbohydrate, fat, and protein – can serve as a source of ATP. (Fat and protein are less important in power performance energetics, since carbohydrate is selectively utilized for this purpose, when supplied in adequate amounts, by the type IIb muscle fibers which dominate this type of activity.) This indispensable molecule is produced during a series of biochemical events that occur after the breakdown of food in the body. For the purposes of this discussion, ATP is produced in three ways: 1) through the regeneration or recycling of previously-stored ATP by creatine phosphate, 2) through non-oxygen-dependent glucose metabolism (glycolysis), and 3) through oxygen-dependent metabolism that utilizes both fatty acids and the end products of glycolysis (oxidative phosphorylation). Conventionally, the first two mechanisms for ATP production are termed "anaerobic" and the third "aerobic". Each of these distinct pathways provides ATP at different rates and contributes a greater proportion of the required ATP under different circumstances.

Energy Utilization. Stored ATP is always the energy source utilized during muscular contraction. During contraction, ATP loses one of its three phosphate groups and becomes adenosine diphosphate (ADP), liberating energy stored in the molecule and allowing its use in muscle contraction. As ATP reserves are depleted, which takes just a few seconds, ADP is rapidly recycled back into ATP by the transfer of a replacement high-energy phosphate ion from a creatine phosphate (CP) molecule back to the ADP. Creatine phosphate thus serves as a carrier of this replenishing energy for ATP.

ATP utilized and resynthesized by this two-part mechanism powers intense, short-duration exercise (less than 10 to 12 seconds) such as sprinting and weight training. If the exercise is longer than this few seconds worth of stored ATP can cover, the ATP that would normally serve to replace that just used becomes the ATP that now must power the exercise. Sources for these slightly longer efforts are 1) ATP produced through glycolytic metabolism, if the effort lasts up to a couple of minutes, and 2) ATP produced by oxidation of fatty acids and glycolytic products, if the effort is of very long duration. However, all the ATP utilized during muscle contraction comes from this stored ATP pool, and the other processes function to replace it there.

The form of energy stored within the muscle is glycogen, the storage form of glucose, which is made up of long branched chains of glucose molecules stuck together. Intense exercise longer than 12 seconds and up to a few minutes in duration, such as longer sprints and high-repetition weight training, requires the breakdown of glycogen molecules into glucose, a process called glycogenolysis. The resulting individual glucose molecules are further broken down through the processes of glycolytic metabolism. Steps in this process generate ATP, and the ATP produced by glycolysis is available as a fuel for continued intense exercise. In addition to ATP, glycolysis produces pyruvate and lactate as end products. These glucose breakdown products can be further used to produce ATP through oxidative metabolism. Lactate is able to move out of the cell and be taken up for use by other cells as a fuel for oxidative metabolism or, in the liver and kidney, as a precursor to new glucose formation. Under conditions of very high energy demand, lactate levels in the blood rise as release outstrips uptake.

Of lesser importance to individuals who train for strength and power is the production of ATP through oxidative metabolism. Lower-intensity rhythmic repetitive exercises that can be sustained for minutes to hours, like jogging, walking, or distance cycling, depend on the processing of fatty acids and glycolytic end products through the Krebs cycle and then the electron transport chain (ETC). Fatty acids are broken down into acetyl coenzyme A (Acetyl-CoA) through the process of beta-oxidation before entry into the Krebs cycle. Pyruvic and lactic acids also enter this system after they are converted to Acetyl-CoA. Both beta-oxidation and oxidative phosphorylation take place in the organelles known as *mitochondria*. Large amounts of ATP are produced by oxidative metabolism. Oxygen is required for this process.

But since a single set of a weight training exercise takes considerably less than a minute, is very intense, and consumes a lot of ATP, oxidative metabolism is not a factor in this type of training. Even though it does operate (all of the various processes of ATP production are always operating), oxidative metabolism contributes very little to the actual performance of a heavy set, since it transpires over a much longer timeframe and yields ATP more slowly. An overview of basic energetics is presented in figure 4-3.

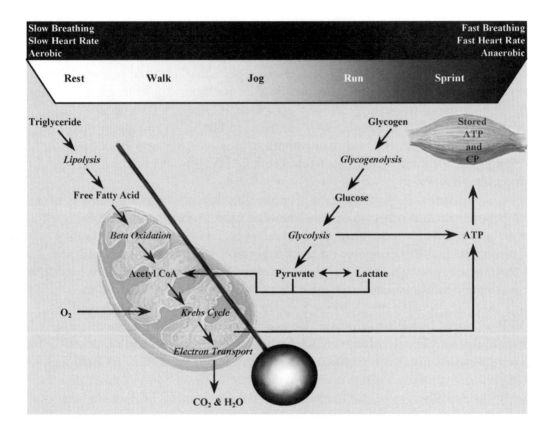

Figure 4-3. The metabolic speedometer. How hard and how long we exercise directly affects which metabolic pathways our bodies primarily use to fuel the activity. All physical activity lies along a continuum, from rest to all-out maximal effort. All activities are powered by the ATP already present in the muscle, and all bioenergetic activity acts to replenish these stores. Low-intensity exercise depends on cardiopulmonary delivery and muscular uptake of oxygen, the ready availability of which enables the body to utilize aerobic pathways and fatty acids as substrates. These aerobic processes take place inside the mitochondria within the muscle cells. As activity levels and energy requirements increase, the ability of oxidative metabolism to meet the increased demand for ATP is exceeded. Weight training and other forms of high-intensity training exist at the anaerobic end of the continuum, utilizing substrate that does not require added O_2. The diagram above represents the relationships between the energy substrates and the metabolic pathways in which they are used in different types of exercise. With the exception of short-duration, all-out maximal effort, no activity uses only one metabolic pathway, so the scale above represents a sliding scale of continually increasing intensity of activity.

There is a huge interest in the supplement creatine monohydrate, so huge that nearly half a billion dollars annually are spent on it by athletes and recreational exercisers. So huge, in fact, that about 50% of all high school football players and about 75% of all strength and power athletes take it routinely for its purported benefits. But the NCAA bans its distribution by affiliated schools and school-associated personnel, and lots of other clinical and consumer protection groups criticize its use and propose that it is both ineffective and unsafe. How can it be both worthy of a ban and ineffective, both biologically useless and unfair to use?

Creatine is a component of the "CP" part of the ATP-CP system discussed in this chapter. It is part of the metabolic machinery that powers short-duration activities such as weight training. It is obtained from meat in the diet, and it is produced in the liver, with about half our daily requirement coming from each source. The daily requirement is determined by body mass; bigger people need to eat more and make more creatine. If we are using 2 grams of creatine a day to support general life processes, we need to consume about 1 gram and our body will make the other gram. The one gram of creatine we need to eat could come from eating two 4-ounce steaks. So providing our bodies with an external source of creatine is a normal human activity. Creatine monohydrate is a stable form of creatine that is manufactured for use as a dietary supplement. It is supplied as a powder, and is suspended in liquid for consumption by stirring it into water or juice. It does not dissolve well in cold liquids, and is not stable for long periods in liquid, so it is best purchased in powder form.

There is more to creatine than simple survival. It is well documented that increasing high-energy phosphate stores in the body improves the ability to produce force. A good analogy is that of a gas tank. Our normal tank is half or 3/4 full. We never really get close to our genetic potential for storage on a daily basis if we are untrained, since we aren't strenuously active and our muscles have no reason to be full. When we start to lift weights or do other power training, our body's stores of creatine increase by about 10 to 20%. Driven by the body's adaptation to new, high-intensity physical demands and facilitated by an increase in food consumption to support the new level of activity, creatine supplies from both internal and external sources increase. Studies have shown that creatine monohydrate supplementation provides a rapidly assimilated source of creatine that optimizes storage beyond the additional 20% driven by exercise and diet, pushing it up to near genetic potential. Our creatine gas tank becomes much fuller.

A huge body of well-controlled research has clearly demonstrated that creatine supplementation is quite effective, with improvements in performance noted in as little as seven days. The real value of creatine supplementation, though, lies not in its short-term performance enhancement but in its ability to assist in recovery between sets and workouts done repeatedly over time. Better recovery as a result of a full creatine tank leads to better quality and quantity of work done during a series of sets and a series of workouts. This leads to better gains in strength and performance. The best research results are always found in longer-duration supplementation studies, precisely because of this.

The second point to consider is safety. Creatine is frequently kicked around in the press by "experts" using individual case studies of diseased individuals who developed further health problems during creatine supplementation, or silly people doing silly things at the same time they were taking creatine. But no study of any duration has demonstrated negative effects of supplementation on healthy athletic populations. A wise man once said, "You can prove anything with one example." The very thing the detractors of creatine supplementation accuse creatine supporters of doing is exactly what the detractors are guilty of: using poorly designed research and faulty logic to make their case. Heed the advice of Nobel laureate Kary Mullis: "It doesn't take a lot of education to check things out. All it takes is access to resources and a minor distrust of everyone else on the planet and a feeling that they may be trying to put something over on you." Go to the library and read the research. Thus enlightened, make your own decision.

Creatine Safety Starting Points

Schilling, B.K., et al. 2001. Creatine supplementation and health variables: A retrospective study. *Medicine and Science in Sports and Exercise* 33(2):183-8.

Waldron, J.E., et al. 2002. Concurrent creatine monohydrate supplementation and resistance training does not affect markers of hepatic function in trained weightlifters. *Journal of Exercise Physiology* 5(1):57-64.

Training-Induced Muscle Adaptations

Weight training elicits numerous changes in both muscle structure and function. If the training program is well planned and the exercises are correctly performed, exercise-induced changes can be beneficial and enhance fitness and performance. If workouts are poorly planned and/or incorrectly performed, gains may be slow or absent, or performance may actually decay. Figure 4-4 illustrates the continuum of responses to different organizations of training programs with respect to reps per set.

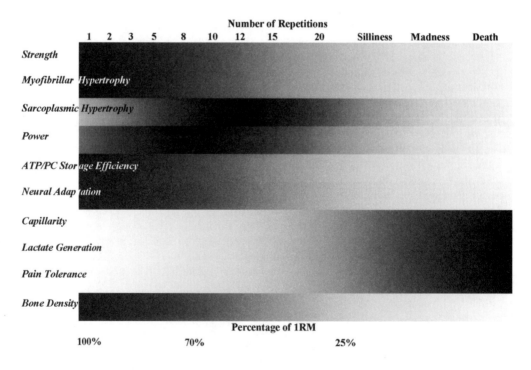

Figure 4-4. The repetition continuum. Different repetition schemes result in different anatomical and physiological adaptations. The program chosen should match the goals of the trainee. Black = great effect, white = little effect. (Rippetoe & Kilgore, 2005)

When it comes to understanding the effects of various repetition schemes in training programs, there is a difference of opinion between those who rely on practical experience and those who have only the academic interpretation of limited research to go on. Several academic sources have proposed that, in essence, all repetition schemes will result in the same gains in strength, power, mass, and endurance – that is, that doing a set at 3RM will yield the same result as doing a set at 20RM. This is in stark, obvious contrast to the observations of practitioners familiar with training athletes for strength, power and mass, and performance. It ignores the basic tenets of metabolic specificity, the same principles that are eagerly applied to endurance training. A 40-meter sprint is a much different race than an 800-meter event. Running a mile is different from running 26.2 miles. Training for these events requires some degree of specificity, and no one would suggest that all running yields the same result. Why would anyone with even a passing interest in the training of athletes suggest that a 3RM squat, which takes a few seconds and exists entirely within the ATP/CP end of the metabolic spectrum, yields the same training result as a set at 20RM that takes 60-120 seconds and exists squarely within the glycolytic middle of the spectrum? There is good quality research that supports the validity of the repetition continuum presented in figure 4-4 and provides for a thorough understanding of the physiologic basis for the concept. That data has the added benefit of more than a century of recorded practical application to back it up. The failure to correctly apply this information results in wasted training time and ineffectively designed programs.

One of the results most closely associated with weight training is an increase in muscle size. This phenomenon, **hypertrophy,** is the result of increased protein synthesis and decreased protein degradation, which leads to an increased accumulation of proteins within the muscle cell and a resulting increase in the size of the whole muscle. There are two basic types of hypertrophy. In **myofibrillar hypertrophy**, more actin, myosin, and other associated proteins are added to those already existing in the cell. More contractile elements within the cell mean more actin/myosin interactions and more force production. This type of hypertrophy is typical of low-repetition, high-intensity training. It adds less mass but produces greater increases in the force generated per unit area of muscle than the second type of hypertrophy, **sarcoplasmic hypertrophy**. In sarcoplasmic hypertrophy there are more cytoplasmic and metabolic substrate accumulations than in myofibrillar hypertrophy. Lower-intensity, high-volume training produces a significant addition of myofibrillar elements but less than that added by high-intensity, lower-volume work.

Bodybuilding-type training utilizes very high-volume repetition and set configurations that cause an increase in metabolic substrate stores in the muscle. The addition of glycogen and high-energy phosphates to the cell causes additional water to be stored. This effect, combined with minor accumulations of fat droplets, enzymes relevant to the additional activity, and a moderate increase in contractile proteins, causes the cell volume to increase. However, since this type of hypertrophy lacks a significant force-production component, it explains why some individuals with smaller muscle mass are stronger than individuals with much more extensive muscular development derived from bodybuilding training.

Concentrations of the enzymes responsible for driving ATP production also increase as a consequence of training. Several researchers in the 1970s independently demonstrated increases in the concentrations of enzymes responsible for catalyzing all three of the ATP pathways discussed earlier. Of primary interest is the finding that concentrations of enzymes driving the resynthesis of ATP from ADP and creatine phosphate, as well as those responsible for glycolytic metabolism, can be increased with weight training. The degree of increase in enzyme concentrations is related to the duration, frequency, and intensity of training. Programs that elicit increased enzyme concentrations enhance performance through more efficient production and utilization of ATP.

Energy stores within the cell also increase in response to weight training. ATP and CP reserves increase by about 20% after a prolonged (multi-month) training program, resulting in more energy immediately available for contraction. Larger stores of ATP and CP correlate with improved power output. Glycogen stores are also increased as a result of prolonged training, which both increases the amount of rapidly available energy and also contributes to muscle hypertrophy.

Measures of contractile properties, such as power output, absolute strength, and rate of force production are obviously improved by training. These changes are likely related to the effects weight training has on the fiber composition of muscle, since the rate of ATP utilization differs according to fiber type. In decades past, changes in muscle fiber types were thought not to occur, but more recent research has shown that shifts in fiber type do in fact occur in response to various types of exercise. Furthermore, even in the absence of a fiber type change, fibers with slow-twitch contractile properties can assume more fast-twitch properties following strength training. Resistance training of four to six weeks in duration has been shown to reduce the number of muscle fibers classified as slow-twitch. This trend away from fibers suited for endurance activity may potentially affect increases in contractile performance. It is also interesting to note that the intramuscular concentrations of ATP and CP are related to the fiber composition of a muscle; if ATP and CP are depleted in the muscle for long durations, there will be a switch from fast-twitch contractile properties to slow-twitch properties. It is also likely that the elevated ATP/CP stores associated with heavy weight training may drive this relationship in the other direction, toward fast-twitch characteristics.

Neural Integration: Stimulating the Muscle to Move

Structure and Function. While the muscle fiber is the basic unit of contraction, without its intricate link to the nervous system, coordinated movement could not occur. The central nervous system is linked to muscle fibers by way of motor neurons. These neurons vary in size and innervate varying numbers of muscle fibers depending on fiber-type and muscle function. Slow-twitch fibers are innervated by smaller motor neurons. Fast-twitch fibers are innervated by larger motor neurons. In terms of speed and magnitude of conduction, think of the motor neurons for type I fibers as drinking straws and those of type II fibers as fire hoses.

The number of fibers innervated by a single neuron depends on the muscle and its function. Large muscles responsible for large-scale movements, such as the rectus femoris muscle of the thigh, have a low ratio of motor neurons to fibers, with a single motor neuron innervating a large number of fibers, up to one neuron for as many as 1000 fibers (1:1000). Muscles responsible for fine motor activity, such as certain eye muscles, may have a high ratio of neurons to fibers, nearing 1:10. The term **motor unit** is used to describe a motor neuron and all of the fibers it innervates, and the term **neuromuscular system** describes the functional integrated whole of the body's nerves and muscles. The motor unit is the basic functional unit of the neuromuscular system, since muscle fibers fire only within motor units and never individually. Heavy, high-velocity training over time improves recruitment, defined as the quantity of motor units in the muscle actually generating force during contraction. A higher percentage of recruited motor units means more force and more power. Average novice trainees can recruit around 70% of their available motor units on the day they start training. Intermediates have increased their neuromuscular ability to recruit motor units and generate force, and by the time they become advanced trainees they may be able to recruit in excess of 95% of the available motor units. Neuromuscular improvement is one of the main reasons strength and power can be gained in the absence of muscle-mass increases, although hypertrophy normally accompanies a strength increase.

The number of fibers innervated by a motor neuron dictates the maximum amount of force the motor unit can produce during contraction. The more fibers contained in the motor unit, the higher the force production. An active motor neuron stimulates all the fibers it innervates to contract. The amount of force a

---

There has been and continues to be debate between various factions of the exercise science community regarding how muscle hypertrophy actually occurs, whether through "cell hypertrophy," the enlargement of individual cells, or through "cell hyperplasia," an increase in cell numbers. In reality, there should be no debate, since the works of Phil Gollnick and Ben Timson clearly demonstrate that cell hypertrophy is responsible for muscle hypertrophy.

Hyperplasia, either through fiber splitting or cell division, is inconsequential and occurs in only one situation. There is a population of undifferentiated stem cells immediately adjacent to the outer cell membrane of the muscle that are referred to as "satellite cells." Weight training can induce microruptures of the muscle cell membrane (not necessarily a bad thing), which then stimulates any satellite cells at the site of the microrupture to differentiate into tiny new muscle cells in an effort to repair the damage and assist in adaptation to the stress that caused the microrupture. These little mononucleate cells start to produce sarcoplasm and myofibrillar proteins as they assume their new identity as muscle cells. This constitutes an alternative version of hyperplasia. But this process is responsible for no more than 5% of muscular hypertrophy, and then only transiently, as the newly differentiated satellite cells quickly fuse with existing muscle cells for zero net increase in cell numbers at the completion of the hypertrophic process.

muscle generates will vary with the number of motor units recruited. If all the motor units in a muscle are recruited simultaneously – an event that occurs only as a result of a planned 1RM in training – maximal force is generated.

Motor units are recruited in a specific order, according to each one's threshold of stimulus required for the contraction to occur. Lower-threshold slow-twitch motor units are recruited initially regardless of the intensity of the exercise. These motor units are associated with the maintenance of normal posture, and as such they fire most of the time the body is upright. Walking increases low-threshold motor unit recruitment, since posture is being maintained while the body propels itself forward. The muscles associated with posture and walking therefore would be expected to have proportionately higher percentages of slow-twitch fibers, and they do. During low-intensity aerobic-type exercise, slow-twitch motor units are preferentially recruited, but as intensity increases higher-threshold fast-twitch motor units get called into contraction. Low-threshold fibers continue to be recruited at high intensities but their contribution is negligible relative to the contribution of the high-threshold fibers. If high power output is the objective of the training program, it must be designed to improve the ability to recruit high-threshold fast-twitch motor units.

It is often noted in novice trainees that strength gains are larger than would be expected as a result of muscle size gains alone. An individual becomes more efficient in neuromuscular function by improving both technical competence and motor unit recruitment. As expertise increases, strength and power gains become more directly related to gains in muscle mass than to neural function, since muscular growth can occur long after technical and neural improvement plateaus. Nevertheless, whether for novices or for elite athletes, a primary training objective should be more complete, coordinated, and effective recruitment of motor units in the working muscle. Neuromuscular efficiency is the easiest, fastest way for improvement to occur, and well-designed training programs optimize its development.

Hormones: Mediators of Physiologic Adaptation

Hormones are compounds produced by glands, and they are integral regulators of the vast majority of the physiological functions in individual cells, the organs, and the body as a whole. Hormones are secreted into the entire body systemically, and their specific function is produced in the tissues that contain receptor sites sensitive to those particular hormones. Each hormone system is capable of responding to external stress, since the body uses these systems to cope with stress and to facilitate adaptation to future stress exposure. As such, hormone systems are an integral part of the mechanisms by which the processes in Selye's theory of adaptation operate. Each hormone has a characteristic effect or effects on specific target tissues (table 4-2). Muscle magazines are filled with ads and articles about hormones and how to manipulate them through exercise, diet, and supplementation to get bigger and stronger, huge and muscular, more massive and powerful. As you might imagine, not all of these ads are exactly accurate.

Hormone Function. Hormones affect physiologic events in two basic ways. First, hormones can change the rate of synthesis of specific substances. Examples of this are an increase in contractile protein synthesis or increased enzyme production. Second, hormones change the permeability of cell membranes. Membranes are selective barriers, allowing certain molecules to pass into the cell while keeping other molecules out. Hormone-induced changes in permeability affect cellular function in many ways, all of them important, since substances outside the cell are usually necessary for the modification of the environment inside the cell.

Training program composition (frequency of workouts, duration of workouts, exercises, sets, repetitions, and rest periods) affects hormone production in the body. Effective program design capitalizes on the body's innate hormonal response to these changes.

Hormonal Adaptations. There has been considerable research in the area of hormone-specific exercise physiology. While exercise in general affects numerous hormone systems, a few hormones have a direct effect on muscle structure and function as they relate to weight training.

Hormone	Function and Characteristics
Testosterone	Promotes muscle growth and development of male sex characteristics; anabolic; increases metabolic rate.
Cortisol	Increases in times of stress; catabolic; associated with decreased performance.
Growth Hormone	Develops and enlarges all tissue types; increases protein synthesis.
Insulin	Drives glucose transport into cells; anabolic.
Glucagon	Drives movement of glucose into blood; catabolic.
Insulin-like Growth Factor I	Mediates growth factor action; anabolic.
Epinephrine	Mobilizes glycogen; increases muscle blood flow; increases cardiac contractility.

Table 4-2. Hormones of specific interest to training.

Testosterone. This hormone has been the center of much scientific and popular attention for many years as its role in **anabolism** – protein synthesis and tissue growth – is well known. It is also associated with bone growth, metabolic rate, glycogen reserves, red blood cell production, and mineral balance. Elevated levels have a beneficial effect, but there is limited experimental evidence that exercise or training of any type elicits increased testosterone production.

Researchers have produced many studies of high-intensity, short-duration exercise such as weight training which show increases, decreases, or often no changes, in testosterone levels over the course of an exercise bout. The inconsistency and lack of clear pattern between these studies may be due to the relatively complex nature of resistance training. Protocols used have varied widely in the volume, intensity, load, rest intervals and total muscle mass involved in the exercises. Each of these factors interacts with the others to influence the nature of the exercise stress and thus the response that is produced. Study design and its interpretation are further complicated by the circadian fluctuations of testosterone which may make changes more difficult to elicit and observe, especially where few time points were selected for analysis.

Although the acute effects of each training session on testosterone levels remains obscure, the cumulative effects of multiple sessions is more clear. Resting levels of testosterone can be significantly reduced following multiple sessions over longer periods (one to eight weeks) of sufficiently high-intensity or high-volume training. Testosterone levels recover to previous baseline or greater levels (that is, they supercompensate) after the training load is reduced to an appropriate level for an adequate period of time. While this reduction of testosterone levels may seem counterproductive on its face, it is an important result of training, part of the process that produces the adaptation to the training. Training programs designed to produce a disruption of normal testosterone levels followed by its recovery have been successfully used to improve performance in advanced athletes (see discussion of testosterone-cortisol ratio below).

Cortisol. In contrast to testosterone, the net effects of cortisol may be more negative than positive for the athlete. The role of cortisol in normal physiology is catabolic – it acts as an anti-inflammatory by dismantling damaged tissues and ushering them in the direction of the excretory pathways, thus making room for the synthesis of new tissue. But when excessive stress (both physical and non-physical) is applied to the body, cortisol production goes up, often in excess of the levels associated with normal anabolic/catabolic balance. In fact, excessive cortisol levels are one of the main influences and contributors to metabolic and structural fatigue after training. Normal cortisol secretion promotes protein degradation and the conversion of proteins into carbohydrates, and conserves glucose by promoting fat utilization. At higher levels it inhibits protein synthesis, promotes hyperglycemia, depresses immune function, produces perceptions of fatigue, and is probably one of the mechanisms that produce the symptoms of clinical depression often associated with severe overtraining. As a catabolic hormone it counters the effects of the anabolic hormones testosterone, growth hormone, and insulin-like growth factor. It would be beneficial for the hard-training athlete to maintain lower concentrations of cortisol. It has been shown that cortisol levels increase with normal training and with any external stress, including the mechanisms that hamper recovery, such as inadequate diet, lack of sleep, and psychological and emotional stress. Resting cortisol levels are significantly increased after long periods of high-volume or high-intensity training, but they return to baseline with adequate recovery, rest, and nutrition.

Cortisol response is also trainable. After a bout of maximal exercise a novice may experience a much greater than 100% increase in blood cortisol levels, whereas maximal exercise in an elite trainee may induce as little as a 20% increase. The novice's cortisol response is more acute on both ends – it comes up higher and goes back down quickly, whereas a more advanced trainee has both a more blunted increase and a slower decrease in cortisol levels. As we progress through the training stages, novice to elite, this is one of the ways it becomes incrementally more difficult to disrupt homeostasis. Proper programming, progressive or periodized, is organized so that it disrupts homeostasis and increases cortisol levels but then facilitates a reduction in resting cortisol levels. This requires that adequate recovery be incorporated as an integral part of the program.

Testosterone-Cortisol Ratio. The relative amounts of testosterone and cortisol may be a more important and practical measure of training stress and recovery than either hormone alone. The ratio of testosterone to cortisol provides a glimpse of the general hormonal balance and removes the complication of accounting for the circadian fluctuations in the systemic levels of each hormone. Although we know that we benefit from higher circulating levels of the anabolic hormone testosterone and lower levels of the catabolic hormone cortisol – a high testosterone/cortisol – it is the depression of this ratio in the body that marks a significant training stress. Data from much research in advanced athletes suggests that a short series of workouts can initially reduce testosterone/cortisol productively. This occurs as testosterone levels decrease while cortisol levels rise. A change in testosterone/cortisol of less than 10% indicates that stress inadequate to force adaptation has occurred; on the other hand, levels that are chronically depressed by 30% or more are associated with overtraining. The goal of programming, in terms of testosterone/cortisol, is to train hard enough to initially reduce its value by more than 10% but not more than 30%, and then provide appropriate loading and recovery to re-attain and then exceed the previous baseline value. The application of this observation to novice and intermediate athletes is unclear, but we suggest that the basic mechanism is in operation there as well, varying only in magnitude, but nonetheless still the probable mechanism. Supercompensation is strongly associated with strength and performance gain, and this concept will be explored further in association with advanced training programming in chapter 8.

Changes in testosterone/cortisol in response to training stimulus are predictable and intensity dependent. Futher, it is likely that these systems adapt predictably to long-term-training, and that these adaptations are both intensity- and volume-dependent. It is also apparent that the recovery of hormonal status after a workout or series of workouts is strongly associated with improved performance. Understanding that both short-term responses and long-term adaptations in hormone levels relate to Selye's theory and the two-factor model – since they are an essential component of the comprehensive recovery processes discussed in chapter 2 – can help us design effective training programs.

Growth Hormone. Human growth hormone is a peptide hormone that has numerous physiologic effects: it increases bone growth, cartilage growth, cell reproduction, and protein deposition in the cells. It stimulates the immune system, promotes gluconeogenesis in the liver, and drives metabolism toward fat utilization. Studies have demonstrated that weight training induces an increase in circulating growth hormone. Concentrations change little during the first few sets of a whole-body workout composed of large-scale multi-joint exercises but increase about twelve sets into the workout. Concentrations peak about 30 minutes after the workout then return to normal approximately an hour and a half later. This data comes from an experiment using a forty-minute workout, and it is possible that longer workouts may elicit a larger or more prolonged growth hormone response. Isolation exercises targeting only one segment of the body are probably ineffective in altering growth hormone levels. The effect of shorter duration higher intensity whole-body workouts has yet to be investigated.

Insulin. A highly anabolic hormone, insulin regulates the permeability of cell membranes and facilitates the transport of glucose and other substances into the cell. This function is crucial for recovery from training, since depleted glucose and amino acids must be replaced so that comprehensive recovery processes can occur. Animal research has demonstrated that hypertrophy can proceed in the absence of insulin, so other mechanisms are also at work, but insulin remains one of the most potent, abundant, and easily manipulated anabolic hormones.

Insulin-Like Growth Factor. IGF-1 is a peptide hormone similar to insulin in configuration. Insulin-Like Growth Factor-1 has a strong anabolic effect in both children and adults. It is secreted by the liver in response to growth hormone, and low levels of GH as well as inadequate protein and calorie intake can inhibit its release. It affects almost every cell in the body, and is a potent regulator of cell growth. Production of this hormone has been linked to weight training in a few studies, but this finding has not been consistently demonstrated.

One study has shown that bathing isolated muscle cells with IGF-1 in a Petri dish induces hypertrophy, but there is no good data showing that IGF-1 can be easily and favorably manipulated with training. It has been observed that IGF-1 is found in milk, possibly contributing to milk's reputation as a growth food for heavy training.

Epinephrine/norepinephrine. These catecholamines have widespread effects all across human physiology as both neurotransmitters and hormones, and are largely responsible for the "flight-or-fight" response familiar to all humans. Epinephrine (EPI or adrenaline) and norepinephrine (NE or noradrenaline) acting as endocrine hormones are produced in the adrenal glands located on top of the kidneys and are secreted directly into the bloodstream. NE is the dominant neurotransmitter released at sympathetic nerve endings. Among many other things, the combined effects of direct sympathetic nervous system stimulation and EPI/NE released into the blood cause an increase in the amount of blood the heart pumps each minute and promotes the breakdown of glycogen. During intense bouts of training, epinephrine concentrations can increase a dozen times over. This may help the body cope with the rapid onset of exercise both by quickly increasing blood supply to the working muscle and by helping provide a rapid energy source (glycogen→glucose→ATP). This response is transient, with exercise-induced increases returning to normal within six minutes of the cessation of exercise.

The bottom line for the athlete is that the body reacts to the stress of training with a specific sequence of hormonal responses. These responses derive from the body's general stress-response/adaptation mechanisms, as predicted by Selye's theory. If the coach designs an appropriate training program and the athlete adheres to it and gets adequate rest and good nutrition, the body will respond – largely through hormonal mechanisms – optimally to training, and improved performance will be the result. Coaches can attempt to employ training methods that induce and capitalize on short-term hormonal responses and long-term hormone-mediated adaptations. However, with very few exceptions, coaches are forced to approach this task by the seat of the pants, as it were. Blood tests are not widely available or useful to the average coach; he must rely on his own observations of his athletes and correlate those observations with the signs and symptoms of what he knows to be the effects of desirable and undesirable hormone responses. Essentially, a coach must make an educated guess as to how to tailor the training program to induce the necessary hormonal changes required to drive improved performance. Later chapters will present some programming models that have been shown to induce productive changes in testosterone and cortisol, probably the two most important hormones relevant to strength training.

Cardiovascular Considerations

When a heavy weight is lifted, several events occur that stress the cardiovascular system. One of the first is that the contracting muscles compress the blood vessels and thus increase their resistance to blood flow. This increase in resistance causes a dramatic increase in blood pressure. There are reports of blood pressure increases as high as two to four times their normal values. These pressures place a tremendous load on the heart, which has to pump harder to compensate and to continue to deliver blood not just to the compressed working muscle but to all areas of the body.

After long-term weight training, the heart adapts to this stress by increasing the thickness of the muscular wall of the left ventricle (fig. 4-5). The increase in heart muscle mass enables the heart to deliver blood efficiently in spite of temporary blood pressure increases during exercise.

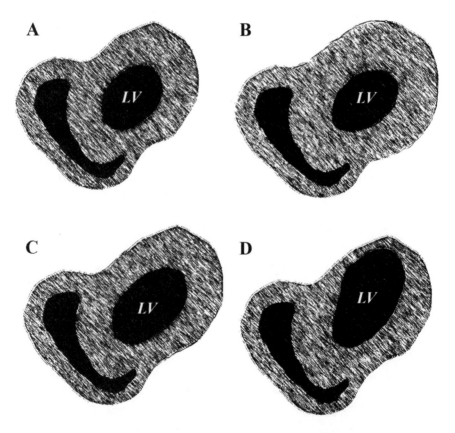

A

B

C

D

Figure 4-5. There are a number of different types of cardiac hypertrophy. The normal, unadapted heart has a "normal" left ventricular (LV) chamber size and muscle wall thickness (A). Long-term resistance training increases the thickness of the muscle walls without significantly changing chamber size (B). Long-term endurance training increases chamber size without increasing muscle wall thickness (C). Pathological hypertrophy results in increased chamber size and reduced muscle wall thickness (D).

Requirements for Cardiorespiratory Fitness. An issue of importance to the strength or power athlete is cardiorespiratory fitness, sometimes confused with aerobic fitness or endurance. Aerobic/endurance fitness relates directly to the efficiency of oxidative metabolism and is not the same as cardiorespiratory fitness – the capacity to efficiently deliver oxygenated blood to working muscles. Specifically, aerobic fitness – the oxidative mechanisms of ATP generation adapted for prolonged, low-intensity exercise – does not contribute to power performance, either directly or indirectly. Exercise scientists trained in academic programs where aerobic exercise is the focus will usually say that aerobic training is necessary for all athletes. Exercise scientists trained in programs where anaerobic exercise is the focus will argue against that point vehemently, as studies have shown that aerobic training actually interferes with maximal strength and power gains.

These arguments should be evaluated with four things in mind. First, cardiorespiratory fitness is primarily a health issue, and competitive athletes do not normally fall within the population that needs to be concerned about heart attack prevention. (The fact is that elite competitive athletes are not concerned about their health; they are concerned about winning.) Individuals with below-average levels of cardiorespiratory fitness are in fact at a higher risk for developing high blood pressure and cardiovascular disease, both of which are certainly detrimental to health and performance. Competitive athletics has already selected against these individuals. People for whom aerobic training addresses a problem that does not exist would be better served by devoting the time to skill acquisition, more complete recovery, or a hobby.

Second, although a degree of cardiorespiratory fitness is needed to more efficiently recover from sets or workouts, supply needed oxygen and nutrients to the working muscle, and carry away waste products fast enough for adequate recovery, a VO_2 max only 2-3 ml/kg/min above normal is adequate for accomplishing this task in strength and power athletes. This is not a tremendous improvement in cardiorespiratory fitness above normal level. In fact, anaerobic training alone, over time, develops aerobic fitness to just above average levels and therefore negates the argument for including aerobic training in power athletes' programs. Limited early-season aerobic work would be sufficient to solve any endurance problems that might be encountered. If power athletes stay in the weight room year-round, there will be no real need for long slow distance work outside the weight room.

Third, even if an increase in VO_2 max were desired, long slow distance-type endurance training is not as efficient a way to obtain it as a more intense approach to training. A concentrated dose of high-intensity glycolytic-type work lasting several minutes, utilizing exercises that incorporate a full range of motion for a large amount of muscle mass, which putatively produces significant O_2 desaturation, has been shown, in practice, to drive improvement in VO_2 max better than low-intensity long slow distance exercise that produces no oxygen desaturation at all. Small scale pilot data from our laboratory has shown that 4 consecutive weeks of multi-modal exercise that elicits depression of blood oxygen saturation to 91% or below, when performed 5 days per week improved VO_2 max by 33.4%. In is interesting to note that in our experiment the longest bout of training was 21 minutes in duration, the shortest was 8 minutes. The popularity of CrossFit and its use of "metabolic conditioning" has demonstrated the value and practicality of developing significantly greater endurance capacity without actually doing traditional forms of endurance exercise.

Finally, research regarding the use of endurance training for strength and power athletes rather strongly suggests that endurance work interferes with all the parameters such athletes are concerned with developing. The most recent research into interference deals with the tendency of aerobic training to reduce the magnitude of anaerobic improvement when the two are done together or in close sequence. And this research does not consider what happens to existing power performance. It has been well known since the 1980s that a program of endurance training will cause large reductions in vertical jump height. For athletes whose sport requires a mix of anaerobic and aerobic/endurance training, studies suggest that separating the two by as little as an hour blunts the negative effect of the endurance workout. The studies, and practical experience, indicate that aerobic training may be included at low volumes and intensities if desired by the athlete or coach, but the question remains as to whether it contributes to effective training and time management. Many athletes have for decades excelled in their sports in spite of the inclusion of endurance training, not because of it.

Research examining aerobic-anaerobic interference typically looks at the effects of long slow distance-type training on strength performance. It is quite likely that the interference between the two occurs due to differences in the nature of the activities and the metabolic pathways involved. We suggest not only that high-intensity glycolytic exercise drives improvements in VO_2max, but that this type of training can be used alongside weight training programs without significantly reducing strength gains.

The distinction between cardiorespiratory fitness and aerobic training is particularly important. Anyone who has ever done a 20RM set of deadlifts knows that there is a cardiorespiratory component to the work. The depression in O_2 saturation produced by this high level of glycolytic intensity is much more disruptive to the homeostasis of oxygen transport and utilization than traditional low-intensity types of aerobic ("cardio") training. This is probably what drives both the moderate improvement in VO_2max seen in traditional weight training programs and the high degree of improvement associated with high-intensity glycolytic exercise.

Genetic Potential

"Genetics" is a term bandied about fairly loosely in sports. A good definition of genetic potential is whether the athlete possesses the active genotype necessary to excel in sport. In simpler terms, does the athlete have a suitable set of genes, and enough of them turned on, to be good in the sport of choice?

There are at least 78 genes associated with fitness and performance. While humans all swim in the same genetic pool, there is a huge amount of variation in both the genes possessed and the genes actively expressed. These variations lead to differences in performance potential. And so, like it or not, here is the rule: DNA → RNA → protein → function. The reality is that genetic potential ultimately affects the performance of every individual.

As an example of how a specific gene may affect performance, consider the ACTN3 gene, a little segment of DNA that ultimately codes for the production of alpha-actinin, a structural protein in the z-line of the sarcomere (see figure 4-1 above). Studies have shown that possession of specific variants of this gene was strongly associated with elite sprint performance. Three variants of this gene have been identified; RR, RX, and XX. Possession of a specific *actn3* profile is strongly associated with either an elite power or an elite endurance performance. In elite sprinters (up to the Olympic level), 50% of the ACTN3 variants present were RR, 45% were RX, and 5% were XX. Elite endurance athletes were markedly different, with only 31% RR, 45% RX, and 24% XX. In light of this data, the RR variant was termed the "sprint" variant and the XX the "endurance" variant. It seems clear that the possession of the two different variants in significantly different ratios is associated with different performance capacities. A vast number of genes code for functional or metabolic proteins that can exert the same type of effect.

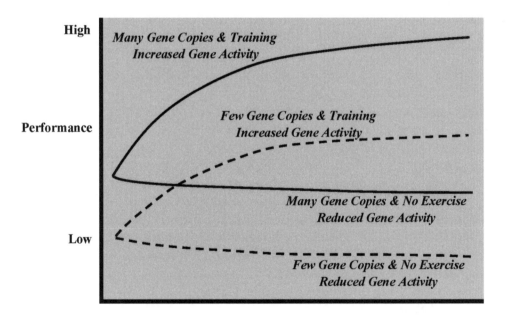

Training Years

Figure 4-6. The effect of gene redundancy on performance potential. Note that an individual with fewer gene copies (dashed lines) will have a lower potential for strength gain that in individual with more copies (solid lines). Failure to train leads to less gene activity and reduced performance.

Occasionally an athlete possesses an excellent genetic profile, is highly motivated to succeed, responds well to training, and improves beyond expectations. These are the exceptions, those rare individuals that can make an average coach look exceptional. But most coaches and trainers must deal with all types of athletes, genetically gifted or not. Athletes cannot change genetic profile unless they are willing to enter into the moral and ethical quagmire of gene doping (inserting exogenous genes into a human to improve performance. It is sad to say that, at the time of this writing, it has been suggested that there was at least one genetically enhanced human competing in the Olympics in 2004, a number that is expected to increase dramatically in future Olympiads.) Only coaches who work at the highest levels of sports have the luxury of working with many gifted athletes. Most coaches must learn to deal with the average athlete, since they will make up the bulk of any normal team or clientele, and must relish the rare opportunities presented by the occasional genetic freak.

Genetic redundancy is a useful feature of our biology. Within every human's genome there are multiple copies of many genes. These duplications function as backup in the event of damage or malfunction. Even though we have multiple copies of genes, not all of them are active at any given time; many or most of the copies are inactive or suppressed. In times of need, the genes can be expressed through various biological processes and can allow for large-scale production of important end products which then affect performance (fig. 4-6). If we stress the body appropriately, we can turn on the specific set of genes that would drive the adaptation to that stress. For example, if a trainee has a number of dormant ACTN3 RR genes, we may be able to use high-intensity, low-volume training to activate those genes while not activating the additional associated ACTN3 XX (endurance) gene variants. This preferential activation will help power athletes attain their fullest performance potential without the clutter of unnecessary aerobic adaptation. Alternatively, an endurance athlete could be preferentially trained with higher-volume, lower-intensity work to activate the ACTN3 XX variant copies they possess in order to make a better aerobic athlete.

The take-home point is that, while coaches cannot alter an individual's "genetic potential," they can program appropriately to capitalize on each trainee's genetic profile, *if* that potential is recognized. An athlete who is genetically favored will progress faster and ultimately reach higher levels of performance if the nature of his potential is correctly identified and trained for. Everyone responds to training in much the same way, through the same mechanisms; only the rate of progression and the magnitude of the result will vary. This is why it is possible to define useful generalizations about training and coaching. But it also means that individualized training is necessary and that you must know your athletes – their strengths, their weaknesses, and the nature of their genetic potential.

Although an individual with only a few copies of a gene such as ACTN3 may not reach the same level of performance as someone with multiple copies of a specific variant, appropriate programming can still produce impressive results. Frequently, individuals with great genetic potential fail to train appropriately, since success has always come easily. A lack of work ethic is sometimes the result of exceptional genetics, and cockiness occasionally allows a genetically gifted athlete who trains inappropriately to be beaten by a less gifted athlete who is receiving proper coaching and programming.

As is often the case, sports preparation can shed light on the human condition. Humans are built to move. We evolved under conditions that required daily intense physical activity, and that hard-earned genotype is still ours today. The modern sedentary lifestyle leads to the inactivation of the genes related to fitness and performance, attributes that were once critical for survival and are still critical for the correct, healthy expression of the genotype. The genes are still there, they just aren't doing anything because the body is not stressed enough to cause a physiological adaptation requiring their activation. Heart, lungs, muscles, bones, nerves and brain all operate far below the level at which they evolved to function, and at which they still function best. Those among us who are sedentary suffer the consequences.

Going Backward: Detraining

When an athlete stops training for a substantial period of time, there will be a regression in strength levels. Although strength is a much more persistent adaptation than endurance (strength declines much more slowly than VO_2 max does), a trainee's ability to generate force can be reduced within a few weeks time and can drop at a rate of about 15% a year depending on individual circumstances. This loss of fitness is perfectly consistent with what we know about the stress-response/adaptation response. In this case, the stressor is a lack of activity, and the corresponding adaptation is detraining.

If an athlete stops training for a period of a few months and restarts training again, he should start back one level below where he was when he stopped. For example, an intermediate trainee who stopped for 6 months would re-start using a novice's program. He would continue using this program until his previous levels of strength were regained, and then move to a program consistent with where he was before he quit training. This process will occur much faster than the first time, due to a group of phenomena collectively referred to as "muscle memory." A combination of persistent neuromuscular adaptation and increased numbers of muscle cell nuclei make the rebuilding process proceed quickly. The replacement of the layoff-depleted glycogen stores and cytoplasmic volume are the main reasons muscle size returns as quickly as it does. In other words, the presence of all the metabolic machinery originally built during previous training and a diminished but quickly replaceable level of the substrate that makes it work are the factors that make regaining previously acquired muscle size and function and fitness occur in a fraction of the time it originally took.

A longer training hiatus requires a different approach. If an advanced or elite trainee "retires," and then a year or two later decides to once again start training and competing, it would be best to begin with a version of a novice program, rather than reducing just one level to an intermediate program. This athlete has regressed far enough away from genetic potential that a short period of simple progression will be useful for reestablishing fitness. After the gains from simple linear progression begin to plateau, the athlete would follow an intermediate program for the short time it would be useful, and then, when improvement plateaus or when the coach judges him ready, he would adopt an advanced training organization again. This entire process might take anywhere from 3 months to a year, depending on the athlete, the sport, and the length of the layoff, but in any case, the process would take a fraction of the time originally invested in the progress from baseline.

It is very important to understand that previously trained athletes returning from layoffs – even relatively short layoffs – must be handled with care. Ambition is useful; greed is dangerous. Athletes with even an intermediate training history have developed a neuromuscular system that is far more efficient that that of an untrained individual; this athlete can still recruit a high percentage of his available motor units, although they are not in shape to be used very hard. This athletic neuromuscular system enables the muscles to generate more force than they are currently conditioned to produce. In practical terms, this means that these trainees are going to be very, very sore, unless marked restraint is used for the first few workouts. The athlete or coach ignores this fact at peril. Extreme cases of soreness, to the point of loss of function, disability, or even rhabdomyolysis (the breakdown of muscle caused by mechanical, physical, or chemical injury that can lead to acute renal failure due to the accumulation of muscle breakdown products in the blood) can and certainly do occur. So coaches and trainees need to resist the urge to push to the limit when returning to training after a layoff. During simple progression we are redeveloping the mechanical and metabolic adaptations within the muscle to match the neural abilities that have persisted over the period of detraining. Patience here is a priceless virtue.

An interesting phenomenon has been noticed in the training of cyclists in the weight room. High-level cyclists, especially good time-trial riders and track cyclists, who have no previous barbell training experience are nonetheless very strong and tend to be able to squat relatively heavy weights even though untrained in the exercise. This presents immediate, potentially serious problems to both coaches and athletes who are not aware of the need to practice restraint.

Cycling lacks a significant eccentric component – a "negative" movement. An eccentric contraction, one in which the muscle lengthens under a load, occurs in most slow barbell movements, since lowering the weight is an integral part of most exercises (this is not necessarily true of the Olympic lifts, which modern equipment allows to be done in a concentric-only fashion: with bumper plates and platforms, we can now drop our snatches, cleans, and jerks without tearing up the weight room). Cycling has no equivalent loading pattern, since a correct pedal stroke either pushes down or pulls up. Never is the pedal resisted eccentrically. So the eccentric phase of the contraction, and the ability of the muscle to lengthen under load, remains untrained. Add to this the fact that cycling utilizes a limited range of motion, one that never approaches the extent of that used in a full squat. A cyclist very well may be strong enough concentrically to come up from the bottom of a deep squat, even without ever having lowered a weight that far. He is therefore in the position of being quite capable of pushing a weight that is relatively heavy for an untrained lifter up from the bottom of the squat while at the same time being completely unadapted to carrying it down.

It is widely recognized that the eccentric phase of a resistance exercise is the part of the movement that produces the majority of the soreness associated with training. A cyclist is unadapted to eccentric contraction but able to generate high concentric force. Extreme care must therefore be used when training these athletes, lest they be crippled by soreness from squatting weights they appear to handle easily. Coaches should recognize the need for light workouts at first, and although this may lead motivated cyclists to become frustrated with the seeming ineffectiveness of the barbell program, it is necessary. These problems may also be the reason many cyclists fail to stick with weight training as part of their sports preparation: the choice between extreme unaccustomed muscle soreness or what is perceived as slow progress on an ineffective and irrelevant exercise is often one that competitive road cyclists refuse to make.

"The radical of one century is the conservative of the next.
The radical invents the views. When he has worn them out,
the conservative adopts them."

— Mark Twain

5 - Training Program Basics

Strength training programs may vary considerably depending on the sport, the goal, the athlete, and the coach. But all strength training is based on the use of a few basic tools. These have been developed over the past hundred or so years out of the experiences of millions of smart folks who paid attention to what worked and what didn't while they were getting strong.

Repetitions

Organized training programs are based on the concept of the "repetition maximum" (RM or max) or personal record (PR). This is the maximum weight that an individual can lift for a specific number of repetitions:

1RM = maximum weight that can be lifted one time

10RM = maximum weight that can be lifted ten times in a single set

All RM tests that are lighter than a 1RM are, by definition, done with a submaximal weight, since a 1RM defines maximal. A 5RM will be done with a weight that is 85 to 90% of the 1RM, and is thus submaximal. It is very heavy relatively – the maximum that can be done for 5 reps – but it is still submaximal to 1RM.

There is no single repetition scheme that is appropriate for achieving all training goals (fig. 5-1). The number of reps per set is important because **different numbers of reps produce different types of adaptations**. This is an extremely important principle of exercise programming, and it often goes unappreciated by those without a background in the subject. Strength, a basic objective of training and an important component of power performance, is gained using lower repetitions (1 to 3) with heavier weights (90 to 100% of 1RM). Muscular hypertrophy is produced by using higher reps (8 to 12 or more) at lighter weights (65 to 80% of 1RM). Power, the combination of speed and strength, is developed by using moderate numbers of reps (3 to 5) performed at maximal velocity with loads between 50 and 80% of 1RM. The speed component of power is developed when each individual repetition is performed at maximum velocity. The load range of 50 to 75% of 1RM allows most people to develop maximum power in each rep. This weight is heavy enough that a high amount of force must be used to accelerate it, but light enough that the velocity is sufficiently high for power production. Power training of this type also increases strength at heavier weights by teaching the neuromuscular system to recruit high-threshold motor units more efficiently. When heavy weights are used, this improved ability to "explode" is useful even at the slower velocities of 1 to 5 RM sets.

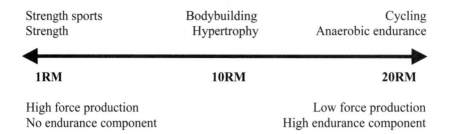

Figure 5-1. The repetition continuum. Different numbers of reps have different training effects, and it is important to match the correct reps to the goal of the trainee (Rippetoe & Kilgore, 2005).

In power sports that involve lengthy competition periods (football, basketball, etc.), endurance represents the ability to produce many consecutive bursts of anaerobic effort, as opposed to the more conventional understanding of the term "endurance" to mean long durations and low intensities. This type of anaerobic endurance is dependent on strength, and for the already-strong athlete is best produced by increasing the number of low-rep sets, rather than by increasing the number of reps per set, since this more closely duplicates the metabolic demands of the sport. An approach would be to condition with multiple short sprints, perhaps 40 reps of 20 meters, as opposed to doing longer distances for fewer reps.

Although endurance is usually associated with aerobic exercise, it is important to understand that there are different types of endurance. Aerobic endurance for long slow distance is one example, but endurance can mean several things. Local muscular endurance – the ability to tolerate the pain that develops in the muscles during intense efforts lasting 30 seconds to several minutes – can be very effectively improved through weight training. High-rep sets are used for this purpose. And by increasing the absolute strength of an endurance athlete, it is possible to quite effectively increase the time to fatigue by reducing the relative effort required for each submaximal contraction. High reps, in excess of 15, can be used effectively for such athletes to increase pain tolerance and the ability to contract while fatigued, and sets of 5 can be used on alternating workout days to increase absolute strength. Even though neither of these rep schemes directly improves any aspect of oxidative metabolism, both do in fact improve aerobic endurance performance.

Sets of more than 15 to 20 reps will significantly improve muscular endurance, but will not produce large strength gains due to the lighter weights necessarily involved, and this is certainly not optimal for any athlete with the primary goal of improving either power or strength. Athletes for whom power must be produced repeatedly for extended periods must still be trained to produce power in the first place, and high-rep sets do not accomplish this. The advantage of using multiple low-rep sets is that both power and strength are trained in the precise metabolic context in which they will be used in competition.

Sets

Most national exercise and credentialing organizations recommend 1 to 3 sets (groups of repetitions) per exercise, irrespective of the fitness goal. This is generally acceptable in that it works better than no exercise at all and therefore improvements will occur for those people who have never exercised before, but results will be better if the number of sets is actually designed to produce a specific result and achieve a definite training objective. Doing one set at 8 to 12 RM will yield about 80% of the potential gains from training in the 8-to-12-rep range. This may be enough to achieve the fitness goal of a typical health club member, or it may be adequate for assistance exercises after the actual barbell workout. It is inadequate for athletes trying to improve strength and power.

As with other aspects of training, the number of sets must produce the metabolic effect desired as an adaptation. One set of an exercise is not capable of producing the stress that multiple sets can produce, because stress is cumulative. If one set is all the work that is necessary to force an adaptation, then the athlete has not been training either very long or correctly, because an athlete's ability to adapt to training stress is itself one of the aspects of physiology that adapts. As an athlete progresses through the stages of advancement, more stress is required to disrupt homeostasis. One set of an exercise – no matter how hard, or long, or heavy – is not enough stress to cause an adaptation in an already adapted athlete. As an athlete progresses past the novice stage, his adaptive capacity becomes advanced to the point where stress must be accumulated, not just with multiple sets during one workout but over several workouts, and training complexity must accommodate this fact. This will require programming more complicated than one-set-to-failure, one set of twenty, or other types of single-set training organizations that might work well for some novices or in bodybuilding and physique activities.

Multiple sets are required to make the best use of a trainee's gym time. Basic exercises that are critical for enhancing sport performance should be done for multiple sets. Depending on the trainee's level of advancement, this could be as few as 3 to 5 sets for novices or as many as a dozen sets for the elite athlete. Numbers of sets, as mentioned above, can accumulate for an emphasis on endurance for sports that involve long periods of time under competitive stress, such as football or boxing. Lighter-percentage sets can be done under controlled rest intervals to simulate the metabolic stress of the sport for a very effective preparatory tool. The possibilities are limitless, depending only on your ingenuity in creating the metabolic conditions necessary for further, specific adaptation.

When referring to the number of sets, a distinction must be made between **warm-up sets**, the lighter preparatory work that readies the trainee for heavier work, and work sets, which accomplish the training objective for that workout. Warm-up sets prepare the tissue and the motor pathway for the coming work. As such, they should not fatigue or interfere with the work sets; their purpose is to facilitate the work sets, not function as work themselves. When properly planned, warm-up sets need not be counted as work, since they will always be light enough that in the absence of the subsequent work sets no adaptation would result from their having been done.

Work sets are the heavy sets that produce the training effect of the workout; they constitute the stress that causes the adaptation. They may be progressive – they may go up five or ten pounds per set until they are all done – or they may be done "across," with the same weight for all sets. Progressive sets are a good way to explore an athlete's capabilities with a load if uncertainty exists about his ability with it. For instance, coming back from a missed week, an injury, or an illness might indicate the need for small progressive jumps at work-set intensity. Sets of 5-rep squats at 285, 295, 305, 315, and 325 are an example of progressive sets for an athlete otherwise capable of $315 \times 5 \times 5$ (5 sets of 5 reps each, all done with 315 pounds on the bar), which is an example of sets across. Sets across is a marvelous way to accumulate total set volume of high quality, since the weight chosen is repeated for all the work sets, producing higher average load at the limit of the trainee's ability.

Rest Between Sets

The time between sets is an important variable in workout configuration. Several exercise organizations recommend 30 seconds to 2 minutes between sets. This also varies with the goal of the training program. If strength gains are the primary training objective, rests of greater than 2 minutes are not only okay but necessary. While partial recovery from anaerobic exercise is rapid (50% of ATP/CP stores recover in 3 to 5 seconds), complete recovery doesn't occur for three to seven minutes, depending on several individual factors such as the intensity of the set, the fatigue and nutritional status of the lifter, as well as the trainee's age, the temperature of the facility, and injury status. Competitive strength and power athletes are often instructed to use rests of much greater than two minutes. In contrast, if muscle hypertrophy is the only concern, rests of 45 seconds or less are best. There seems to be a link (although not necessarily a causal relationship) between lactic acid production from resistance exercise, hormonal status, and increases in muscle mass. Between-set rests of about 45 seconds would be optimal in maintaining this relationship. If a training regimen is undertaken to increase muscular endurance, very little, if any, rest should be taken between the sets of different exercises.

It is also important to consider which sets the rest occurs between. Warm-up sets function as preparation for work sets, and they should be approached with this in mind. The lightest warm-ups will not be heavy enough to produce any fatigue, and no rest need be taken longer than the time it takes to load the bar for the next set. As they get progressively heavier, more time should be spent between warm-up sets. As a rule, warm-ups facilitate work sets; they should not interfere with them. If three heavy sets across are to be done after warm-up, 15 warm-up sets done as fast as possible up to 5 pounds away from the work set would be inappropriate, since the fatigue of inappropriate warm-up would interfere with the work-set intensity.

Workout Frequency

The American College of Sports Medicine (ACSM) prescribes training two days per week for improving "muscular fitness." Many exercise organizations propose a three day per week schedule, yet the vast majority of elite weightlifters train six days per week, with multiple workouts per day. Why such a discrepancy? First, the ACSM's guidelines are minimal recommendations for the sedentary, completely unadapted-to-exercise general American public, not for athletes who have been training for years. Second, textbook recommendations often fail to account for individual differences in ability, level of training advancement, training objective, and all other parameters that may influence the ability to recover from more frequent training. Finally, elite athletes are highly adapted to training and can not only tolerate, but in fact require, much higher training loads than novice or intermediate trainees to sufficiently disrupt homeostasis and facilitate further adaptation. This level of training stress cannot be administered in three sessions per week without overwhelming the athlete's recovery ability; it must be distributed more uniformly over the week. This will require many more than three workouts per week and possibly multiple daily workouts for some athletes. These specific details are addressed in subsequent chapters.

Careful selection of the exercises included in a series of workouts can enable the trainee to recover more efficiently and therefore perform more work per week. Basic guidelines are a good starting point, but every trainee is different. Table 5-1 offers some basic guidelines regarding workout frequency. Experimentation with various workout frequencies is the best way to determine each trainee's capacity and optimal workout frequency.

Level of ability	Novice: fewer workouts Advanced: more workouts
Level of fitness	Poor: fewer workouts Excellent: more workouts
Desired level of achievement	Lower: fewer workouts Higher: more workouts
Individual time constraints	Does the athlete have the time available to do the workouts?
Motivation	Does the athlete have the necessary motivation to stick with a really tough program?
Bodyweight	Smaller trainees seem to recover from intense workouts more efficiently than larger athletes.

Table 5-1. Factors involved in determining the number of workouts to include in a training program.

Too few workouts per week will not adequately stress the body, and no positive adaptation will occur. A common way to organize training among recreational lifters and bodybuilders is a "split" routine, where one body part or "muscle group" is worked each day, until the entire body has accumulated a workout. If "chest" is trained only once a week, even though training may occur several days per week, "chest" will not receive enough work to constitute overload, and optimal adaptation cannot occur. By the same token, "chest" will usually include triceps, since the bench press is the favorite chest exercise; if "shoulders" involves pressing, "arms" get their own day too, and "back" really means lats and therefore lat pulldowns or chins, it is possible to expose the triceps to four or more workouts in a week. This is an example of poor training organization producing a schedule that includes both inadequate and excessive exercise frequency.

It is also worthwhile to note that the incidence of training injury is not significantly increased with greater strength training frequency. However, it is quite high with more than five aerobic workout days per week, particularly monostructural (single-activity) workouts. These kinds of aerobic exercise programs involve thousands of identical and repetitive movements over a short range of motion, and are thus inherently different from weight training, even when weight training workout frequency is very high. The end result is a higher incidence of repetitive use injuries in endurance training than in strength training.

Exercise Selection

The combinations of exercises included in a workout and in a long-term training program directly affect progress. The most important consideration is to select exercises that have functional application to the training objective. The exercises included should develop the muscle mass, strength, or power of the athlete in ways that apply to the sport or event he is training for. They should produce strength and power in ways relevant to performance, using the muscle groups involved in the sport in ways that are metabolically relevant. It is not necessary, or even desirable, that exercises exactly mimic or duplicate the skills or movement patterns of the sport. It *is* necessary, though, that exercises adequately prepare the neuromuscular system for the range of motion, power requirements, strength requirements, and endurance requirements of the sport. Specific sport skills are acquired in sport *practice;* fitness for sport is enhanced by appropriate strength and power *training* outside of sport practice. And the whole panoply of athletic performance characteristics can be enhanced by "general physical preparation," or GPP, the practice of general movement skills which may not be specific to the sport but which enhances its performance nonetheless. Sprints, jumping, gymnastics skills work, rope climbing, and intense recreational sports unrelated to the primary sport are examples of productive GPP.

Virtually every single effective exercise program for sports performance will include the following rather short list of weight room exercises: squat, press, deadlift, bench press, clean or power clean, jerk, snatch or power snatch, and chin-ups or pull-ups. These movements and their simple variations can be used in various ways to satisfy all the requirements for exercises that contribute to performance. It is imperative that their performance and correct use be mastered by both athlete and coach.

The next consideration in exercise selection is how many times per week an exercise, or type of exercise, should be done. To make exercise selection more logical, it is best to consider specific groups of related exercises. For an Olympic weightlifter, there would be four basic groups: 1) snatch-related, 2) clean-related, 3) jerk-related, and 4) squats and deadlifts. An athlete in a less specialized sport concerned with strength and power might use three categories: 1) squats and squat variants, 2) pressing and pressing variants, and 3) pulling, which includes deadlifts, cleans, and snatches. The example here for a weightlifter can also be used as a basic template for power sports, such as field events. Football players would use the less-specialized template, since there is a significant strength component in addition to the power demands of the sport. There is a great degree of possible variability within each of these templates. For weightlifters on a three-workouts-per-week schedule, two workouts might be devoted to more technically demanding snatch-related exercises and one day to clean- and jerk-related exercises, and then the emphasis could be reversed the following week, with two clean and jerk workouts and one snatch workout. Squats and pulling strength movements would be included in workouts on all three days, since athletes need strong hips and legs. Football players should also squat all three days, and could alternate bench presses with presses and deadlifts with cleans.

Note that this represents a whole-body workout every time, the preferred approach to training. It is not productive for athletes to think in terms of body parts or muscle groups, as bodybuilders do. The human body functions as a system – in both sports and life – with all its component parts operating together in coordinated synergy. It makes no sense to separate it into its constituent components for training when the desired result of the training is the improvement of the whole system. It does not function that way, and it cannot be effectively trained that way.

Workouts should consist of three to five exercises, appropriately selected from the template groups. Athletes seldom need more exercises than this, but if circumstances warrant, say, six exercises, it may be more effective to do them in two workouts per day rather than all in a single session. Few coaches and athletes are afforded the luxury of unlimited time in the gym, so if six exercises are required and they must be done in one workout, try to do them efficiently.

Workouts should not consist of ten to fifteen exercises. If they do, there are two possibilities. They could be composed of too many core exercises, like squats, cleans, snatches, deadlifts, and chins, along with benches and presses, and will produce overtraining. Or they are composed of ten different isolation movements like leg extensions, leg curls, three kinds of dumbbell curls, two kinds of dumbbell flyes, and two kinds of calf raises, and are a waste of time. Three to five correctly chosen and performed exercises are all an athlete needs, and should be able to do, in one workout. Any energy left over for arm exercises means energy *not* used where it should have been, and is typically a sign of an unfocused athlete or a badly designed program.

Exercise Variation

It is normal to vary the individual exercises and total number of exercises included in a training program at several levels: the individual workout, the training cycle, and according to the advancement of the trainee (fig. 5-2). For the novice, effective workouts are short, basic, intense, and progressive. Exercises are chosen to accomplish the program's specified goal in the most efficient manner possible. This means large-scale, multi-joint exercises involving large muscle masses working in a coordinated manner. It therefore requires that coaches be effective teachers of movement skills and that athletes become better at learning them. Among other things, novices are developing motor skills that will allow them to handle a larger variety of exercises later in their training careers. As they proceed from the novice

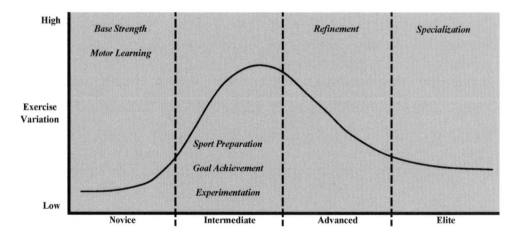

Figure 5-2. The selection and total number of exercises used in a training program varies by advancement level and the goal of training. Initially the beginner has few exercise skills and the primary purpose is to teach basic technique and develop basic strength, so only a few exercises are included. As the trainee develops strength and motor control with free weights, additional exercises can be added. The intermediate trainee benefits from a wider variety of exercises to reach his sports preparation objectives. The advanced trainee will have already selected a sport and is a competitive athlete. This allows the coach to narrow the exercise selection to those exercises most relevant to the sport. The elite athlete is an accomplished expert, competing at a high level, and uses only those exercises that have proven to be necessary and useful for continued performance at that level.

stage to the intermediate stage, the number of exercises in the program increases. This is because they have gained strength and motor skill and can now tolerate and directly benefit from a wider variety of exercises.

During the late novice and the intermediate stage, an athlete who will ultimately proceed to advanced or elite levels defines the course of his career, choosing a sport to train for and compete in. Many decisions are required of the athlete at this point. Strengths and weaknesses, abilities and interests, time and financial restrictions, and the support of family and friends are gauged. This involves experimentation with training and its application to the chosen sport, and it requires a greater variety of exercises than a novice either needs or can tolerate. An intermediate's skills are developing as fast as his strength, power, and recovery ability. It is at this time, when the ability to learn is peaking, that an athlete benefits most from exposure to new movement patterns and new types of stress. For these reasons, exercise variety for intermediates is higher than for novices.

It is also higher than for advanced athletes, who already know the things an intermediate is learning and who have by definition developed in their competitive careers into specialists at one sport. These athletes use fewer exercises, because they know exactly which ones are relevant to competitive success and know how to manipulate their well-developed stress/adaptation mechanisms. Elite athletes are accomplished competitors, experts in their sport, and are well into their careers. They have developed highly individual training programs that might involve only four or five exercises but that very specifically develop critical aspects of their already highly-adapted muscular, neuromuscular, and psychological abilities.

Variation in exercises improves the stress/adaptation response to training, thereby delaying the inevitable performance plateau as long as possible. Essentially, the purpose of exercise variation is to make the body treat each workout as if it were a new stimulus, so that further adaptation can occur. From a psychological perspective, it also reduces the boredom that can accompany monotonous workouts and further stimulates progress by keeping motivation levels higher. Motivated trainees tend to push harder, contributing to the quality of the stimulus on the stress/adaptation system.

Exercise selection must be based on a thorough understanding of both the benefits and limitations of the exercises and the requirements of the sport for which they are being used. A few basic principles should be kept in mind whenever designing weight training programs for sports. First, the exercise must fit the sport biomechanically. The vast majority of sports that use weight training as a conditioning tool rely on the coordinated effort of all the muscles in the body as they generate force against the ground and apply that force through the upper body; effective weight training exercises for these sports should do the same. Large-scale structural exercises – squats, presses, cleans, deadlifts, bench presses, and snatches – provide the best quality, biomechanically applicable work for sports that require strength, power, balance, and agility. Exercises that attempt to divide the body into segments for separate training are much less effective, since it is the coordinated use of all the segments working together that produces the sport-specific movement. Whole-body exercises have been shown to produce superior results, through their ability to train the system as a coordinated whole as well as their capacity to perturb homeostasis and affect the entire hormonal milieu.

The second principle for programming weight training for sports is that the exercise must benefit the sport metabolically. If the sport requires brief, explosive bouts of high power generated by the whole body, the chosen exercises must be capable of producing this adaptation. If the sport requires pulses of explosion for several seconds repeated over a longer period of time, the exercises must challenge the depth of the ATP-CP system's ability to provide for this. If the sport demands muscular endurance at intensities near anaerobic threshold for extended periods, the exercise must be capable of producing this stress in a controllable, programmable way. All these requirements are predicated on the athlete's strength, which must be adequate to the task before more elaborate preparations are necessary.

Meeting the demands of sports with this degree of specificity involves more than just matching sets and reps to the expected loads; the exercises themselves must be capable of producing these specific qualities of the expected stress in ways that fit the mechanical requirements of the sport. It is not enough to do 50-rep sets of leg extensions if hill climbing on a bicycle is to be prepared for correctly, since more muscles than the quads are involved in the sport. Heavy preacher curls do not prepare a defensive lineman for the job of moving a guard and making a tackle, since the biceps are probably the least important muscle group in the kinetic chain that accomplishes the job.

Third, the exercise must be workable within the context of the program – the time and equipment available, the skill levels and maturity of the trainees, and the ability of the coach to teach and administer the program. A $10,000 barbell-based weight room in the hands of an experienced coach is infinitely superior to a $300,000 collection of exercise machines run by an inexperienced trainer. Every situation is different and few are ideal, but at a minimum the program should include as much barbell time as possible, and the complete absence of machines should not be considered a drawback to the success of the program.

Adding variation to the program is accomplished within the context of function. New exercises should have a purpose other than just being new. For example, for an Olympic lifter, reasonable squat variations might be high-bar (Olympic) squats and front squats. The leg press would not be reasonable because it is not a functional movement – it does not provide either the biomechanical specificity to sports or the capacity to produce the systemic stress necessary to be considered functional. If leg presses are done at all, it should be only as an assistance exercise, not as a variation of the squat, and as such they would occupy a different place in the workout hierarchy.

If an intermediate trainee needs to add another workout – a medium or light day – to his week, or if the decision is made to cut heavy pressing work back to twice per week and substitute a variant for the third day, it might be appropriate to introduce a dumbbell exercise as the variant workout. This is what is meant by "variation," where the quality of the workout remains high due to the careful choice of substitute exercises that accomplish the same purpose as the basic movement but in a slightly different way.

For the novice lifter, each training day of a three-day week should be a heavy day, since this is consistent with linear progression. As intermediate status is achieved, more variation becomes necessary, and light and medium days become part of the week. New exercises should be initially included on light and medium days because the neuromuscular novelty of these exercises will produce beneficial adaptations at lower intensities. This way, a light day of training can produce a significant training stimulus while still allowing for recovery from the preceding heavier workouts.

It is important to note that with any new exercise, the weight that can be used increases quickly, much like the general response seen in a novice trainee. Adaptations in neuromuscular efficiency and motor coordination are responsible for much of this early improvement. After this early progress tapers off, the variant exercise is no longer a variant, and can then join the standard exercises for inclusion on heavy days. In this way the intermediate increases his training repertoire as more exercises accumulate.

Exercise Order

Workouts should be ordered in a way that allows the most important exercises to be done first. "Important" is obviously a relative term, and the most important exercise to a novice is very likely different from that for an advanced athlete. Basic strength for a rank novice is the primary training consideration, and this means that squats should always be done first. Between strength movements that use some or most of the same muscle groups, it is useful to insert exercises that use other muscles so that some measure of recovery can occur. Bench presses or presses are commonly done between squats and deadlifts, so that the best performance can be obtained from both of these lower-body exercises done in the same workout. If power cleans are to be done, they can usually be performed effectively by novices after the short break from squats provided by benches or presses, since these trainees are not yet proficient enough at power cleans that a small amount of fatigue will adversely affect them. Any other assistance work would be done after the structural exercises, if time and energy levels permit, since their inclusion in the workout is not as critical to the basic effects of training.

As the trainee advances, other considerations complicate the scenario. If power becomes a primary training objective, as it will for Olympic lifters and throwers, the emphasis will shift to those exercises and they will be performed first, with squats moving to the end of the workout. As a general rule, the faster the movement, the more precise that movement must be, because of the decreased amount of time during the rep in which position adjustments can be made; and the more precise the movement must be, the more important it is to do it without the interference of fatigue. For intermediate and advanced athletes, snatches, cleans, jerks, and their related movements should be done early in the workout, with slower strength-focused movements done later.

Fatigue decreases the precision with which motor unit recruitment patterns can be managed and has a direct bearing on the skill with which a movement can be executed and practiced. Movements that depend highly on skill of execution – those for which technical components are more limiting than strength level for determining the 1RM – should be done first in the workout, before fatigue has blunted the unimpeded contribution of efficient force production to the movement. A snatch is limited by the ability of the lifter to execute the movement in a technically correct manner more than by the absolute strength of the athlete. But if the athlete's strength is compromised by fatigue, the ability to apply that strength in the correct way will interfere with the technical execution of the lift, since correct technique depends on the ability to deliver maximum power to the bar at the right time in the right position, all of which are affected by the ability to produce maximum force, the very thing that fatigue affects (fig. 5-3).

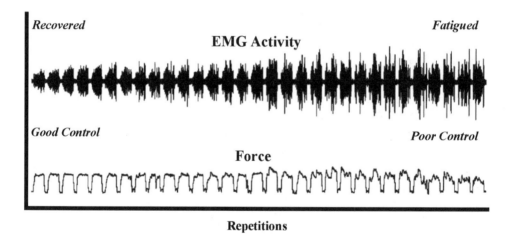

Figure 5-3. Electromyogram (EMG) and force production tracings from a high-rep set. Note that the muscle fatigues as more repetitions are completed and that motor control erodes with fatigue, as evidenced by the amplitude scatter of the EMG tracing. This effect can result from a single set, as presented here, or can be the cumulative result of repeated sets.

Speed of Movement

There is a persistent belief among the public, many personal trainers, some coaches, and even among many exercise scientists, that weight training exercises must be done slowly. The intentional use of slow movement in weight training reflects an inadequate understanding of the nature of efficient power production, the physics of work, and weight-room safety.

A slow cadence increases the time under tension (how long the muscle spends in contraction) and is thereby thought to increase the amount of work the muscles do and the resulting amount of muscular development. An examination of the physiology of power production, though, is enlightening. The vast majority of research demonstrates a clear relationship between high movement speed and the ability to generate power both at that speed and at all slower speeds. Conversely, exercising at a slower speed develops strength only at that speed and does not improve power at faster movement speeds. Complete power development across the whole range of movement speeds requires high-velocity loaded movement.

This is because high power production depends on the recruitment of a maximum number of motor units to generate the high amount of force necessary to produce that power. More power requires an increased efficiency in the number of motor units firing during contraction and – most importantly for the person interested in more muscle – a resulting increase in the actual amount of muscle tissue involved in the work. As more high-threshold motor units are recruited to generate more power through increased force production, more of the muscle fibers in the muscle go to work, using more ATP that must be replaced through active metabolic recovery processes. Studies have found that longer duration repetitions with a longer time under tension actually demand less metabolic work when compared to the fast moving repetitions. This is because only the lower-threshold motor units are recruited and fatigued by lower-movement-speed exercise. It is true that the motor unit fatigue produced during sustained contractions or with higher repetitions (8 to 12 or greater) produces a "burn," a sensation that we may believe to be an indicator of high-quality stimulation. But the fact is that more muscle tissue is recruited and worked by higher-velocity movement than by slow exercise speeds. In the interests of both muscle mass and power training, higher velocity works better.

The commercial emphasis on exercise with machines may be the source of a lot of the misinformation about weight training, due to considerations other than the physiology of exercise. Because of their construction, weight machines generally have limitations in their use, one of which is that if the stack is dropped, the plates may fracture. Over the decades since the invention of weight machines, this limitation has resulted in the dogma that a specific exercise cadence (a count of 2 up and 4 down or something similar) is needed for optimal results from weight training. This also controls the noise level in the spa. Thus, the conventional wisdom developed from the desire of spa management to extend the life of their machines and make for a more placid business environment, not from exercise science or experiential evidence. The practices that benefit health club management are not necessarily the ones that contribute to your increased development and performance.

Safety also gets dragged into discussions of movement velocity, under the assumption that fast is dangerous, as in driving a car. But just as in driving, it really depends on the ability of the operator. The more experienced an athlete becomes with barbell exercises, the more efficiently and safely he can perform them at higher speeds. Squats can be dangerous for novices at high speeds, but for advanced athletes high-speed squats are a very productive power exercise. If technique is correct, all multi-joint exercises can be performed in a way that enhances power production. **Safety is the result of correct technique, at any velocity.** High-speed exercise is necessary if power is to be trained. This obviously means that power training is not inherently dangerous; if it were, the only powerful athletes would be the ones that were born that way. Bad technique is inherently dangerous, whatever the speed or load. Good technique increases safety, and that should be the emphasis in every weight room.

The correct movement velocity of an exercise should be determined by the movement pattern of the exercise and the effect the exercise is intended to produce, not by arbitrary notions of intensity or safety. Many exercises cannot be performed slowly. A slow clean is not a clean; in fact, a clean cannot be performed without an explosion at the top that converts the pull to a catch. On the other hand, some single-joint exercises cannot be performed both quickly and correctly. A barbell curl cannot be performed rapidly through the entire range of motion. In fact, one might argue that the more slowly an exercise must be executed, the less valuable it is for sports training. Also, the closer a weight is to 1RM, the slower it moves; this is true for any exercise, regardless of its nature. A heavy snatch comes off the floor more slowly than a light one, although it will still be faster than a heavy deadlift. Movements that are limited by absolute strength will approach zero velocity in a true 1RM, and will always be slower than a 1RM explosive movement. Many factors affect movement speed, and blanket statements about what is best are seldom useful – except for this one: faster is almost always better.

Warm-up

Warming up is an essential component of training, but it need not be a tremendously creative affair, with lots of arm waving, hopping, wiggling, and calisthenics. Once again, the warm-up should fit the workout, and if weight training is the workout, then the warm-up should prepare the body for weight training. Preparation is both muscular and neuromuscular: it elevates the temperature of the muscles and associated tissues, making them more flexible and less prone to injury, and it improves muscular contractile properties while at the same time allowing the movement pattern to be practiced so that it is familiar, comfortable, and more automatic at work set weights. Begin with a simple five minutes on an exercise bike or rower; other types of aerobic exercises, like treadmill walking or the elliptical trainer, are less desirable since they involve an inadequate range of motion and less muscle mass. Five short minutes with a gradual increase in intensity elevates body temperature and prepares the body to exercise. Then move directly to the first barbell exercise. Do the complete range of motion for that exercise with an empty bar first, for as many sets as necessary to warm the range of motion (this might be as many a five sets for an injured athlete, or a creaky old masters guy). Then increase the weight in even increments for 3 to 5 sets until the trainee is ready to handle the work set weight. After the work sets, repeat the process (without the aerobic part) for every exercise in the workout.

In more experienced trainees, warm-up reps can be tapered down to two or even to a single rep for the last warm-up set, saving gas for the work sets. Novices who need the motor pathway practice should stay with the full number of reps all the way up, until skill level permits the taper.

And it is very important that the athlete understand the proper role of warm-ups: they *prepare* for the work sets; they do not *interfere* with them. If the last warm-up set is too heavy – i.e., too close to the weight of the work set – it will fatigue rather than warm. The warm-up sets are valuable in that they ready the body for the work sets, but they do not themselves make anything stronger. If $295 \times 5 \times 3$ are the bench press work sets, 285×5 is not a good idea for the last warm-up. If 295 is heavy enough to constitute an adaptive load, 285 will reduce the likelihood of succeeding at all 15 reps of work since it is close enough to be tantamount to another heavy set done before. By the same token, if $295 \times 5 \times 3$ will actually go for all 15 reps, 285×5 will not produce a strength increase, because that adaptation has already occurred or 295 would not be feasible.

Flexibility is traditionally defined as having complete range of motion around a joint. It is probably more usefully described as the ability of the muscles that limit motion around a joint to extend beyond their resting length, which affects the range of motion around the joint. Stretching increases flexibility by increasing the ability of the muscles to lengthen, and it should not be thought of as acting on the connective tissue of the joint itself. Stretching has traditionally been included as part of the pre-training, pre-event preparatory ritual. It is thought that stretching before exercise prepares the joints to move through their complete range of motion, thus improving performance and reducing the incidence of injury. A great deal of money has been spent on posters and books dealing with how to stretch effectively, and it is nearly universally accepted among exercise professionals that stretching must precede exercise. But hang on...

An examination of the scientific and medical literature paints a different picture. The majority of the data available indicates that pre-training stretching neither reduces the frequency of injury nor effectively improves flexibility, the two areas in which it is supposed to provide benefit. Studies of marathon participants failed to show a difference in injury rates between athletes who stretched before the race and those who did not. But wait, there's more!

Evidence from studies on vertical jump and broad jump performance indicates that pre-event stretching actually *reduces* power output, and other studies suggest that this is true for other explosive activities, such as weightlifting, as well. This may be due to a reduction in the effectiveness of the stretch-reflex portion of the concentric contraction caused by proprioceptive reset during the stretch.

If pre-training stretching doesn't increase flexibility or reduce injuries, what does? Proper warm-up safely does both. The loaded human body moving through its maximum range of motion actually provides a stretching stimulus for the antagonist muscle groups, the very ones that are tight. (The agonists cause the motion around the joints, while the antagonists resist or decelerate that motion. A lack of extensibility in the antagonists is the usual cause of flexibility problems.) A number of studies have shown an increase in flexibility as a result of complete-range-of-motion weight training. Improvements in hip and knee flexibility on the order of 40% or better are commonly experienced. This is because proper form requires complete range of motion of the involved joints and, if proper position is maintained, the weight puts the body into a properly stretched position at the bottom (or top) of each rep, exposing the antagonists to a stretch stimulus each time the load is moved. This obviously requires good form, and good coaching. Properly done, each weighted rep provides a better stretch than an unweighted traditional stretch, because the complete range of motion is easier to reach with the help of the weight. More importantly, and most especially for the hamstrings, the postural position of the back – the very critical lumbar extension that must be maintained to fully stretch the hamstrings – is best accomplished with a loaded spine, since the load gives the spinal erectors some resistance to contract against to maintain proper lumbar curvature. It is common to see athletes attempt to stretch the hamstrings with a rounded lower back; this cannot be done effectively.

If traditional stretching exercises are desired, they should be done at the end of the workout, when the muscles are warm and the stretch will not interfere with performance. There are several methods of stretching currently practiced, but the only type of stretching really needed, beyond the active flexibility work inherent in full-ROM strength training, is static stretching. Move the joints into a position of mild discomfort and hold the position for 30+ seconds. Repeat 2 to 3 times for maximum benefit. Problem areas – hamstrings often need extra attention from both very young and older lifters – should be stretched after every workout.

But a more critical question might be: how flexible does an athlete need to be? If full range of motion in all the positions encountered during training and performance can be properly expressed under load and during skill execution, the athlete is sufficiently flexible. Training through a full range of motion and the correct practice of sport skills will maintain flexibility, just as they have established it to begin with, and an attempt to further increase flexibility is at best a waste of time.

"Never attempt to teach a pig to sing;
it wastes your time and annoys the pig."

–*Robert A. Heinlein*

6 – The Novice

Programming for the novice is the most important task a coach will encounter, and the most important task an athlete can undertake. Done correctly, it sets the stage for a lifetime of proper training habits, long-term progress, and athletic achievement far above what would be possible without it. Insufficient attention to detail, and to the trainee's response to training during this phase, can cost valuable progress that may not be recoverable later.

In one very important respect training novices is easy: virtually anything that makes a novice work harder than bed rest will produce positive results. As a result, many people have an erroneous impression of the quality of their training system. Single sets, multiple sets, high volume, high intensity, super slow, supersets, giant sets, gnarlmonster sets – quite literally anything resembling a training program will produce better results than no program at all in novice trainees. The ignorance of this simple fact has produced profound confusion among both academics and coaches in the strength and conditioning profession, with many coaches believing that there is only one right way to train all athletes, and many academics believing that research conducted on untrained eighteen-year-old males is relevant to all populations, including athletes.

Most research into weight training has been done on the untrained populations commonly found in college weight training courses – unfit young adults eager to earn bonus points by participating in a study. Unfit and inexperienced people are by definition far removed from their genetic potential for athletic performance. Older adults, middle-aged women, large populations of nurses, active 30-year-old walkers, and any other relatively sedentary population that has never trained with weights for any significant period of time or with any degree of organization – the groups most commonly studied – will be quite distant from their genetic potential for strength and power. The subjects used in these experiments, and all novice trainees for that matter, will exhibit large increases in fitness and performance following a short series of exposures to weight training, *regardless of the nature of that exposure*. The literature provides many, many examples of statistically significant increases in fitness within a very few weeks using virtually any training program. Figure 6-1 illustrates the steep slope of performance improvement for the novice trainee. It is quite easy to produce fitness gains in a beginner.

These studies may be valid for the populations studied, depending upon the training acumen of those designing the study protocol. Quite often, however, even this is not the case, since researchers inexperienced in the weight room sometimes design studies using unrealistic, impractical methods that an experienced coach would consider bizarre. But this is not really the problem. Frequently, the data acquired from these essentially novice populations has been generalized as valid for all training populations, from novice to Olympian, from healthy to diseased, young to old. It would be a gross understatement to characterize this as merely inappropriate. *The results of a study done on a specific population – one with specific characteristics that make it very different from other specific populations – apply only to that specific population.* These results cannot be applied to other populations, because their differing characteristics will change the results. In the same way that a training program must be specific to the sport that it is designed to produce an adaptation for, the program must also be specific for the athlete's level of adaptation.

The very essence of training is the correct application of the stress/adaptation cycle, and the outcome of this cycle is extremely dependent on the physiological characteristics of the individual to whom it is applied. As the characteristics of the individual change, so must the stress, if the adaptation is to continue. Novices eventually become "trained" and thus move to the intermediate, advanced, and possibly elite stages. Diseased populations respond differently depending on their pathologies. The elderly adapt to stress less efficiently; children and adolescents adapt more efficiently, but only to certain stresses; males respond differently from females; motivated athletes progress faster than casual trainees. Specific training organizations are necessary for each population and for each stage of life and of fitness, and the blanket application of one program across all populations is absurd.

Yet we claim above that all novices respond to any stress by adapting – an apparent contradiction. The point is that in an unadapted trainee, any stress serves to cause an adaptation, but a program that makes optimal use of the novice trainee's ability to adapt quickly is better than a program that doesn't. And as the novice trainee becomes more adapted to stress and more closely approaches the limits of genetic potential, the stress must become more and more specific to that individual's level of advancement in order for adaptation to continue.

The Basics of Novice Programming

The result of the universal "novice response" is that there are nearly as many training programs for beginners that produce at least marginal improvement as there are coaches. They all produce results because the beginner adapts to an increased training load quickly, in as little as 24 to 72 hours (fig. 6-2). This means that, as long as the novice training program provides overload at some point, performance improvement will be the result.

This actually means that any programming model fits within the context of Selye's General Adaptation Syndrome theory when applied to novices. Any stress causes an adaptation, because so little adaptation has already taken place.

So what's the fuss? If everyone is right, can't we all just train? Actually, everyone is right, but some are much more right than others. And some are right only accidentally. Being "more right" means basing the training program on the optimal recovery rate of the athlete being trained. To be most effective and efficient at improving fitness for novices, a program must progressively increase training load as rapidly as tolerable so that meaningful results happen in a useful timeframe – and that they can continue beyond the trainee's universal novice response.

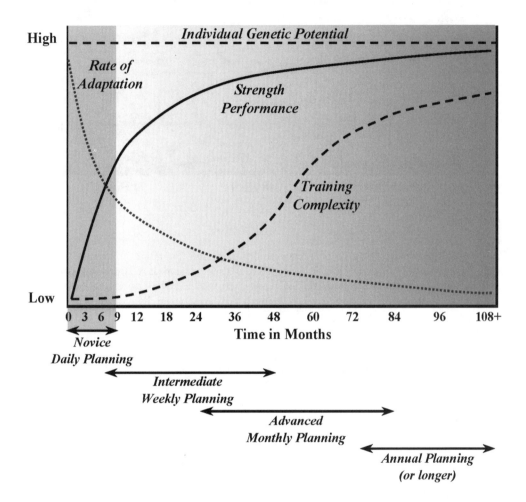

Figure 6-1. The generalized relationship between performance improvement and training complexity relative to time.

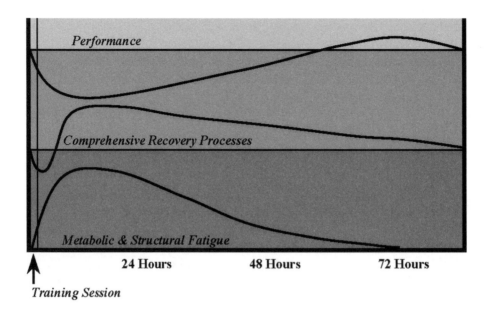

Figure 6-2. The two-factor model of the human responses and adaptations to a single bout of training. During and immediately after training, there is a suppression of comprehensive recovery process (Selye's stage 1). Shortly after training ceases there is a general increase in recovery (Selye's stage 2). An important observation here is that during the period when fatigue has increased as a result of training, there is a negative effect on performance.

Most people arrive at this conclusion intuitively. In gyms all over the world, inexperienced people training by themselves know they can successfully add weight to the exercises they did last time, and most will do so unless told they can't by someone who is supposed to know more than they do. Most individuals enjoy testing themselves with heavier loads or more reps. They derive a sense of pleasure and accomplishment from the improvement, and only become frustrated with exercise when improvement stops. Simple progression is everyone's friend. It works well. It's how weak people can get very strong very fast.

Up to a point. The keys to maximum efficiency in using simple progression are selecting the correct amount to increase the load each time and timing these increases to coincide with recovery from the previous training session. This is where the role of a coach becomes important: applying the discipline of a program to an eager trainee who might otherwise not exercise discipline or the judgment that comes from experience.

Novice trainees adapt to stress more quickly than is usually recognized by the typical strength and conditioning academic or coach. As illustrated in figure 6-2, the best time to train again after the first session would be somewhere between 48 and 72 hours later: train Monday, rest Tuesday, train again at the same time on

Wednesday or Thursday. The goal is to drive adaptation as quickly as possible. In a rank novice, a 48- to 72-hour recovery can generally be expected, meaning that 2 to 3 workouts per week will generate excellent results (fig. 6-3).

All successful, productive training relies on the body's innate ability to adapt to stress. Novice training may very well be the athlete's first exposure to truly hard work done in a planned, logical, progressive manner. This regimented approach to work is not necessarily fun, but the results it produces are something that motivated people find rewarding and encouraging. The desire to test one's limits is harnessed for the first time in a program of this type, where hard work is done in a logical manner to produce a predictable, directable outcome. Athletes' responses to this phase of training – in several different ways – determine their ability to move to the next level.

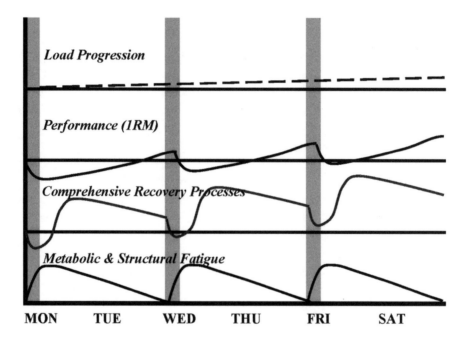

Figure 6-3. A week of simple progression training according to an integrated Selye/two-factor model would look like this.

Novice trainees, by definition, have little or no weight training experience. Having been a member of a health spa, using the machines at the Y, or curling with the plastic-coated weights in the garage doesn't count. Novices lack the motor skills to perform the basic barbell exercises that form the core of the program, and they must learn proper and safe exercise execution. The novice is also unexposed to systemic exercise stress and has not developed the ability to respond to the demands of exercises that cause whole-body adaptation. Since the trainee is both inefficient and unadapted, only a few basic exercises should be used, and they should be repeated frequently to establish the basic motor pathways and basic strength. The squat, deadlift, press, and bench press should be learned first, with the power clean and the power snatch introduced as skill and ability permit. These core strength and power exercises develop the foundation of strength, flexibility, and motor control that will allow for the later inclusion of more demanding exercises, because they utilize all the muscles in the same coordinated fashion that more advanced exercises do.

It may be tempting for individuals who are very fit from other activities to assume that that fitness translates to the barbell exercises. Even fit individuals who have not trained with weights before are novices and their programs should be designed accordingly. More importantly, even people who have trained with weights extensively but who have never followed a program that drives progress in a linear fashion are still novices with respect to their response to linear programming. Progress through the novice stage occurs very rapidly for everyone since an increase in weight every workout generates the fastest possible progress mathematically, and this therefore constitutes the most efficient possible use of training time. But if the trainee is placed immediately into an intermediate program, the rapid initial improvement of the novice will not occur, since the weekly workload increase is slower for the intermediate than the every-workout increase for the novice. The fit trainee can tolerate incremental increases in loading every 24 to 72 hours just like a deconditioned person, and rapid initial progress is the objective of a well-designed program.

There are two important differences for the very fit novice. First, a very fit trainee might be able to make bigger initial incremental increases through the novice phase than a poorly conditioned person. Second, and as a result, the period of time before intermediate-type training programs are necessary will probably be shorter, since the initial progress has occurred more quickly. This is because a very fit person, although unadapted to barbell training, is closer to his genetic potential than a completely unconditioned person and thus has less far to go.

Basic Program Variables

The first goal for the novice should be the development of basic usable whole-body strength. At this stage in a trainee's development, even short-term goals unrelated to getting stronger are irrelevant. Sports performance, general fitness, and improved appearance all depend, first, on the acquisition of basic strength. It is the foundation for all other physical improvement, and it must be the trainee's first concern.

Exercises. The core of the novice program comprises just a few "big" exercises to develop the novice trainee's strength base: the squat, the press, the bench press, and the deadlift. After a few weeks of successful training – or sooner, depending on the aptitude of the athlete – the power clean can be added to the program. Power cleans are considered a core exercise for most sports, but they not are included in a beginner's program until the basic strength and motor skills have developed enough that they can be done with reasonable form. The four basic exercises have been used for many decades by strong men and women to improve basic strength, and no substitute exists for them. Together they form a complete package of loaded movements that stress the whole body in exactly the patterns that get used in sports and in life. It is critical to a program's success that everyone involved learn to perform and coach these exercises correctly.

Once the basic exercises have been mastered, accessory exercises can be added into training. The most valuable assistance movements are those that improve any weaknesses in the basic exercises or otherwise benefit their performance. To the extent possible, they should also be multi-joint, since more muscles involved in an exercise make it both more functional and a better use of training time.

A coach who is responsible for a large number of beginning trainees at one time, such as a PE teacher or a public school sports coach, should consider using only the four basic exercises. The power clean does not lend itself well to some programs due to the limitations imposed by time, experience, and equipment.

The technical demands of the power clean are such that many trainees will require individual attention from a coach experienced in solving the problems encountered in Olympic weightlifting-derived exercises. Sometimes neither the time nor the expertise is available for this. Cleans and snatches are best coached by people who have been trained to do so by competent coaching instructors. Complex multi-joint movements have lots of potential for error, and they are harder to get right than slower lifts because the errors happen faster and are thus harder to observe. Coaches who lack the experience to work with athletes on the clean and snatch serve their charges better by not teaching things wrong. Cleans also tear up the floor in the absence of bumper plates, since heavy cleans will get dropped. This is unavoidable, and if the equipment is not available, power cleans will be a costly exercise to perform.

For these reasons, in certain contexts and for certain coaches, it might be prudent to leave power cleans out of the program and concentrate just on the correct execution of the four basic strength exercises. Focusing on these four exercises without the power clean accomplishes several important things:

- They develop an excellent strength foundation.
- The elimination of the power clean expedites the teaching process.
- Training will be more inclusive, since differences in existing motor skills will not be as significant a factor in learning the slow lifts.
- Time can be managed more effectively.
- Performance-related fitness will still be significantly improved.

Back extensions and their derivative the glute-ham raise are very useful for adding extra work on the spinal erectors and hip extensors, as is the Romanian deadlift, a special version of the stiff-legged deadlift that starts at the hang position rather than at the floor. The classic barbell row is a good builder of back strength when done properly, starting each rep off the floor like a deadlift and finishing each rep touching the abs (they are, however, not a substitute for power cleans). Chin-ups (with hands supine) and pull-ups (prone hands) are the staple upper-body assistance movements, since they work the entire arm and the upper back muscles in a way that closely duplicates the pulling and grasping functions of the arms and hands in sports and work. Chin-ups also build a nice-looking set of arms, since biceps get used more in this version of the movement, thus satisfying the normal male concerns about arm appearance while at the same time being a more useful exercise than curls. Arms should probably be included in the program – a certain amount of "beach work" will get sneaked in anyway, and lots of chins do the job better than any other exercise.

Focused abdominal exercises may be the most important assistance movements to include. The lower back is supported from the anterior by the abs, and ab work, done correctly, protects and assists lumbar stability. "Done correctly" means that the abs are strength-trained, as opposed to endurance-trained with high reps and low resistance. Weighted sit-ups or some version of them, knees-to-elbows from a hanging position on the chin-up bar, and exercises that isometrically load the abdominals in a fashion similar to their normal postural-support function, are preferred over exercises (e.g., crunches) that do not adequately stress the muscles in a way that actually applies to their role as spinal supporters.

Reps and Sets. Figure 5-1 illustrates the continuum of physiological responses to varying repetition and intensity schemes. Absolute strength is gained by using very low reps (1 to 3) per set, mass is increased with higher reps (10 to 12), and local muscular and systemic endurance is developed with even higher reps (20+). For the novice, a repetition scheme that is right in the anaerobic middle works best: sets of 5 reps. Fives are close enough to the strength end of the continuum to provide tremendous increases in strength, the primary goal of the novice. Fives are also enough reps to develop a tolerance for elevated work levels, and provide for a good amount of hypertrophy so that muscular weight gain occurs too. This mix of adaptations provides a very good fitness base that allows for progress. Fives are optimal for the novice; they effectively stimulate strength gains and other forms of progress without producing sufficient muscular or neuromuscular exhaustion to cause technique deterioration at the end of the set.

Some assistance exercises, when finally integrated into the program, will be done with higher reps. Chin-ups and pull-ups, for instance, might be done with up to 15 reps before weight is added. They function as an arm and upper back exercise, and are useful for satisfying most trainees' desire for rapid positive effects on their physiques. They are also a very good basic strength indicator; a trainee who cannot do many chins needs to work on them, since chinning strength is closely related to pressing strength and improving a weak chin-up/pull-up will improve the pressing movements.

The number of sets to be done varies with the athlete's circumstances: first workout ever, or second month of training; sore from the previous workout, or fresh as a garden tomato; perfect form, or in need of technical practice to hone a skill. It also varies with the exercise being done: core lift or assistance exercise; presses, which do not tap in too deeply; or heavy deadlifts, which are hard enough at 5RM that one set is plenty for most people. These decisions must be made on an individual basis each time, but it is possible to establish some general guidelines. As a rule, work sets for squats, bench presses, and presses should be three sets across (three sets at the same weight) for novices, but as much as five sets across or as little as one work set might be appropriate, depending again on the circumstances.

The number of sets per exercise is the sum of the warm-ups and the work sets. Warm-up sets are done as necessary, more if the trainee is sore, inflexible, or older, fewer if he is already warm from previous exercises. Warm-up sets add to the total number (and total work done), which might, in atypical cases, be as high as twelve sets if extensive light warm-up sets and three work sets across are done.

As mentioned in chapter 5, sets across have several advantages. They allow sufficient tonnage to be accumulated to produce the necessary adaptive stress, more than is possible with only one work set. But they also allow a coach to observe enough reps to analyze any form problems a trainee might be having, and then observe the effectiveness of the correction in the next set. Gross technique problems can be seen immediately by anyone familiar with the movement; less pronounced or intermittent form problems need more reps for diagnosis. Sets across provide that opportunity.

Scheduling. For a novice trainee, the adaptation to a new training load occurs within 24 to 72 hours. Three days per week yields a training session every 48 hours with one 72-hour interval at the end of the week (the longer break following what might be a harder workout). Three days per week fits well into most people's work schedule, an important factor for most novices just getting started, trying to integrate a training schedule into their lifestyle.

Monday, Wednesday, and Friday are the most obvious training days for most people on a three day-per-week program. In fact, Monday and Wednesday are the busiest days in all gyms everywhere, Monday being referred to as Guilty Conscience Day since so many people show up on Monday to apologize to themselves for Friday's missed workout. Depending on the facility, this might be an excellent reason to use a Tuesday/Thursday/ Saturday schedule, or a Sunday/Tuesday/Thursday one.

Depending on individual scheduling flexibility, recovery ability, and personal preference, a trainee might decide to use an every-other-day schedule, where each week is different but each break between workouts is the same 48 hours. This schedule does not allow for a longer break between two harder workouts, and works best if two different daily workouts are being alternated, an option we will explore later.

Workloads. Any novice learning a new exercise, regardless of training history, apparent fitness level, aptitude shown on previous exercises, or protestations to the contrary, should begin with *an empty bar*. And that empty bar may need to be a lighter one than the standard 20-kg/45-lb type, depending on the trainee. For the novice, the law is: learn first, and then load. There will be plenty of time to put weight on the bar later; the first task is to learn the movement pattern without having to worry about how heavy it is. *Heavy* always competes with *correct,* and at this point *correct* is much more important. The vast majority of the time, a trainee will learn the movement well enough that the load can be increased during the first workout, but it is important that a good command of the movement pattern be established before any plates are added to the bar. This process may take three sets, or it may take three workouts, depending on both coach and trainee. Do not rush this process: this is not the place for impatience. If the first workout for a 150-pound trainee progresses through the empty bar for three sets of five, then 75 × 5, 95 × 5, and 115 × 5, and then ends with 135 × 5 × 3 sets, all with good form and the bar speed on the work-sets slowing down *just a little*, it is a very good first day.

This is enough work to disrupt homeostasis and bring about Selye's stage-1 response. The trainee has done more work than he is accustomed to already, and adding more weight is pointless on the first day of training. If the trainee has worked through the entire range of motion of an unfamiliar exercise, he will experience some muscle soreness. The goal for the first workout should be a little soreness, but not so much that daily tasks are markedly impaired. It accomplishes absolutely nothing for a novice trainee to wake up the day after the first workout with crippling soreness, and many, many people are discouraged to the point of quitting when faced with what they think will be a second workout with the same result. An exercise professional will never let this happen intentionally, although it is sometimes unavoidable.

After the first workout has established the trainee's strength level, subsequent workouts should progressively increase the work-set weights of all the exercises. This should occur at every workout. Weight is the only variable in the progression that is adjusted up. The number of reps is fixed by the physiologic effects that the training program is designed to improve, as discussed earlier, and if five reps is the assigned workload, rest cannot be decreased without compromising the ability to do all the reps. The increments by which the weight of the work sets increase are determined by both the exercise and the ability of the trainee.

As a general rule, the smaller the number of muscles the exercise involves, the longer it will take for the trainee to get stronger at it. Exercises that use large numbers of large muscles, such as deadlifts and squats, get strong much faster than upper body exercises like the bench press. Exercises such as the press, clean, and snatch, which use a lot of muscles but are limited by the contribution made by smaller muscles or technical proficiency, get strong more slowly as well. Chins and assistance exercises that involve only one joint get stronger very slowly, and progress on them is expected only on a monthly basis.

People of different sexes, sizes, ages, levels of experience and athletic ability, and levels of motivation make progress at different rates. As Selye's theory predicts, those populations most capable of adapting to external stress will make the fastest progress. People whose hormonal, dietary, rest, and motivational circumstances are optimal for recovery from physical loads – well-fed young men on sports teams, for example – will make more rapid gains than any other population when subjected to intense training. All other groups will progress more slowly, and will attain commensurately lower levels of absolute performance, although their relative performances may certainly be comparable.

So, for young males who weigh between 150 and 200 pounds, deadlifts can likely move up 15 pounds per workout, and squats 10 pounds, with continued steady progress for perhaps three weeks before slowing down to half that rate. Bench presses, presses, and cleans can move up 5 to 10 pounds for the first few workouts, with progress on these exercises slowing down to 2.5 to 5 pounds per workout after only two to three weeks. Young women tend to progress on the squat and the deadlift at about the same rate as young men, adjusted for bodyweight (which would mean 5-10 pounds instead of 10-15), but more slowly on the press, bench press, clean, snatch, and assistance exercises. Progress can be made for quite some time, and specific strategies to maximize it and delay the onset of a training plateau should be employed as progress starts to slow. These methods are discussed below.

Linear progress, for as long as it is possible, is the most efficient way to utilize a novice's training time, since every workout yields a strength improvement. This is true even if the increases are very small; two pounds per week on the press still adds up to 104 pounds per year, pretty good progress if you can make it. As progress begins to slow – i.e., as work sets become harder to do and to complete – or as reps begin to get missed, smaller incremental increases should be used. Smaller jumps will allow for more linear progression, so that more progress is accumulated before a radical change in programming is necessary.

The Starting Strength Model

As outlined in *Starting Strength: Basic Barbell Training*, a novice starts with three or four basic whole body exercises and after warm-up does three work sets (except for the deadlift) at a weight that is based on the performance during the previous workout. When the prescribed sets and reps are completed at the assigned weight, the load is increased for the next workout. This is very simple, and it works for quite a while for most beginners. In the presence of adequate rest and nutrition, it would be unusual for someone to fail to add quite a bit of muscle and strength before any changes to the workout are needed at all. In fact, the failure of a novice to progress on this simple program means that it was not followed precisely.

For a rank novice, the simplest of workouts is in order. This short program can be followed for the first few workouts:

A	**B**
Squat	Squat
Press	Bench Press
Deadlift	Deadlift

The two workouts alternate across the Monday-Wednesday-Friday schedule for the first couple of weeks, until the freshness of the deadlift has worn off a little and after the quick initial gains establish the deadlift well ahead of the squat. At this point the power clean is introduced:

A	B
Squat	Squat
Press	Bench Press
Deadlift	Power Clean

After this program is followed for a short time, chin-ups and pull-ups can be added, along with back extensions or glute/ham raises for a break from pulling every workout. This somewhat more-complicated program looks like this:

A	B
Squat	Squat
Press	Bench Press
Deadlift/Power Clean	Back Extension
	Chin-ups/Pull-ups

In this variation, the deadlift and power clean alternate every time workout A is done, and the chin-up alternates with the pull-up likewise. The 2-week schedule would look like this:

Week 1

Monday	Wednesday	Friday
Squat	Squat	Squat
Press	Bench press	Press
Deadlift	Back extension	Power clean
	Chin-ups	

Week 2

Monday	Wednesday	Friday
Squat	Squat	Squat
Bench press	Press	Bench press
Back extension	Deadlift	Back extension
Pull-ups		Chin-ups

The squat, bench press, and press are done for 3 sets of 5; note that the bench press and the press alternate in all variations of the program. The deadlift is done for 1 set of 5 reps every fifth workout, due to its harder nature at heavy weights, and alternates with the power clean, which is done at 5 sets of 3 reps across. Squats continue each workout uninterrupted; this is possible because they start lighter than the deadlift due to a longer range of motion but are less fatiguing due to the inherent stretch reflex at the bottom. Unweighted chin-ups or pull-ups are done to failure for 3 sets unless the trainee can complete more than 15 reps per set (unlikely for a rank novice), in which case weight is added. Chin-ups use a supine grip (and thus more biceps), while pull-ups use a prone grip. If the athlete can maintain his chin/pull-up numbers as his bodyweight increases, he is actually getting stronger.

This is a reasonable exercise selection for a novice, and a reasonable weekly plan. It can be followed for several months if careful attention is paid to the increments of increase, rest, adequate nutrition, and the elimination of activities that compete for recovery resources during this important period of rapid strength increase.

Back-off Periods. Inevitably, progress will stall. There are two basic scenarios, one in which the trainee does everything right but still fails to stimulate further progress and another in which progress stalls or regresses because of greed for quick progress or because of a lifestyle factor that affects recovery. In either case, something must be done to salvage the novice's ability to use simple linear progression and milk all possible progress from the first level of training advancement.

The first scenario assumes proper application of all the progression principles, adequate attention to recovery, sleep, and nutrition, and proper technique on all the exercises. This may be a bit of a stretch, since few novice trainees execute all parts of the plan without flaw. But for purposes of illustration, we'll make the stretch, we'll use the bench press as an example, and we'll ignore the effects of the press workout done on alternate days to simplify the example (a factor that would obviously have to be considered in an actual situation of this type).

If the trainee correctly follows the simple progression program, does not get greedy, and eats and rests correctly, then he will be able to add weight to the bar at every workout for quite some time. He might start by adding weight in 5-pound increments at each bench press workout and progress to 1- to 3-pound increases. At some point, adding weight will cause missed reps in one workout (usually in the last set), followed by all three sets of 5 completed at that weight the following workout. Finally, he will begin to miss the last reps in the work-sets for two to three workouts in a row.

Quite a few things could be changed about the workout, but the correct approach will accomplish two things. First, it will offer the highest probability of restoring linear progress as quickly as possible and, second, it will keep the trainee as close as possible to his most recent 5RM, thus avoiding the loss of hard-won progress. The trainee needs a change but will do best with a change that disrupts the essence of the program as little as possible. A slight back-off in training weight with the immediate resumption of slow and steady progress identical to what has taken place in previous months is appropriate.

Any time a trainee working very hard is allowed a bit of extra rest and recuperation, performance will increase. This is evidence not of a dramatic unexpected increase in overall physical ability, but of the increased ability to display it on a given day. It's not that he's actually stronger; he's just not tired. "Peaking" for a contest or testing procedure works the same way: no dramatic increase in strength occurs at a peak, just the ability to demonstrate the strength that is actually present as a cumulative effect of the training program. And, in this case, this is exactly what is necessary. A trainee at this stage is not terribly "stuck" and will not take much unsticking to get back on the road to progress. A little extra rest will always allow a small increase in the weights that can be handled afterward, and the accumulation of strength through progressive loading can resume from there.

For example, say work-set weights for the bench press have been $165 \times 5 \times 3$ (three sets of five reps at 165 pounds) on Monday, $167 \times 5 \times 3$ on Friday, $170 \times 5 \times 3$ on Wednesday, 172×4, 172×4, 172×3 on Monday, and then the same for the next bench workout. The following Wednesday the same workout would be done, with an 8-to-10% reduction in training load, and then a return to incremental increases from there. So the work sets would be $160 \times 5 \times 3$ on that Wednesday, $165 \times 5 \times 3$ on the next bench press day, and 170 on the next one. These will be perceived as light weights, and the temptation to do extra sets must be resisted if the unloading is to do its job. It will take about two weeks to get back to the previous level of performance, the precise number of workouts depending on the weight being used and the jumps in weight between workouts. At this point the weight that was missed, 172, should be used at the next workout. The following workouts with 175, 177, and on up, can be done just as if the little "detour" never happened. The extra rest and recovery – the small "peaking" effect from the temporary reduction in training load – should allow success with a weight slightly above that which the trainee was successful with previously, and the act of lifting this heavier weight should spur further progress for several more workouts.

The second scenario, in which progress stalls because of impatience or other external factors, is different. Here, the trainee has actually regressed slightly, or possibly more than slightly. The build-up of fatigue is more pronounced, and the back-off should therefore be more drastic. The first example had the trainee dropping his bench press poundage back from 172 to 160. Assume that the second trainee is also stuck at 172, except that instead of getting 4 reps for 2 to 3 workouts in a row, the last workout with 172 netted only 1 or 2 successful reps. In this circumstance there is really no point in backing off only 8 to 10%, because that would still be somewhat difficult and it would not allow sufficient rest and recovery. The first back-off workout should be very light and easy, and lower in volume than a normal workout. For example, 3 work sets of 5 reps at 160 should be reduced to only one set of 5 at 145. Another approach might be to warm up normally, using standard incremental sets up to the last warm-up, and then stop, doing no work sets at all and letting the warm-up sets serve to maintain the motor pathways.

The second and third workouts will depend on how much work the trainee was doing when progress stalled. If he was at 3 to 5 work sets, then in the second workout he would warm up to 10% below the point where progress stalled, and

Small plates are necessary for small jumps, and small jumps are necessary for progress. An understanding of this very practical matter is fundamental to continued improved performance under the bar.

As training progresses, the ability to adapt to the stress of training slows, as discussed at length previously. What were once easy 10-pound jumps for sets of 5 reps become difficult 5-pound jumps for 5 reps. With standard 2½-pound (or 1.25kg) plates, sets of four is the inevitable result. The object is to use sets of five, for the physiologic effects produced by five reps, and training is designed around a certain number of reps for this specific reason. So it is necessary to be able to make incremental increases while holding the reps constant, and this requires that the increments be small enough that an adaptation can occur during the time allotted. A novice trainee who has correctly followed the program will eventually not be able to adapt to 5-pound jumps between sets.

But that trainee *can* get strong 1 pound at a time, or 1.5 pounds or 2 pounds at a time, depending on the exercise. Certainly for small-muscle-group exercises like the press, bench press, and even chin-ups, small jumps are the only way progress will accumulate smoothly. And if a 2-pound jump is loaded, it will have to be loaded with 1-pound plates. Several companies make small plates, in both pounds and kilos. Or they can be made in the garage out of 2-inch washers glued, taped, or welded together in varying increments. Or 2½-pound plates can be shaved down at a machine shop. In pounds, the range should be ½, 1, and 1½; in kilos, 0.25, 0.5, and 0.75.

It is also important to understand how the small plates relate to the rest of the equipment. Standard "Olympic" barbell plates are castings, and castings are inherently inaccurate. Even good-quality calibrated plates, which are milled to tolerance, are not dead-on. When loading a bar, which will itself have a small error, with several plates, all of which have a small error, it is likely that the face value loaded weight is not actually what is on the bar.

This is not important for warm-ups, or for back-off sets, or for anything else during the workout that does not represent a measured incremental increase over the previous workout. But when the load on the bar is supposed to be 173.5 pounds, and it actually weighs 175.5 due to plate error, the target has been missed. It may not be possible, or even necessary, to have dead-on plates; it is possible to have the same big plates on the bar as last time, so that the *increase* made with the small plates is exactly what it is supposed to be. That is the concern anyway – that the amount lifted today be exactly the specific intended amount more than last time. If training is done in a commercial gym or school weight room, number or mark the bar and a set of plates so that they can be identified for use at every workout, and buy and bring with you your own small plates. This way, the amount of the increase can be exactly what it needs to be, the increase will be exact every time, and progress can be better ensured.

then do that weight for one set. This prevents detraining but still allows some rest. The content of the third workout will depend on how the trainee feels. The warm-up and first work set should be the same as the second workout, but a decision should be made after the first work set. If the weight feels light, as such a weight should, and the trainee feels good, then he should do three sets across there. If the weight feels heavy or he still feels tired, then he should again stop after one work set and try again the next time. When possible, usually within two short workouts, training can proceed with three normal work sets being done at 10% lighter than the pre-stall work sets, progressing right back up to and through the previous loads.

One aspect of back-off workouts is that, to the extent possible, intensity should not drop more than 10% for more than one workout. This is an important concept to follow if the back-off period is to be kept short and new personal records for 3 sets are to be set afterward without much time elapsing. Again, the key feature of novice training is linear progress – the ability to steadily increase the weight on the bar at each workout – and every effort should be made to keep this from stopping.

The reason intensity is kept relatively high while the volume of training is dropped is to maintain neuromuscular efficiency, the ability of the neural system to fire the motor units in a way that allows all the muscles to work together to efficiently display strength in a movement pattern. Basic muscle strength remains relatively constant (fig. 8-4, pg. 148) even with reduced training. Neuromuscular efficiency, however, is much more influenced by short-term changes in training. This is why we keep intensity relatively high and cut volume drastically: high intensity develops and maintains neuromuscular efficiency, while high volume with low intensity does not. Keeping the weight within 10% of where it was while drastically dropping volume maintains a high state of neuromuscular readiness, while at the same time allowing for some additional recovery. It allows the trainee to resume personal record (PR) performance after the back-off period.

This back-off method is an important tool that will be used throughout the trainee's career, from novice through advanced. For each different rep and set scheme and level of fatigue there is a different "ideal" way to do it. But the basic concept is simple: rest, but don't detrain. The more fatigued the trainee, the more his performance has dropped, the longer the progress lasted before reaching a sticking point, the more gains that were made, and the longer the training history, then the longer the back-off period will have to be. A novice who has trained three months and then simply stalled in his progress and not regressed will need only a short back-off period and a moderate reduction in load, while an advanced athlete who has trained seven years, has hit a serious wall at the end of a very hard training cycle, and has regressed quite a bit due to fatigue over his last 2 to 3 workouts will need a much longer back-off period and much lighter workouts to begin it.

Once a back-off period has become necessary, other changes can be made in the program that are appropriate for the more advanced novice. The squat can go from three days per week to two, with the introduction of lighter squats at 80% of Monday's work set weight into the program. They provide a break in the intensity due to the unloading, which helps to prolong linear increases. The program would now look like this:

Week 1

Monday	Wednesday	Friday
Squat	Light squat	Squat
Bench press	Press	Bench press
Back extension	Deadlift	Back extension
Chin-ups		Pull-ups

Week 2

Monday	Wednesday	Friday
Squat	Light squat	Squat
Press	Bench press	Press
Power clean	Back extension	Deadlift
	Chin-ups	

Deadlifts are still done for one set of five, although more sets could be added due to their reduced frequency in the program. Deadlifts are very easy to overuse; they are important for basic strength, but too many sets make recovery difficult because of the weights that can be used and the amount of stress they can produce cumulatively. Chins and pull-ups should have improved, or at least kept pace with added bodyweight. If chin/pull-up reps are consistently above 10 on all of the three sets, they should be done every other workout with weight, either hung from a belt or with a dumbbell held in the feet, so that failure happens at 5 to 7 reps. This will increase the reps on the bodyweight-only days and increase arm and shoulder strength for the presses. Any other assistance exercises should be done after the basic program exercises, and then for no more that three sets.

A simple recycling of the training intensity will work once, and maybe twice. If training has been going well in the context of proper progressive programming and proper recovery, more than two training intensity back-off periods usually will not be productive. A need for a third usually indicates a need for more complex programming. If, however, there were problems the first and/or second time through, with progress stopping suddenly because of lack of rest, improper or inadequate diet, or greed for unreasonable incremental increases, one more back-off period might fix a sticking point. After the second back-off period, an honest evaluation of training status is warranted.

This is a rough outline of the first three to nine months of training for most novices. Starting with three work sets, the weight increases steadily until progress stalls. The weight drops 10% to get unstuck, the exercises are changed slightly, and progress is made again until another plateau occurs. Finally the point is reached where the amount of work needed to disrupt homeostasis exceeds that which the trainee can recover from between workouts, and more elaborate programming is needed. Key to this novice level of training advancement are the workout-to-workout increases that are possible during these first months. The trainee has made rapid progress and is now much stronger than he would have been had simple linear progression not been used.

At some point, usually between the third and ninth month of training, the standard variations on linear progression will have been exhausted, and training will need to be organized into weekly periods instead of the workout-to-workout periods that characterize the novice phase. At this point, the trainee can be considered an intermediate.

"Loyalty to petrified opinion never broke a chain or freed a human soul."

—Mark Twain

7 – The Intermediate

After several months of steady linear-progression training, with no layoffs and uninterrupted steady progress, all trainees will get stuck. This is the normal, inevitable result of progress having advanced the trainee closer to the limits of genetic potential. By this point both strength and muscular bodyweight have improved quite a bit. So has the trainee's ability to recover quickly from heavy training, but this is offset by the fact that increased strength levels allow heavier and therefore more taxing loads. This more advanced trainee is more efficient, in both recovery and in the ability to tax recovery capacity. And with increased efficiency comes change: simply increasing the workload at each workout can no longer be relied on to spur continued progress. When the training overload of a single workout and the recovery period allowed for by the 48- to 72- hour schedule does not induce a performance improvement, the novice trainee needs a change of program. A single training stress constitutes an overload event for a novice, and this overload and the recovery between that training stress and the next one is enough to disrupt homeostasis and induce a gain in strength for the beginner. Once this is no longer the case, the trainee is no longer a novice. His program must be adjusted accordingly.

An important characteristic of intermediate trainees is that they have specific training goals developed from their experience at the novice level. The high school kid who simply wanted to "learn how to lift" and get bigger and stronger for sports might now realize that he wants to concentrate on training that will increase his performance in the shot put. The 35-year-old who started off wanting to get back in shape might have been bitten by the bodybuilding bug, and now wants to concentrate on muscle size. Even competitive athletes who knew from the start that they were training for a sport – but as wise novices to weight training decided to begin with a novice program – will find that this is the time to tailor their training to their now more-specific needs.

Simple progression works for months when the trainee is new to a program of organized training. At this level, the amount of work that disrupts biological equilibrium and results in an adaptation – the overload – can be applied in one workout. As the trainee adapts to the stresses of training, he becomes capable of applying enough stress in one workout that he will not be recovered from it before the next one. A "heavy" load for an athlete at this level is relatively more stressful on the body than a "heavy" load for a novice, and so requires a longer recovery period. At this point, if progress is to continue, training must be reorganized into periods of work that constitute a recoverable overload for the trainee at this level of adaptation. This involves training periods that include more than one workout – enough work to accumulate into sufficient stress to constitute an overload event and enough built-in recovery time to allow adaptation to take place. At the intermediate level of adaptation, training organized in week-long periods functions well for this purpose (fig. 7-1).

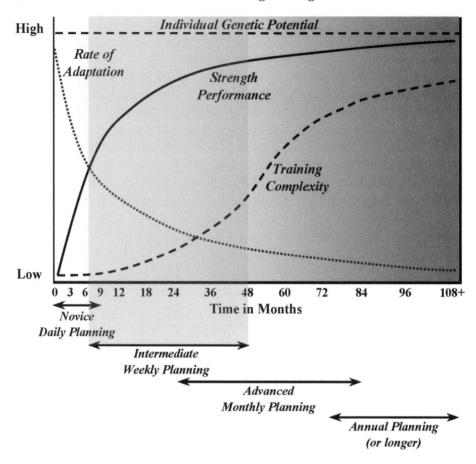

Figure 7-1. The generalized relationship between performance improvement and training complexity relative to time.

There is nothing magical about one week of time. It might very well be that 96 hours (4 days) might suffice to allow enough work to accumulate and be recovered from, since the previous work/recovery period was 48 to 72 hours. But it is likely that more than 4 days will be necessary, because only one workout in 72 hours has probably been barely sufficient – in terms of both sufficient stress and sufficient recovery – for some time. The trainee has not suddenly flipped a switch and become unable to produce an overload/recovery in 3 days, so increasing the cycle period to 4 days will probably not really solve the problem. Five days might, and 6 days probably will, but given the fact that society is organized along weekly timeframes, one week works most easily into most people's schedules.

The intermediate program must differ significantly from the novice program. A novice using 3 sets of 5 repetitions on the squat three days per week will find that those 3 sets are sufficient to stimulate progress, and that recovery from that quantity of work occurs quickly enough that each subsequent workout can be done with heavier weight. A novice bench press program might be 3 work sets of 5 reps on Monday and Friday, with the press done on Wednesday. An intermediate lifter using 3 work sets of 5 reps on Monday will not receive sufficient stimulation to spur progress. Five sets might be enough, but it also presents a problem. Doing 5 work sets across at an intensity high enough to drive progress may exceed recovery when done twice per week. Some variation of the work must be introduced to accommodate the intermediate trainee's need for both more work and sufficient recovery from that work (fig. 7-2).

There are many ways to accomplish this and produce the desired variation across the week. Three methods will be presented later in this chapter, all proven to work well for different applications. But first, let's look at the general principles guiding intermediate programming.

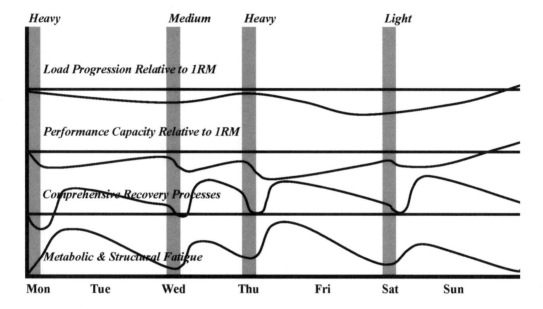

Figure 7-2. Two-factor model of an intermediate trainee's responses and adaptations to a series of training stresses over a week's duration. While similar to the single-day cycle of the beginner, note that fatigue does not dissipate between each training session (gray bars) nor do recovery processes catch up until the conclusion of the week. This defines the difference between the beginner and the intermediate trainee. The workout load presented here is a Starr-model heavy-medium-heavy-light organization that would repeat the following week.

General Considerations

Exercises. The most important consideration for programming at the intermediate level is the selection of exercises, which will be determined in large part by the trainee's choice of sport or training emphasis. If powerlifting is the sport of choice, training will based around the squat, bench press, and deadlift; if it is weightlifting, the snatch and the clean and jerk will form the basis of the program. Athletes training for heavy field events will incorporate power exercises such as clean and snatch variants into the basic strength program. Those interested primarily in hypertrophy will use more isolation exercises at higher reps along with the basic strength-based program.

It is likely that athletes in sports that are less dependent on strength – the lighter field events, sprinters, basketball and baseball players, non-grappling martial artists, etc. – will never have a need to advance much beyond this initial phase of intermediate training. Strength acquisition is perhaps the most important part of any athlete's preparation because it has such a profound impact on the ability to efficiently develop and express all the other parameters of athletics. But these athletes are engaged in activities that are more dependent on skills acquired in the *practice* of their sport than the strength and power provided by *training* in the weight room under the bar. One reason it is important to identify training goals is that the level to which a trainee is intentionally advanced depends on the need for such advancement. The degree of specialization in exercise selection is therefore also determined by the need for more than basic strength enhancement. A javelin thrower might opt for a 3-day program that involves squats, presses, cleans, snatches, and chins; any more complexity than this is unnecessary and would take away training time better spent on this highly practice-dependent sport.

Exercise selection will, to a certain extent, determine sets and reps. The basic strength exercises – squats, presses, bench presses, deadlifts – can be used at a variety of rep ranges, from singles to sets of twenty. This is one of the reasons they are so useful: they can be used throughout the repetition continuum to obtain the entire range of physiologic response, from absolute strength to power to hypertrophy to endurance.

Less versatile are the weightlifting-derived movements, the snatch and the clean and jerk, and their variants the power snatch, the power clean, and hang snatches and cleans. These exercises, referred to as the "quick lifts," are seldom used at high reps in programs specifically designed for strength or power development because their technique-dependency renders them less valuable under conditions of high-rep fatigue. The fact that they cannot be done slowly is both an asset and a limitation. It is common to restrict snatches and cleans to singles and doubles, occasionally using sets of 3 reps for cleans, the thinking being that since fatigue causes technique to break down the reps should be restricted to 3 or less so that fatigue is not the limiting factor. However, high-rep snatches and cleans and their variants have been used quite successfully for a long time as very good conditioning exercises, in part because the full-body nature of the movements produce an output-demand and quality of fatigue that are hard to duplicate with other training modalities.

Assistance exercises will be used by intermediate-level trainees. These movements are more valuable here than at any other period in a training career. An intermediate trainee is developing a feel for the direction he wants his training to take, and assistance exercises are a necessary part of learning the ropes. There are thousands to try, but only a few are valuable. The most useful assistance movements are functional in nature (they utilize normally encountered human movement patterns), use multiple joints, incorporate a balance component, and contribute to the performance of the basic exercises. Chin-ups satisfy these criteria, for example; wrist curls do not.

Front squats can be used by intermediate trainees interested in Olympic weightlifting as a squat variant; they are regarded by some not as an assistance exercise but as another core lift, in our view their omission of significant hamstring involvement limits their consideration as such. Chins and pull-ups are quite useful upper-body exercises that support pressing strength and functional arm strength for sports that involve throwing or pulling with the hands. Romanian deadlifts (RDLs), a deadlift variant that starts at the top instead of on the floor, and barbell rows (pulled from the floor on each rep) can be added at this stage of training. Lower-back-specific exercises such as glute/ham raises and reverse "hyperextensions," are used by intermediate trainees to improve trunk stability for the basic movements, along with weighted sit-ups. These exercises can be varied along the repetition continuum depending on the result desired, but generally they are used at higher reps than the basic strength movements, since their role is to support the function of the basics, not replace them.

Sets and Reps. The number of sets will also vary with the exercise. The bulk of the work should always be focused on the exercises that produce the majority of the disruption in homeostasis. This means that the core lifts will receive the majority of the work in terms of sets per week and time devoted to them, since they deliver more results for the time spent doing them. Cleans and snatches, being used at lower reps, will need more sets per week to equal the amount of work; to match the reps from 5 sets of 5 squats with that from cleans, you would have to do 8 sets of 3 cleans to be nearly equivalent.

Assistance exercises using higher reps per set might accumulate more total reps than the core lifts. If squats are done for 5 sets of 5 across after 3 warm-up sets of 5, and 5 sets of 10 glute/ham raises are done afterward, more reps of glute/hams have been done than squats. But in terms of total volume (weight x reps) – and in terms of their contribution to homeostatic disruption – the squats have been worked far harder.

So, within the framework of the exercises used, our training goals will generally determine the nature of the sets and reps. Strength work needs up to five sets of 1 to 5 reps on the core lifts, hypertrophy calls for five sets of 12 to 15 reps, and power work requires five to ten sets of 1 to 5 reps at weights light enough to move fast. Cleans and snatches will be done with five to ten sets of 1 to 3 reps. Assistance exercises will be done with higher reps, usually 10 to 15, and fewer sets, usually three to five.

Scheduling. At the intermediate level, the weekly schedule conforms to the trainee's individual needs with regard to continued progress, not to the calendar. At the advanced level, quite often the training cycle will be tailored to a competitive schedule, but intermediate trainees are still making relatively rapid progress and they should be allowed to do so as long as possible with minimal interference from scheduling factors external to the training program. If a competitive calendar is superimposed on the training program at the intermediate level, the disruption to both the competitive performance and to the training schedule itself will be relatively minimal. High school football players are often in this position: they are making good progress on a training program despite the fact that football season is on, and with adequate rest and nutrition are able to do both, to the benefit of both. Intermediate trainees are not so far along in their training that an occasional game day will destroy the delicate balance between stress and recovery; the balance is not yet that delicate, as it will be at the more advanced, specialized levels.

As a general rule, squats will be done at every workout – 3 days per week – until the trainee goes to a 4-day-per-week schedule. Squats at 80% of the heavy day work set weight are done as the unloading day workout. As proficiency increases, the percentage moves up to 87 to 90% for medium-day loads. The pressing movements are still alternated for shoulder balance, with presses and bench presses alternated every other workout. This results in a two-week cycle, one week pressing twice and the next week benching twice. The deadlift and the clean will alternate as well, and as the trainee advances and the deadlift gets very strong, RDLs, stiff-legged deadlifts, and eventually power snatches may be substituted for deadlifts every other workout to allow for more recovery if necessary. Assistance exercises should be used only once or twice per week, placed in the schedule so as to create the maximum benefit without interfering with the execution of the core lifts by causing excessive soreness or fatigue. Chins, for example, if done too hard the workout before a heavy bench press day, would be counterproductive.

The time allotted for a training session will obviously vary with the number of exercises, sets, and reps. Rest time between sets should be adequate for recovery but not enough to allow "cooling off," or a decrease in preparedness for the next set. Too much time between sets represents wasted training time and, in institutional contexts, an inefficient use of the training facilities. Too little time between sets causes failed reps and missed work sets and defeats the purpose of training. Make sure that enough time is allotted that the whole workout can actually be done in one session. Any workout that takes longer than two hours probably involves too many exercises, too many sets, or too much talking.

Intensity. In intermediate programming, the intensity of the work varies across the week (table 7-2, pg. 131), and this means that for the core lifts and the quick lifts, the percentage of 1RM and the numbers of reps must be calculated for each workout. Using the progression outlined in table 7-1 (pg. 130), a little math, and some experience and common sense, weights for the work sets of the core lifts and quick lifts can be assigned across the week. Light, medium, and heavy correspond to different percentages, depending on the number of reps used for the exercise, as the table shows. If several sets across are to be done, the weight will have to stay a little below the corresponding RM to allow for accumulating fatigue: 355×5 done as a 5RM would need to be reduced to 335 or 340×5 for 5 sets across.

The Intermediate

While a measured 1RM is nice and makes workload calculation easy, an accurate evaluation of daily performance is better, because minor variations in technique, recovery, and daily status are the realities of training human athletes. This is one of the most important functions of the coach, and one of the best reasons to have one. Performances vary for many reasons, and human response is not an exact science. A coach with a good eye can judge a "relative maximum," the weight the individual trainee can lift on a given day under specific individual circumstances. This coach/athlete interaction involves a great deal of experience and feedback from both the coach and trainee. In that context, "heavy" could be defined as the point where technique begins to break down, or the point where the more experienced trainee says it is. "Medium" could mean that technique is well maintained and the trainee feels like he's working hard but lots of "room" is left. "Light" should always mean that form is perfect and several sets across at that weight would not amount to a significant training stress. This is somewhat similar to using the RPE (rating of perceived exertion) scale in aerobic exercise programming, but RPE depends entirely on the subjective judgment of the trainee, and this is not always useful, especially in the weight room. It takes an experienced coach to be able to apply this method effectively. For trainees without access to high-level coaching, the percentage of 1RM classification works well.

As training progresses and strength and power are developed, the rate of improvement slows down. The closer the trainee is to his genetic potential, the slower the progress toward it will be. The squat may advance 5 pounds per week, instead of 5 pounds per workout, and the bench may go up only 2 pounds per week, if that much. The more an exercise depends on smaller muscle groups, the more slowly that exercise will get strong. It is prudent to keep this in mind. There is no point in getting frustrated when the press moves up only one pound. Any steady progress is good progress for the intermediate trainee, and this becomes more true as the athlete advances and progress inevitably slows.

There will be many times over the months and years of using this weekly training model that a change within the program will be required to continue adaptation and improvement. Many things can be done to accomplish these changes. Reps and sets can be varied as needed, and will be changed by the observant coach or the perceptive trainee to accommodate changing conditions as they arise. Warm-ups will vary almost daily, in accordance with soreness and minor injuries; more work sets should be added as they can be successfully handled and until the need for more sets finally justifies an additional training day. Exercise selection and frequency can be varied. As noted in table 7-1, workout frequency will change progressively, but it's also possible that training frequency will need to be decreased temporarily as a result of a brush with overtraining. And the workouts themselves can be manipulated to produce varying physiologic effects by controlling the rest time between sets.

There is a tremendous amount of possible variation in training stress that can be used to drive adaptation for a long time. Only the creativity of the coach or trainee limits the possibilities, as long as the physiologic requirements of the goal are kept in mind and trained for.

As training progresses in intensity and volume, the role of the coach changes from that of a teacher of movement patterns to a consultant in movement, and from that of the planner to the planning advisor. The maturing trainee will eventually have enough experience – from being coached and helping coach others with whom he trains – that the kind of coaching he needs will change. A more experienced trainee needs the coach's eye to check what he himself cannot see, since he has been taught the movement correctly and has months of experience doing it correctly. Technique needs just checking or cueing, not ground-up teaching, at this point. The coach becomes a source of advice about the application of the program instead of the controller of all its elements. Coaching input becomes more subtle, and should become more precise regarding detail as the trainee acquires finer skill. The coach should provide input about exercise variation after all the exercises have been taught correctly, guidance about load and intensity variation after it has been determined how the trainee responds to it, and constant, absolutely necessary reminders about technique on all the lifts, long after technique has been learned.

Variation. The intermediate stage is the place where most athletes make their biggest training mistakes. It is very true that many novices start out on terrible programs, training with no reason or logic, or adopting programs that are designed for more advanced trainees which prevent them from progressing as quickly as they could. But the magical adaptability of the novice is often strong enough to overcome even the poorest of decisions. Beginners can seemingly make progress under even the worst of circumstances. But for the intermediate trainee, progress is harder to come by, and the body is much more particular about what it responds to when it comes to improving an already-honed performance. Many intermediate trainees get caught up in an endless cycle of changing routines, constantly messing around with the weekly schedule of exercises, sets, and reps. In an effort to feel that progress is being made, they often talk about changing even their core goals. How many times does someone in the gym (or, for godsakes, on the Internet) who hasn't really progressed in years talked about how they are going to concentrate on "cutting" now instead of "bulking"? Most often, that person still just wants to get bigger and stronger, but after a long period of no progress and hence boredom, frustration sets in and the goal is changed to something perceived as more attainable. Or someone stuck on the bench press for months decides to just quit doing it and instead focus on the IsoLateral DynoPressMaster. People can ride the merry-go-round of different exercises, different routines, and different set and rep systems for years with no real progress.

The proper way to include variety in the program is to use it in ways that reinforce training goals, so that different types of training during the week have a functional purpose. This means that the variety lies in the way the basic exercises are applied, and not in a bunch of new exercises. Sets of 5 on the basic exercises will always be useful as a part of most every program, and constructive variations will involve different interpretations of sets, reps, and movement speed. If an athlete is training for a sport that requires speed and power production, including some additional explosive-type exercises is a good idea. After the novice stage, some sort of training that involves moving a moderate weight quickly is very useful for these trainees. For those whose main goal is increased muscular weight and size, keeping a higher-volume day in most training cycles is necessary. For those who want increased strength, and especially an increase in strength-to-weight ratio, keeping the higher-volume workouts out of most training cycles might be smarter, with the concentration on power training and lower-volume, higher-intensity training.

The coach uses the training log kept by every serious trainee as an important source of data for determinations regarding staleness, overtraining, the effectiveness of newly added exercises, and the overall effectiveness of the training program. Sometimes it may be necessary to make large-scale changes in the program due to an unexpected lack of response, the inability to recover from the program because of individual lifestyle factors outside the trainee's control, or a change in the athlete's training goals. The log reveals trends in both training and schedule compliance that have a definite bearing on progress. It should also include the athlete's impressions of that day's workout, useful cues discovered, and any other subjective information that might serve a purpose later. It might also include notes about sleep, diet, and other information pertinent to recovery. It is an essential tool for both trainee and coach, and as such is not optional.

The best way to log workouts is to follow a column format, top to bottom, using a small enough hand that the whole workout fits in one column, and that at least four or five workouts fit on one page. This way it is possible to display up to three weeks training data on two open pages, so that trends over time are visible.

This means that a good quality book will be needed. It should be a good enough book to last at least a year, so use a notebook with a decent binding. It need not be expensive, but it should be better than a spiral. Spiral-bound books don't last very long because the pages tear out easily. The best training logs are ledger books with relatively plain paper, but simple composition books, the kind with the mottled covers, work just fine.

A specific example might be the trainee who is mostly interested in gaining muscular weight. He has completed the novice stage, and has finished a training cycle with 5 sets of 5 for one workout and dynamic effort sets for the other. He wants to gain weight, so he will keep the 5 sets of 5 portion of the workout and add in a higher-volume workout for the second session. The choices might be 5 sets of 10 across, 5 sets of 12, or even 3 to 4 sets of 15. The first set of the 5 might be a 10RM effort, with the last 4 sets done to failure and the rest between sets controlled so that full recovery does not occur. Or each set might be done for all 10 reps, with enough rest between to ensure this. Rep schemes for the volume workout could change for each of the next few cycles, while the 5 sets of 5 keeps pace with and drives improvement on the volume training days.

Another example might be the trainee who is mostly interested in speed and power. As workouts are added or variety is introduced, singles, doubles, and triples will become more important. Dynamic effort sets are an invaluable component of this type of training, as are cleans and snatches and their derivatives. Experimentation in subsequent training cycles would include multiple sets across of heavy singles or doubles, and 3 sets of 3 across or ascending or descending in weight through the work sets, along with a continued emphasis on sets of 5. The focus is always on force production, with high volume only a secondary consideration.

The problem is that most people, at various points in their training careers, lose sight of the basis for all productive training. They forget that the goal is *always* to produce a stress that induces adaptation through recovery and supercompensation and that, as advancement continues, the increased timeframe of this response must be factored in. Variety for variety's sake is pointless. All training must be planned, and success must be planned for. All the variety in the world is no substitute for correct planning.

The following are a sample of the many possible interpretations of basic weekly programming. They are meant to be used a guide to your own discovery of a solution to the problem – a starting point on the way to understanding this most important period in the development of a strong athlete.

The Texas Method

This method uses a sharp contrast in training variables between the beginning and end of the week. High volume at moderate intensity is used at the first of the week, a light workout is done in the middle for maintenance of motor pathways, and then a high intensity workout at low volume ends the week. A classic example of this variation would be a squat program where, after the warm-ups, Monday's workout is 5 work sets of 5 across, Wednesday's is lighter – perhaps 5's at 80% of Monday's load, and Friday's is a single heavier set of 5. It looks like this:

Monday
Squat, 5 sets of 5

Wednesday
Squat, 2 light sets of 5

Friday
Squat, 1 heavy set of 5

This simple program is probably the most productive routine in existence for trainees at this level. (As with all the following example programs, the sets enumerated are work sets, with adequate warm-up sets of increasing weight and decreasing reps done beforehand.) It is usually the first program to use when simple linear programming doesn't work anymore. The trainee in transition from novice to intermediate is unable to make progress with either a (not sufficiently stressful) workload that he *can* recover from enough to do 2 to 3 times per week, or conversely, a workload that is stressful enough to induce the stress/recovery/supercompensation cycle but that he *cannot* recover from quickly enough to be able to do 2 to 3 times per week.

In the Texas method, the first workout of the week is the "stress" workout, the lighter midweek workout comes during the recovery period, and the last, higher-intensity/lower-volume workout is done when the trainee has recovered enough from the first day to show an increase in performance. Both the Monday and Friday workouts increase in weight each week by 5 pounds. The total weekly training volume and training stress is low enough that as each week begins the trainee has no accumulated fatigue from the previous week, yet the one "stress" workout on Monday is high enough in volume to trigger an adaptation, the heavy single set on Friday provides enough intensity that neuromuscular function is reinforced without fatally upping the volume, and each week produces a small net increase in strength.

This is the simplest level of periodization, and this is the first appropriate time to use it. While the trainee was making progress with simple linear progression, this type of variation would have wasted training time: more progress was being made each week using the simple incremental increase every workout than could be made with this smaller weekly increase punctuated by the mid-week offloading. But at the intermediate level, the trainee's ability to progress that fast has diminished, and in order for progress to continue, the midweek offload and the Monday/Friday load variation become necessary.

Most intermediate trainees will be able to make progress for months on programs set up like this one. Different set and rep schemes can be used, as long as the basic template of a volume workout, a light workout, and an intensity workout is followed.

Here is another example of this basic intermediate template, this time for pressing exercises:

Monday
Bench press, 5 sets of 5

Wednesday
Press, 3 sets of 5

Friday
Bench press, 1RM, 2RM, or 3RM

Like the sample squat workout, this bench press workout uses a high-volume session on Monday, a related but less-stressful exercise (because lighter weights are used) on Wednesday, and a high-intensity session on Friday where training volume is low but PRs are attempted. Once again, the plan is pretty simple. The Monday workout should be stressful enough to cause homeostatic disruption. Any trainee who has gotten to this point in training should be able to make a pretty good guess at what is needed, and sets across is a proven strategy, one that has worked for many people for decades. The second training session is a different exercise that contributes to the development of the primary muscle groups being trained, working the muscles and joints involved through a different range of motion, but at a load that does not add significantly to the disruption caused by the first workout. In fact, this light workout might stimulate recovery by increasing blood flow to sore muscles, in effect reminding them that they will have a job to do on Friday. The third day should be an attempt at a personal record (whether for 1, 2, or 3 reps) on the first exercise.

Again, this is the key to intermediate level training: workout-to-workout progress is no longer possible, since much of the distance between completely untrained and total genetic potential has been covered in the novice months. What is possible is weekly progress, and Friday's workout is the opportunity to demonstrate it. Every effort should be made to choose weights carefully so that the PR can actually be done. Much is riding on the trainee's ability to stay unstuck during this phase of training. The reps each Friday do not have to be the same; it is quite useful to try for a max single, double, or triple on Friday, and rotate between all three. There is enough difference between singles and triples that the variation helps with staying unstuck.

When a program like this is started, the goal is to make progress on both Monday and Friday, just as in the novice program. When all the prescribed sets and reps on Monday are accomplished, raise the weight for the next week. If a new 1RM is set Friday, next week try for a new 2RM. In essence, linear progress is still being made, but the line is now being drawn between Monday and Monday and between Friday and Friday, instead of between Monday and Wednesday.

Very often, after several weeks of progress with personal records getting more difficult on Friday, the cycle can be sustained for a few more weeks with nothing more than a slight reduction in Monday's workload. Cut back the number of sets, or even the weight on the bar a little, and progress on Friday's workout can usually be maintained. The object is to make Monday's workout stressful enough to spur progress, but not so stressful that it interferes with Friday's PR.

It is always possible to exceed recovery, just as it is always possible to understimulate. Balance between the two must be achieved, or progress does not occur. The novice has little chance of chronically exceeding recovery ability unless heinous abuse occurs, in the form of crazy numbers of sets and reps due to inexperienced or absent supervision. And if any increase in weight at all is occurring each workout, progress is being made, although slower progress than might be possible with more aggressive loading. (The novice can exceed his lifting ability – the limits of strength – in which case the weights chosen cannot actually be done for the prescribed reps and sets. This error will also lead to no progress, but is so obvious that it can and must be immediately corrected.) The intermediate phase of training, then, is the first opportunity for the serious misapplication of training variables that would result in an imbalance between stress and recovery.

The ability of the body to recover from a workload increases with training, but even with the same sets and reps, the workload increases as strength – and the weight on the bar – goes up. The novice squatting 200 pounds for 3 sets of 5 was challenged by the task of recovery from that workload. Now, the intermediate lifter squatting 300 pounds for 5 sets of 5 several months later is still being challenged. Of course 200 pounds for 3 sets would be very easy to recover from at this point, but doing that doesn't accomplish anything since it now does not constitute an adaptive stimulus. Can 300 pounds for 5 sets be recovered from as easily as 200 pounds was months ago? Maybe, maybe not. That is why Monday's workout has to be adjusted as necessary, and not always adjusted up in a simple stepwise manner as with earlier workouts. Sometimes as strength goes up, a set must be dropped from the workout, or the percentage of max slightly lowered to keep residual fatigue from creeping in. The more advanced the trainee, the finer the line between not enough and too much.

Stalled Progress. In chapter 6 we discussed two possible remedies for stalled progress in a novice's linear training cycle. Those principles can be applied at the intermediate level as well, specifically to the task of keeping Monday's training stress from going too high or too low.

If progress simply stalls, with no reduction in the ability to complete Monday's workouts but an absence of personal records on Fridays, the stress needed to spur progress is probably not being applied on Monday. Often an increase or slight change in Monday's workout will restore progress. Adding a set is a good idea. Or, holding the total number of reps constant while using more lower-rep sets with slightly higher weight also works well. For example, Monday's 5 sets of 5 (25 total reps) with 300 pounds becomes 8 sets of 3 (24 total reps) with 315 pounds. The addition of one or two higher-rep sets done after the regular work sets is another option; these are referred to as **back-off sets**. The trainee doing 5 sets of 5 with 300 pounds could follow that with a set of 10 at 250, or even at 225 if done with a pause or some other alteration that makes the reps harder at lighter weight.

The possibilities are endless, but they should not all be explored at the same time; stress should be added in small increments.

If, however, actual regression occurs, not only in Friday's workout but with staleness carrying over into Monday, then usually the workload on Monday is too high, and residual unrecovered fatigue is creeping in. Possible solutions could be to eliminate excessive warm-up volume, to drop a set or two from the sets across, reduce the work-set weight, or reduce the reps in the work sets – from 5 sets of 5 with 300 pounds to 5 sets of 4 with 300, for example.

With intelligent, careful use, it is not uncommon for this type of program to yield many months of continual progress.

Dynamic Effort Sets. A valuable training tool that fits very well into the Texas method template is dynamic effort (DE) sets, as popularized by Louie Simmons in his Westside method. The authors are grateful to Louie and his athletes for this extremely important contribution to the strength training portfolio.

High-intensity training, that is, using a very high percentage of your force production capacity, is very productive but difficult to recover from in large doses. Any reps done where maximal force is applied train the efficiency of motor unit recruitment. The most common way to generate maximal force is to use maximal weights – 3, 2, or 1RMs. The problem with using maximal weights is that it is extremely taxing and hard to recover from. Lifting heavy weights is obviously a useful thing, but heavy weights must be respected and used properly and sparingly or chronic injuries can develop. Tendinitis, ligament injuries, bursitis, tendon avulsion injuries, cartilage damage, and long-term changes in bony anatomy can accompany the misuse of heavy weights at low reps.

Another way to increase the number and efficiency of motor units recruited to generate force is to generate that force quickly and explosively, requiring the coordinated, simultaneous firing of high numbers of motor units. DE sets increase neuromuscular efficiency, in effect making it easier for the body to regularly recruit this larger number of motor units by teaching the neuromuscular system to do it on demand. The most useful way turn on more available motor units each time the bar is lifted is to use a lighter weight, somewhere between 50 and 75% of 1RM, and push the bar as fast as possible. This has advantages over using maximal weights: it allows far more reps to be done, practiced with, and recovered from, and it can be used for long periods of time without injury due to the lighter weights involved and the reduced stress on joints and connective tissue.

A proven way to use this method is with timed sets, usually done with about 10 sets of 2 or 3 repetitions with a short, controlled rest between the sets moving the bar *as quickly as absolutely possible* for each rep. It cannot be stressed enough that even though this type of training is usually done with lighter weights, each repetition must be done with maximum effort. The magnitude of the force production is determined by the degree of *acceleration* of the load, not the amount of weight on the bar, and acceleration is completely volitional – the lifter must actively try to move each rep faster than the previous one. Herein lies the difficulty: this level of focus is hard for many people to maintain, and it must be maintained for all ten sets or the benefit is lost. A 65% weight is of no use moved slowly, but, when moved explosively for 20 reps in 10 minutes, it becomes a very powerful tool for the development of strength and power.

When beginning this type of training, it is normal to continue to use 5 sets of 5 on Monday and replace Friday's workout with DE sets. A lifter ready try this on the bench press might have done 250 pounds for 5 sets of 5, 270 for one set of 5, and might be assumed to have a 1RM of around 300. A good first week for this type of program might be 240 for 5 sets of 5 on Monday and 185 for 10 explosive triples on Friday, with one minute between sets. The weight to use for the sets is the most weight that allows all 30 reps to be done explosively. If even the last rep of the last set slows down, the weight is too heavy. In fact, the first time this workout is used, the last set of 3 should be noticeably faster than the first set.

The object is to maximally accelerate the bar and complete each set as quickly as possible. It is normal to take 2 to 3 workouts to find the correct weight, and then stay at that weight for several weeks while the weight increases on the sets-across workout. For instance, 185 on the bar for Friday's DE sets might work for 4 to 5 weeks, while normal progression on Monday's workout carries the weight incrementally back up to and past the previous 250 for 5 sets of 5. Remember, the object on Monday is heavy weight for sets across that goes up a little each week, and the object on Friday is moving the same weight as last Friday *faster*.

This is probably the best way to utilize this method the first time. It's the hardest to screw up, and the very act of trying to accelerate the bar, even without increasing the weight every week, will improve the ability to fire more motor units, which helps drive progress on the 5 sets of 5.

DE sets can be used with most multi-joint exercises, although different exercises customarily use different reps and sets. Squats use 2 reps, usually for 10 sets, while bench presses and presses typically use sets of 3, again for 10 sets; both are done with a one-minute rest between sets. Deadlifts work well with 15 singles on a 30-second clock. Weighted chin-ups have even been done this way. It works best to take each set out of the rack on the minute, re-rack it quickly after the set, and focus on the next set during the rest.

DE sets work well within the general intermediate template, because at first the ability to do relatively light weights fast will be underdeveloped, and the speed workout will not be that stressful. The speed workout is substituted for the PR workout on Friday, with the high-volume workout remaining as the primary stressor on Monday. The unique neuromuscular stimulus of this type of training should allow steady progress on Monday's workout for a while without subjecting the body to more stress than it can recover from. But as proficiency at DE sets increases, this workout can become stressful enough to be used as the main stressor on Monday, with a lower stress workout, possibly several heavy singles across, at the end of the week.

The Split Routine Model

The three-day-a-week, whole-body workout plan that has been used up to this point is a very effective way to organize training. In fact, most people would be well served by continuing this basic program design through their whole training career. It is an efficient use of time, and it provides a complete workout. There are, however, reasons to change from this model.

One possible reason is simple boredom. Training should be fun, and more progress will be made if it is. Different people have different psychological needs for variety. For some, the prospect of continuing on for years and years training the whole body three times a week is not welcome. These people will respond better to a program that varies more during the week, one that varies every week, or even every workout, as CrossFit programming does.

For some, a shift in goals or the need to combine gym workouts with more specific training for a competitive sport will prompt a change. This could be caused by time constraints, or by the need to avoid the systemic fatigue that a whole-body workout causes so it doesn't interfere with sport-specific training. Split routines address this problem by dividing the workload into more manageable segments along the lines of functional differences in the exercises.

A good example of a weekly schedule change would be that of a competitive shot-putter changing from 3 days a week to a 4-day-a-week program, as follows:

Monday
Squats and pressing exercises

Wednesday
Pulling exercises such as cleans and snatches, and other back work

Thursday
Squats and presses

Saturday
Pulling exercises

This can be appropriate for several reasons. Trainees involved in sports like the shot put normally do technique-oriented training several days a week, throwing various implements and using some form of plyometric training and sprint work. Good quality technique training is difficult the day after a whole-body workout, just as thirty throws would interfere with squats, pulls, and presses if done within an hour or two of practicing the shot put. What many would consider the most important exercises for the shot put – dynamic pulling exercises such as snatch, the clean, and related exercises – are placed by themselves so that the trainee can devote an appropriate amount of attention to them.

Many competitive powerlifters use a training schedule like this one:

Monday
Bench press and related exercises

Tuesday
Squatting and deadlifting exercises

Thursday
Bench press and related exercises

Friday or Saturday
Squatting and deadlifting exercises

For the powerlifter, the split serves a different purpose than for the shot-putter. The specialized equipment used in the sport lengthens time it takes to train each lift. Training all three lifts in one session would often mean an enormous stress on the body and a 4-hour session, something neither desirable nor possible for many people. The bench press is best trained the day before the squat so that it is not affected by the fatigue produced by squatting and deadlifting. As related movements, squatting and pulling exercises can be combined. With the focus on very heavy weights and the use of squat suits, bench press shirts, and wraps in the sport, these two lifts cannot be trained heavy more than once per week by most competitive lifters. Since the same basic muscle groups are used, it is convenient to have a heavy squat/light deadlift workout, and another that is heavy deadlift/light squat.

The Starr Model

A different model of weekly periodization described by Mark Berry in 1933 called for three training days per week and variation in workload among those days. In this model, the whole body is worked every day using many of the same exercises, but the amount of weight varies each day: a medium day, a heavy day, a light day. Various permutations of this model have been used for several decades, one of the most popular being the version presented by Bill Starr in his 1976 book *The Strongest Shall Survive*. Starr's was a similar three-day-per week model, with the loads ordered from heavy to medium to light, a slightly different application of the load/rest relationship than in the Texas method described earlier in this chapter. Another version was used by Dr. Mike Stone as early as 1976 and outlined in a number of his publications from the National Strength Research Laboratory at Auburn University in the early 1980s. Stone's method uses a simple load variation among four workouts per week (rather than the three of previous incarnations). Both the Starr and Stone models call for varying the exercises between days in addition to varying the load. Dr. Stone's model is perhaps the most completely researched and frequently cited periodization program in Western sports science literature. It works very well in its early three- and four-day stages for most strength and power athletes. Other coaches have adapted this program for Olympic weightlifters, adding a fifth and a sixth day as the athlete advances and adapts to an ever-increasing training load (table 7-1). For general strength development and powerlifting, a 5-to-6 day program is excessive, but due to the nature of weightlifting training – most importantly the marked reduction in the amount of eccentric work provided by an emphasis on the snatch and the clean and jerk – the extra days do not provide the type of stress that more absolute strength work would, and thus the longer schedule can actually be recovered from.

Adding a day for the purpose of increasing training volume is actually different from doing a 4-day split routine as described above, where the four days are essentially two workouts that have been divided into four. When increasing training volume from a three-day schedule, another complete day is added and the entire body is trained, as on the other 3 days, but at a different intensity.

Monday	Tuesday	Wednesday	Thursday	Friday	Saturday	Sunday
Three Days per Week						
Medium	Off	Heavy	Off	Light	Off	Off
Heavy	Off	Heavy	Off	Light	Off	Off
Four Days per Week						
Heavy	Medium	Off	Heavy	Light	Off	Off
Heavy	Heavy	Off	Heavy	Light	Off	Off
Five Days per Week (Olympic Lift Emphasis)						
Heavy	Medium	Heavy	Off	Heavy	Light	Off
Heavy	Heavy	Heavy	Off	Heavy	Light	Off
Six Days per Week						
Heavy	Heavy	Medium	Heavy	Heavy	Light	Off

Table 7-1. Progression of the variations of training frequency and intensities. Note that each time a day is added, it is medium in intensity. Each schedule is used for a few weeks or months until progress stalls, before attempting the next, more demanding, level. Notice that there is only one "light day" included in each weekly series and there is at least one complete day off each week. The 5- and 6-day versions of the program assume an Olympic weightlifting emphasis. Assuming 3 months to adapt to each new frequency/load, this table would represent about two years of training and progression in both volume and intensity.

It is extremely important to understand that the addition of training volume in the form of extra training days works only as long as recovery is being carefully managed. Adding an additional day to a program that is already producing overtraining would obviously be a bad idea, so the Starr model must be carefully applied to the right situation. If it can be determined that overtraining is not the cause of an athlete's plateau, the careful addition of the fourth workout can prompt progress to resume. If it does not, a review of the recovery milieu should reveal the problem, and the program should be reevaluated accordingly.

So far, we have used the terms "heavy," "medium," and "light" very loosely, but it is most useful to consider loads as percentages of 1RM, since this is a quantifiable value for each athlete. In general, "light" is any load less than 70% of 1RM, "medium" is greater than 70% but less than 85% of 1RM, and "heavy" is a load greater than 85% of 1RM (table 7-2), but this depends entirely on the number of reps done with the weight.

		Relative Intensity		
		Light	*Medium*	*Heavy*
	100	---	---	1
	90	---	1	3
Intensity	**80**	3	5	8
(% of 1RM)	**70**	5	8	10
	60	8	10	15
	50	12	20	25+
		Low	*Moderate*	*High*
			Adaptive Stimulus	

Table 7-2. The difficulty of a repetition scheme is a function of both the intensity and the volume used. The numbers in the table represent reps. A set of 3 repetitions with 90% 1RM is heavy, as is a set of 15 with 60% 1RM. As such, 60% for 15 reps cannot be considered a recovery workout any more than 90% for 3 reps can. Recovery during periodized training requires a reduction in relative intensity. For example, if sets of 3 are being used to train for strength, 90% would be a hard workout, and 70% for 3 reps would be considered an easy workout that will allow for recovery.

The heavy/medium/light concept seems simple enough. More complex, though, is its correct application. Doing one set of 3 with 70% is light work and will facilitate recovery as "active rest" if used as part of a light-day workout. But what happens with 5 sets of 10 at 70%? Each trainee at the intermediate level has a specific training goal: strength, power, or mass, and each of these goals has a specific repetition range associated with it. Each range also has an intensity (%1RM) associated with it that is a maximal stress. For example, a trainee should be able to do three sets of 10 with about 75% of 1RM. This would be difficult, so its *relative intensity* is high for the repetitions. Knowing this, offload or recovery days can be planned for by reducing the intensity without changing the reps. If 3 sets of 10 reps with 70% constitutes the heavy day, offload would be 50-60% of 1RM for three sets of 10. But if 80% for sets of 5 is the work, 70% for sets of 10 is not offloading, and it will not facilitate recovery. It is important to understand the relationship between repetitions and intensity, how to manage that relationship correctly, and how trainees respond to it (refer back to table 7-2).

Notice that we introduced the concept of 1RM testing and application for the first time in the discussion of intermediate trainees. As useful as 1RM is for trainees at this level, it does have its limitations for athletes in other situations.

Novice trainees cannot use a 1RM to determine anything, because 1) they cannot perform a true one-repetition maximum effort, and 2) if they could perform a 1RM, it would not be valid for exercise programming.

Novices, by definition, lack the motor skill to perform a valid 1RM on any barbell exercise. They have been performing the movements only a short time and have not had a chance to develop the motor pathway of the movement to the point where the effort can be the focus instead of the movement pattern. So, by definition, any heavy one-rep attempt at any barbell exercise by a novice is submaximal. Such a test proves nothing, tests nothing, and is dangerous enough for inexperienced trainees that it is not worth the risk.

One very good reason that the percentages calculated from such a test are invalid for determining work loads for the novice is the fact that novice trainees get stronger every time they are exposed to an effort they have not previously performed. If the test itself makes the trainee stronger, then the test has functioned as a training stimulus and the assumption that the value obtained is actually a 1RM is wrong. If a novice's ability improves every time he trains, he is essentially a different athlete than the one for whom the test is supposed to determine workloads.

Older athletes over 40, even at the intermediate level, need to be cautious when attempting 1RM, especially for purposes of determining programming percentages. It is one thing to risk an exposure to a heavy weight in a contest environment, since that is the purpose for training for the event. It is quite another for a masters athlete to test an actual 1RM as a diagnostic for further programming. If done using correct technique, 1RM can be tested during a heavy-day workout without a great deal of risk for an experienced athlete, and the results of a 1RM are more accurate than a sub-max RM test. But any 1RM effort is by definition less that perfect technically – if it were absolutely perfect a little more weight could be used. Masters competitors have enough problems already, among them chronic injuries being trained around, inelastic ligaments and tendons, and less efficient recovery abilities. Sometimes it might be better to rely on the subjective perception of the older, experienced athlete for information about absolute strength regarding his programming, depending on the acumen of that particular individual.

If the occasion arises that makes strength testing necessary, which should be done, 1RM or multi-RM? A multi-RM test done within the parameters of the workout program, using the same reps that the program is using at that time, is useful for determining program effectiveness. It provides a test result and does not disrupt the volume/intensity scheme the way a series of heavy singles would. But in the context of an effective program, a trainee is never far removed from a maximum multi-rep effort anyway, so this information is readily available without the test. The result of a formal 5RM test will not usually be more than 3 to 4 percent higher than 5 heavy reps done in the course of training.

All exercise testing carries a small amount of risk, but which is safer? A 1RM test is no more dangerous than a multi-RM for an open age-group competitor. A failed 1RM does not occur because it fatigues the muscle; the muscle simply cannot generate enough force to move the weight through the complete range of motion of the lift, and the spotters take it or the weight is dropped. In the absence of an active injury and assuming good technique, a 1RM is not inherently dangerous for an experienced lifter. Contrast this to a multi-RM test that uses repetition to muscle fatigue and subsequent failure. Not only is an additional factor (fatigue) added to the test (which now tests stamina in addition to strength), but the trainee is exposed to a larger, longer testing load. Neuromuscular fatigue and big loads handled to true 5RM intensity are more potentially dangerous than simple failure with one rep.

> The process of executing a 1RM test is fairly straightforward. After a warm-up, a series of progressively heavier attempts is made. Weight increases should be relatively small, and the test should include about 10 to 12 total reps. For a multi-RM test, the number of reps should be consistent with the current training program – it is unwise and ineffective to attempt a 5RM when sets of 5 have not been trained for several weeks. Weight should be added progressively after each successful set, with judgment exercised so that the last set before the final 5RM does not produce sufficient fatigue to adversely affect the results.
>
> It should be understood that a 5RM test yields a 5RM; and a 5RM is not terribly useful for predicting a 1RM. Many factors influence the efficiency with which an individual converts a 5RM to a 1RM, and it is not an exact science. There are many formulas that have been developed, none of which can take into account the factors peculiar to the individual test situation: the neuromuscular efficiency, experience, fatigue, mood, and sex (see chapter 9) of the athlete, not to mention the differences with which individual exercises convert from 5 reps to max single. If a 1RM value is required, then 1RM must be tested, since there is no other accurate way to produce or calculate one.

Remember, the goal of any model of weekly periodized training is to produce a disruption in homeostasis through the cumulative effects of training days, and then allow supercompensation to occur with the inclusion of the light day and the rest it provides. The light day is an absolutely essential component of the program; it is a recovery day. A light training load should not be enough to induce an overload and disrupt homeostasis, and it is not really a part of the overload event. It should be light enough to allow for recovery while at the same time providing enough work through the movement pattern to keep it fresh. Failure to include the light day indicates a lack of understanding of the actual workings of the program. A 70% day may seem too easy and appear to be wasted time, but the offloading it provides is necessary for progress. The average gym member focuses on how he feels during and after each workout – "I caught a most excellent pump today, my man!" – while the athlete trains for long-term improvement. Do not yield to the temptation to push up the percentages on light days. Remember this: you don't get strong by lifting weights. You get strong by *recovering* from lifting weights.

Recovery begins immediately after each workout, as the body begins to repair the damage done by the stress so that adaptation can occur, and all the significant damage is done during the heavy workouts. Light days do not add to the damage. They aid recovery from it by increasing blood flow to the sore areas, working the joints through the ROM, and helping with fatigue the way nature has been dealing with it for millions of years – by forcing recovery during unavoidable continuing activity. The light workout is therefore embedded in the part of the week in which recovery takes place. In this model, it does not matter what day of the week the light day falls on. A light day on Friday means that by Monday a trainee should be recovered and ready for more. If the light day is on Monday, the trainee should be recovered and ready for a larger load on Wednesday or Thursday.

Intensity Variation. It is imperative in the Starr model to vary training stress during the week in some form or another. Varying the intensity – the percentage of 1RM lifted – is only one way to do so. Doing the same heavy-day workout in a weekly schedule that calls for 2 heavy days per week will not work very long. When a week contains multiple heavy days, different ways to train heavy must be used each time or staleness will result. In the example above, 5 sets of 5 across on Monday with one heavier set of 5 reps on Wednesday is an excellent way to vary the quality of the heavy day and keep the intensity high. Using different numbers of reps at the same high relative intensity works well: for a week with three heavy days, a good organization would be 5 heavy sets of 5 across on Monday, one heavy triple on Tuesday, and 5 heavy singles on Thursday. The critical factor is the variation among the heavy workouts, keeping the overall training stress high while changing up the quality of the work done.

Rest between sets is a variable that lends itself to manipulation quite readily. In the earlier discussion of dynamic effort sets, we noted that control of the rest time is an important variable. All training facilities should have an analog clock with a sweep second hand for this purpose. Sets that would otherwise be easy can be made very hard by limiting recovery between sets to a minute or less, such that only partial recovery is possible and each following set is done in a climate of accumulating fatigue.

As discussed above, speed of movement is a variable that can be manipulated very effectively, especially if power production is a primary training consideration. A high bar speed with an exercise traditionally done slowly produces a much higher power output, allowing the squat, press, bench press, and deadlift to be trained at a high rate of force production while using a relatively light weight. This work increases neuromuscular efficiency because of the amount of force necessary to accelerate the weight to high velocity, but it lacks the heavy skeletal load that accompanies weights closer to 1RM, thus stressing the ligaments less than heavier weights otherwise would and contributing to better and easier recovery.

Some exercises are by their nature more demanding than others, in terms of their effects on recovery. Heavy, limit-level deadlifts are very stressful on the entire physiological system, making sets across at a high percentage of 1RM a bad choice for the deadlift because of their effects on the rest of the training week. One heavy set of deadlifts usually produces sufficient stress without the need for more sets. Conversely, the stress produced by even very heavy power cleans is of a different quality, since the factors that limit the amount of weight in the power clean do not involve absolute strength and therefore do not stress the contractile components of muscle, the ligaments and tendons, and the nervous system at the level the deadlift does. Heavy cleans produce their own unique type of stress, related to the impact involved in racking the bar, but it is quite different from that produced by a heavy deadlift. As a general rule, exercises strictly dependent on absolute strength for their execution at heavy weights are harder to recover from than technique-dependent exercises that are limited by skill of execution and power production and that are typically done without a significant eccentric component. This is why the Olympic lifts can be trained with a higher frequency than the power lifts, and why training programs for athletes must take into consideration the relative intensities of the primary components of the program.

Whatever the method used, higher intensity work must be varied if it is to be used for long periods of time in the context of weekly programming. If variation does not occur, and good choices are not made about how to approach training stress variation, progress will slow prematurely.

Frequency Variation. The obvious way to increase volume during the training week in the Starr model is to add workouts. Add training sessions one at a time and hold the volume constant for several weeks or months, until progress slows at that volume, at which point you can add another day. The tremendous number of possible combinations of workouts per week and light-medium-heavy loading make this model of training useful for 2 to 3 years, possibly longer than either of the other two models. When introducing an additional workout, initially add it as a medium-intensity day. Later, as the trainee adapts to the load, the relative intensity of the additional day can be increased.

Progression through the number of workouts per week requires close observation of how the trainee tolerates each addition. Some trainees initially appear to handle a fourth training day with ease, but then crash two to four weeks later: work tolerance goes down, performance decreases, nagging injuries or pain become evident. This point may be the upper limit of the trainee's work capacity, the point beyond which overtraining will occur. Some offloading must happen for a short time, either by changing a heavy day to a light day or by eliminating a single workout (not the light one) for two weeks or until the trainee feels normal again. Failure to do so could easily result in a first exposure to overtraining, costing valuable training time and producing frustration and possible chronic injuries that could interfere with long-term progress. The way this first exposure to excessive overload is handled is crucial to later dealings with overtraining issues. Correct offloading and recovery now teaches the importance of recovery in the grand scheme of training and establishes a precedent for an intelligent approach to handling overtraining.

Most athletes will not need to even attempt training schedules of more than four days per week. There are few sports that benefit from more than four days of training outside their specific practice requirements. Powerlifting, as it has been traditionally trained, does not typically use more than four days per week, although some more progressive lifters have gotten good results by doing so and the paradigm is changing. But field sports, Highland games, strongman competition, and team sports that use barbell conditioning will not normally need or desire any more gym time than a four-day program provides. So anyone interested in five or six days of training is probably a competitor in one of the barbell sports – weightlifting or powerlifting – or is a physique competitor.

For these athletes, each increase in training volume must be carefully gauged. As training progress slows each time volume is added, the cause of the plateau must be correctly evaluated to make sure that the slowdown is not caused by a non-volume-related training variable. It might be that the intensity is too high on one or more of the heavy days or too low on more than one of the heavy days, or that proper recovery is not being attended to. If the cause of the plateau is determined to be other than training volume, progress should be restored by fixing these problems before volume is increased again.

Very fit trainees who tolerate the five- and six-days-per-week schedules may further benefit from doing two workouts on one or more days per week. Dr. Keijo Hakkinen has shown that strength gains may be more efficiently produced by dividing up a day's training volume into two workouts instead of one. This system is used in many national team training situations where the athlete's schedule is completely free of outside constraints on time and recovery. Instead of spending two to three hours in the gym at one time, an hour or so two or more times a day allows the body to experience additional recuperation between training stresses. In collegiate programs and in professional sports situations, it is the strength coach's job to be there to help, and the athletes' responsibility to do everything they can to improve. But most athletes will not be able to conform to a schedule like this due to obvious conflicts with school, work, and family. In high school programs, the schedule is determined by the available time, not by what would be ideal for training.

The intermediate trainee can use this programming schedule for quite some time. There is a great deal of room for progression, with variations in both sets/reps and workout intensities as strength improves and the number of training sessions increases systematically. The limit on the number of workouts per week for this model of periodization is highly individual. Personal schedules, family commitments, work, and the ability to physiologically and psychologically adapt to high training volumes all play a role. At some level, the ability to increase training volume to the maximum tolerable level may determine the ultimate success of the athlete. Five heavy training days and one light day repeated every week for three months is something from which very few people can recover adequately; most will be overtrained on such a demanding schedule. The vast majority will not get even this far before overtraining becomes a major problem. Only the most genetically gifted athletes who are also able to devote all necessary time to training and recovery can function at this high level of loading without gigantic problems. The ability to do so indicates that the athlete can function and progress at the extremes of human ability, the very quality necessary for elite-level performance.

If it is determined that the trainee has reached the end of the usefulness of weekly training organization, advanced programming methods are warranted.

8 – The Advanced Trainee

The advanced trainee is one for whom a weekly training organization is no longer working. At this level of advancement, an overload event and subsequent recovery from it may take a month or more. Furthermore, each overload event may be designed to produce a different type of overload, such that several of these longer periods taken together produce cumulative effects that they would not produce separately.

Arguably the most important step in the stress/adaptation cycle is the recovery – without it, adaptation does not occur. For the novice, a simple day off between workouts is sufficient. For the intermediate, several days are required, during which a couple of low-impact workouts are performed to preserve skill and conditioning and to demonstrate increased performance. For the advanced trainee, the rest phase can be one or two weeks of decreased training load, comprising several workouts that are low enough in volume to allow fatigue to dissipate but high enough in intensity to maintain the skills needed to demonstrate peak performance. Because of the interplay between stress and adaptation of different physical skills at different times, the advanced trainee is almost always in the process of trying to rest some particular physical quality while working to develop a different one. This makes for a complex training milieu, and care must be taken when setting the stage.

Periodization is the term most frequently used when referring to the organization of weight training programming into periods of time longer than the interval between two workouts. Its central organizing principle is the variation of volume and intensity in order to obtain a training objective. One of the most commonly referenced models of periodization is attributed to Leonid Matveyev and is so entrenched in the literature that it is often referred to as "classical" periodization. Conventional wisdom holds that Matveyev's model is the only way to program resistance training for everyone, regardless of their level of training advancement.

The concept of periodic variation in training volume and intensity has been around for quite some time. It is quite probable that the training of ancient Greek athletes involved the use of periods of heavier and lighter training, especially considering the fact that the scheduling of games was dependent on the cycles of war and agriculture. At the turn of the last century, the term "photoperiod" was used to describe the phenomenon observed among athletes performing better in late summer and early fall. It was assumed that the amount of sunlight exposure contributed to the improved performance, and so the most stressful training was done in spring and summer.

As early as 1933, Mark Berry was using weekly variations in programming for his bodybuilders and weightlifters, and wrote about it in several publications. In the 1950s, Lazlo Nadori, a sports scientist and coach in Hungary, developed a model of periodization for his athletes. The development of this particular model was unique to Hungary and was separate from the evolution of Soviet block periodization, since no translations of his work into Russian were done. In the 1960s, Russian weightlifting coach Leonid Matveyev developed his concepts of periodization, and his 1971 book provides several different models for a diversity of sports. The one of these that is now known as "classical" periodization was intended for beginners. Later in 1981, Matveyev's book, *"Fundamentals of Sport Training"* was translated into German and English (many thanks to Dr. Bernard Burton for procuring a copy of this rare book for the authors). Having written the first periodization book available in the West, he became known as the father of periodization by default.

Also in the 1960s Matveyev's hated rival Yuri Verkhoshansky developed his system of conjugated loading, openly stating that periodization was crap. But since his conjugated loading system was also periodized, it must be assumed that he really just thought Matveyev's approach to periodization was crap. In 1982, East German sports scientist Dr. Dietrich Harre edited *Principles of Sport Training,* which is essentially a fusion of the works of Nadori and Matveyev. A couple of years later, Frank Dick, the head of British track and field, "liberally recreated" Harre's book in English. Tudor Bompa, the Romanian author of the famous text *Periodization,* was trained in the East German system, and his first and subsequent texts are essentially reiterations and adaptations of Harre's adaptation of Nadori and Matveyev. And here we are today with no new thoughts, no new systems, and no real explanations of periodization since the last century. What we do have is a large misunderstanding about what periodization is and how to use it.

The fact is that, from Mark Berry's observations in the 1930s forward, the basic features of training for advanced athletes preparing for a competition have always been these two things:

Thing 1 – The closer an athlete is to individual genetic potential, the more important the cumulative effects of a series of workouts become (fig. 8-1).

Thing 2 – Training for more advanced athletes must be organized into longer periods of time, and those periods progress from higher volume and lower intensity toward lower volume and higher intensity (fig. 8-2).

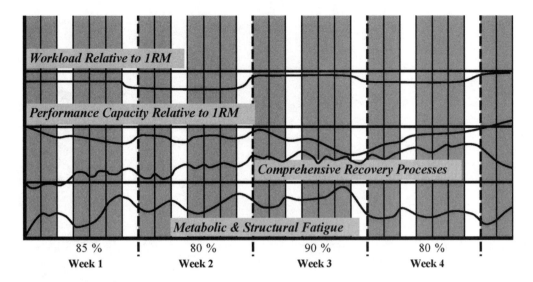

Figure 8-1. Thing 1. The advanced trainee responds to periodized programming over a longer period of time than either the beginner or intermediate trainee. Gray bars indicate training days, white bars are days off.

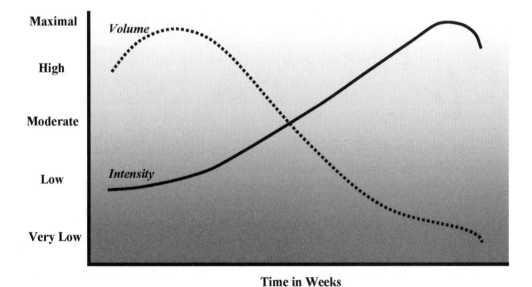

Figure 8-2. Thing 2. There is generally an inverse relationship between volume and intensity during a single training cycle for the advanced trainee.

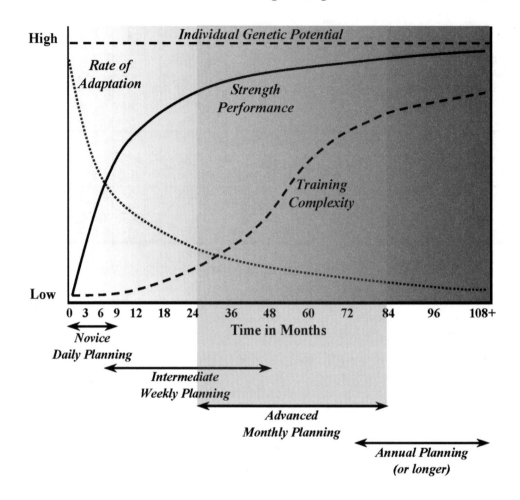

Figure 8-3. The generalized relationship between performance improvement and training complexity relative to time.

As simple linear progression directs the novice's workout-to-workout training, and as simple weekly variation directs the intermediate's training, Thing 1 applies to athletes whose response to training has advanced to the point that several weeks at a time must be considered in their programming. Thing 2 is a function of the fact that advanced athletes compete, they do so at specific times, and their training has to allow all aspects of performance to peak at those particular times. A novice is not a competitive athlete, at least not in any serious sense. An intermediate may compete, but performance at the intermediate level is still progressing quickly enough that each weekend represents a peak anyway. Advanced athletes produce a peak by appointment only, and that peak must be scheduled in advance and trained for precisely and accurately.

There are many ways to set up programs that fit within these parameters. Advanced programs are by their very nature highly individual matters, since no two athletes at this level are the same. They must be carefully developed according to the athlete's training history, personal tolerances and abilities, and the schedule of both the athlete and the sport.

With this in mind, four basic versions will be presented here. First, a very simple pyramid model that illustrates the general principles involved in longer programming models. Second, one that works well for barbell sports in particular, the Two Steps Forward, One Step Back model. Next, the Building Blocks model, which uses four-week periods, each devoted to a different aspect of physical preparedness, to accumulate all of the necessary elements at meet time. And last, the Hormonal Fluctuation model, which uses a 5- to 8-week period of very intense training to force an adaptation through specific manipulation of the endocrine system.

The Pyramid Model

The best way to jump into longer training cycles is with a very simple model, with a structure that consists of nothing more than a pyramid that lasts for a two-month period. This example uses the squat, and a lifter whose 1RM is 400 pounds, 5RM is 365, and 5 sets of 5 max is 340.

Week 1		**Week 3**	
Monday:	$300 \times 5 \times 5$	Monday:	$330 \times 5 \times 5$
Wednesday:	$250 \times 5 \times 5$	Wednesday:	$250 \times 5 \times 5$
Friday:	$300 \times 5 \times 5$	Friday:	$330 \times 5 \times 5$
Week 2		**Week 4**	
Monday:	$315 \times 5 \times 5$	Monday:	$335 \times 5 \times 5$
Wednesday:	$250 \times 5 \times 5$	Wednesday:	$225 \times 5 \times 5$
Friday:	$325 \times 5 \times 5$	Friday:	$345 \times 5 \times 5$

These first four weeks make up the "loading" portion of the cycle. The total weekly training volume is much higher than the trainee has previously done, with five sets of five across for two heavy days per week rather than just one, and one offloading day. This volume is such that the trainee should experience some residual fatigue and may not make a PR for 5 sets of 5 by the end of week four. In fact, by Friday of week three the trainee might have trouble completing the prescribed sets and reps. But if fatigue has not accumulated, if recovery is occurring well, and all the reps of the fourth week's sets are finished, it would be useful to milk this process for another week, establishing significant new PRs for 5×5, before entering a peaking phase.

The four weeks that follow – the peaking phase – are dramatically different:

Week 5		**Week 7**	
Monday:	340 × 3 × 3	Monday:	380 × 3
Wednesday:	250 × 5	Wednesday:	250 × 5
Friday:	350 × 3 × 3	Friday:	390 × 3
Week 6		**Week 8**	
Monday:	360 × 3 × 3	Monday:	350 × 3
Wednesday:	250 × 5	Wednesday:	250 × 5
Friday:	370 × 3 × 3	Friday:	400 × 3

As in the loading phase, another week can be added if warranted by recovery and progress in order to get the most out of the cycle.

Reducing the volume and total training stress in this second phase allows gradual recovery from the previous high-training volume. During weeks five through eight, the trainee is actually "resting" from the previous high-volume work, and as fatigue dissipates and adaptation occurs, improved performance is attained. Weeks one through four are, in essence, doing the same job as the Monday high-volume workout in the Texas Method intermediate program, placing enough stress on the body to force adaptation, and weeks five through eight function like the Texas Wednesday and Friday workouts, allowing for rest and adaptation and the demonstration of increased performance. But for the advanced trainee the process is stretched out over a much longer timeframe.

It is possible to successfully repeat a simple pyramid cycle like this several times, with virtually no changes other than an increased load. A trainee who completes this cycle might start the next cycle on week one, with Monday's workout weight set at 315 × 5 × 5, and end up with 415 × 3 at the end of week eight. This process could carry forward for many months, possibly longer.

Usually, a week or two of "active rest" or less-frequent training with moderate weights is a good idea between cycles to assure that the trainee is rested and ready to undergo another period of stressful training. After finishing the above cycle, squatting twice per week for two weeks with 2 or 3 sets of 5 at 300 pounds would be appropriate.

The effectiveness of the pyramid cycle is not limited to sets of 5 and 3. Loading could be 3 sets of 10. Peaking could be one set of 5. The important thing is to do sufficient volume during the loading phase so that fatigue is accumulated, enough to make performance at or near PR levels difficult but not impossible. A good rule of thumb is that if levels of 90% or more of 5RM cannot be performed during week three before any reduction in training volume occurs, the workload is probably too high. If the trainee is at or above PR levels at the end of the loading period, an increase in loading for the next cycle will probably work.

This simple example of the basics of longer programming can obviously be applied to all the lifts, not just the squat. There are also more complicated plans, each useful in its own particular set of circumstances.

The Two Steps Forward, One Step Back Model

A second model, a variation on one used by USA Weightlifting's former national coach Lyn Jones with some of his athletes, manipulates the workload in four-week blocks, with progress made by connecting a series of these blocks using progressively higher loads. Each block starts with a week at a baseline load of moderate intensity. The second week moves average intensity up 10%. The third week is an offload or recovery week where average intensity is reduced 5%. This lighter week enables a 10% increase in load in the fourth week. The next four-week cycle begins at an intensity 10% greater than the previous cycle's starting point. Each of the series of four-week blocks prepares the trainee for the next, progressively heavier, block. Although each block may have a slightly different goal in terms of a particular narrow range of sets and reps, this model lacks the large magnitude in goal variation that is the primary feature of the Building Blocks model that we will discuss in detail later in this chapter. Each four-week cycle is slightly different, but they flow seamlessly toward the contest date with the object of improving the specific aspects of performance required that day.

The TSFOSB model is not expected to achieve a measurable improvement in 1RM every four weeks. An advanced trainee will experience an improvement in performance with each four-week cycle, but the slow rate of improvement in the advanced trainee may be imperceptible over a period as short as four weeks (note the shallow slope of the performance improvement curve in figure 8-3). Each block functions as an overload event, but the adaptation to the overload may produce an improvement small enough that it can be easily measured only in the cumulative. Research suggests that a trainee at this level may improve only 10 to 20 pounds on the basic exercises in up to a year's time – less than two pounds per month – depending on the individual and the exercise, a quantity small enough to be buried in daily variation.

As a result, 1RM is not tested at the end of each cycle; the 1RM that the trainee was capable of in the very first week is used as a reference point throughout several connected cycles. And loads beyond 100% are not included. For example, if the previous cycle was programmed for 90%-85%-95%-90%, it would be tempting to follow the pattern and assign 100%-95%-105%-100% for the next four weeks. However, the cycle is too short to produce a successful 105% effort. This improvement in four weeks would be 40 pounds on a 400-pound squat, an unreasonable expectation. Such progress is possible for a novice or an intermediate trainee, but these adaptive capacities have already been exhausted by this point or advanced programming manipulation would not be necessary. What actually should happen is that the four-week block starting with 100% tapers for the remainder of the cycle toward final testing or a competition done at the end of week four. The new 1RM performed at the meet or test would serve as the benchmark for the next series of four-week cycles.

Setting up a four-week block of training in this format is fairly simple. Four-week blocks will usually be strung together into a longer period during which volume decreases and intensity increases, so it is necessary to identify the target date in advance and count back from there (this is a common feature of all contest-oriented programming). The number of weeks between the starting date and the target date determines the number of four-week segments and governs the selection of volumes and intensities. The example below is for 12 weeks using three four-week blocks. In a perfect world, four such series with one week's active rest after each would fill out a year's training schedule. But things usually do not work out this way, and shorter or longer programs can be designed using the same principles.

For the following example, the program's overall goal is power and strength. Each cycle throughout the training year can and should have a different goal. Simple repetition of the same program over and over will produce staleness and leave many aspects of performance undeveloped.

Exercises for the cycle are chosen based on the focus of the cycle, and the focus of each workout. The following three-day-per week example incorporates power development exercises (power snatch, power clean) and strength exercises (squats, presses, deadlifts). There are four exercises on two of the days, and three on the other, allowing for some daily variation. The whole body should be trained every workout, since large-scale stress on the whole system is more effective at driving adaptation than exercising a small amount of muscle.

The goal in this cycle is to develop power and strength for a weightlifter, so a repetition range from singles to sets of five is appropriate. The exercises used should be appropriate for this rep range. One way to manipulate the volume is to vary the numbers of reps and sets. Since the trainee is well adapted to volumes of up to 5 sets of 5, we can use 5 work sets as an initial target, and then vary the number of sets to produce onload/offload. Volume starts high and progressively goes down through the four-week blocks. This means that the sets of five will be done first in the program. The triples, doubles, and singles will come toward the end of the cycle.

In this model, loads are determined according to specific percentages of the trainee's 1RM. For example:

Week	1	2	3	4
Repetitions	5	5	5	3
Sets	5	5	4	5
Percent 1RM	70	80	75	85

Using percentages of 1RM for advanced athletes is no problem, since all advanced athletes have sufficient experience with the exercises to know their current 1RM values within a few pounds, even if a 1RM has not been performed recently. The percent of 1RM used can vary within a workout or workouts but should average out to the programmed percentage over the week. And a more advanced athlete might need to use more than the 5% offload in week three. Small alterations are acceptable as long as they remain within the general guidelines.

When calculating intensity, consider only the heaviest sets in the workout. Do not use warm-up sets in programming calculations, because the sometimes-necessary extra warm-up will skew the calculation down and give an inaccurate picture of the actual intensity of the workout.

Using week three as an example, the TSFOSB model uses work sets at 75% of 1RM for sets of 5 across. To calculate the work sets, we multiply each of our hypothetical 190 lb. athlete's best lifts by 0.75, as follows:

Power snatch:	$198 \times 0.75 = 148$ lbs.
Power clean:	$264 \times 0.75 = 198$ lbs.
Press:	$175 \times 0.75 = 131$ lbs. (use 130)
Bench press:	$275 \times 0.75 = 206$ lbs. (use 205)
Back squat:	$405 \times 0.75 = 303$ lbs. (use 305)
Deadlift:	$450 \times 0.75 = 337$ lbs. (use 340)

Now, we make a few changes to tailor the workout to the lifts and the lifter. Due to the nature of the quick lifts, power snatches should be done for doubles and power cleans for triples, instead of fives. The main pulling assistance movements, the snatch and clean high pulls – essentially the same form as the full movement, especially the shrug, but without the rack at the top – will use weights that are 20% heavier than the full version of the lift. This is because partial movements can be done heavier, and must be done heavier if the benefit of position-holding strength off the floor is to be obtained. Straps are normally used for these movements as well, to save the hands for the main lifts. Deadlifts are very hard to recover from if used for sets across, so only one work set will be done, at about 80%, since the volume is reduced. The work sets for the week will then be as follows:

Day	Exercise type	Exercise	Load
1	Technical/fast	Power snatch	$148 \times 2 \times 4$
	Upper body	Press	$130 \times 5 \times 4$
	Lower body	Back squat	$305 \times 5 \times 4$
2	Technical/fast	Power clean	$198 \times 3 \times 4$
	Fast	Clean pull	$231 \times 5 \times 4$
	Upper body	Bench press	$205 \times 5 \times 4$
	Lower body	Deadlift	365×5
3	Technical/Fast	Power snatch	$148 \times 2 \times 4$
	Fast	Snatch pull	$175 \times 5 \times 4$
	Upper body	Press	$130 \times 5 \times 4$
	Lower body	Back squat	$305 \times 5 \times 4$

To introduce some daily variation within the week, it is useful to alter the squat loads. The day 1 back squat weight is increased by 5% and the day 3 load is decreased by 5%. This does not affect average intensity, and it produces a more balanced, less monotonous week. The day 1 back squat will be $320 \times 5 \times 4$ and the day 3 back squat will be $290 \times 5 \times 4$. Such minor changes should be made as needed, along with any others that seem necessary to the execution of the program, as long as they remain within the guidelines and intent.

There are a few details that remain to be addressed, two of which are assistance exercises and stretching. **Assistance exercises** are not directly related to the movement patterns of sport performance, but support other exercises that are. Examples of these would be all types of abdominal work, low-back exercises such as back extensions, and chins and pull-ups. These types of exercises are important, as they contribute to trunk stability during sports performance and to the execution of basic barbell exercises. Strengthening these areas will also reduce the chance for injury. The programming of assistance exercises is done separately, and they are not included in the volume and intensity calculations for the overall workout. Generally, these exercises involve smaller muscle groups, and are done with fewer sets and higher reps than the core movements. When done appropriately, they are not stressful enough systemically that they add enough work to perturb the rest of the training program.

By this point in an athlete's career there should be no need to do any special flexibility work prior to training. Issues of correct exercise performance and range of motion should be long resolved. But if a need for flexibility maintenance still exists, stretching should be done at the end of the workout for best results and the least interference with the power movements.

Once all these calculations have been performed for all the weeks in the program, the whole cycle is laid out. The final program with assistance exercises and warm-up sets included for the 75% week looks like the following:

Day	Exercise type	Exercise	Warm-up sets	Work sets
1	Warm-up			
	Technical/fast	Power snatch	88-88-110-132	$148 \times 2 \times 4$
	Upper body	Press	45-75-95-115	$130 \times 5 \times 4$
	Lower body	Back squat	135-185-225-275	$320 \times 5 \times 4$
	Assistance	Chin-ups	Bodyweight	Failure $\times 3$
	Assistance	Back extension	Bodyweight	20×3
	Abs	Weighted situps		
	Stretch			
2	Warm-up			
	Technical/fast	Power clean	88-132-154-176	$198 \times 3 \times 4$
	Fast	Clean pull	198-220	$231 \times 5 \times 4$
	Upper body	Bench press	45-95-135-175	$205 \times 5 \times 4$
	Lower body	Deadlift	135-225-275-315	365×5
	Abs	Twist		
	Stretch			

3   Warm-up

Technical/fast	Power snatch	88-88-110-132	$148 \times 2 \times 4$
Fast	Snatch pull	154	$176 \times 5 \times 4$
Upper body	Press	45-75-95-115	$130 \times 5 \times 4$
Lower body	Back squat	135-185-225-260	$290 \times 5 \times 4$
Assistance	Pull-ups	Bodyweight	Failure $\times 3$
Assistance	Back extension	Bodyweight	20×3
Abs	Weighted situps		
Stretch			

The volume and intensity variation within the four-week block follows the intra-cycle relationship that has volume decreasing and intensity increasing between blocks. The full twelve-week cycle is detailed below. The final block of the twelve-week series maintains the increased intensity and decreased volume relationship for the first two weeks, and then both volume and intensity are reduced by 10 to 20% in the final two weeks. This allows for cumulative recovery and supercompensation prior to the event or test.

Week	1	2	3	4
Repetitions	5	5	5	5
Sets	5	5	4	5
Percent	70	80	75	85

Week	5	6	7	8
Repetitions	3	3	3	3
Sets	5	5	4	5
Percent	80	90	85	95

Week	9	10	11	12
Repetitions	3	1	1	1
Sets	4	5	4	4
Percent	90	100	85	80

If an athlete stops making progress using this model after a year or so, there are a number of possible reasons. The offload weeks may not be sufficient for recuperation. Increase the magnitude of offload to 10 or 15% while maintaining the programmed increases: instead of 70%-80%-75%-85%, for example, try 65%-80%-60%-85%. Or break up longer workouts into two workouts separated by at least four hours. This allows the body additional recovery during the training day and, depending on other daily activities, may be what some athletes need to cope with an intense training program.

If these simple fixes do not work, the athlete may be experiencing the consequences of increased performance ability and work capacity, a need for longer recovery periods following longer periods of more intense training closer to genetic potential that other programs can provide.

This type of cycle, where the degree of variability is low and the main parameter that is manipulated is intensity, has much in common with intermediate level programming, in that it is very simple in terms of the variables manipulated and the degree of manipulation. It works well for athletes at a certain level of advancement in a sport like weightlifting with very narrow performance characteristics. More metabolically complicated sports require more elaborate programming.

The Building Blocks Model

The building blocks model provides that elaboration. It is common to see references to "phases" of training, defined as a period of time spent developing a specific component of the training necessary for the sport. Phases might typically be assigned to develop hypertrophy, strength, muscular endurance, power, and technique, with a competition scheduled at the end of these phases when all components are brought to bear on the contest. This particular order is designed specifically to develop these five important performance characteristics in the order in which they persist most effectively over the time (fig. 8-4), hypertrophy being most persistent and least relevant to performance (unless the contest is physique) and technique being the most relevant and most sensitive to the temporal proximity of the contest.

The concept of **adaptation persistence** plays an important role in contest preparation for some sports. Beyond the well-recognized fact that strength is more persistent than cardiovascular endurance, few training references have observed which parameter is more persistent once developed. This hierarchy can be logically derived from an analysis of the mechanisms involved in the adaptation, as well as from coaching observations of athletes over time (fig. 8-4).

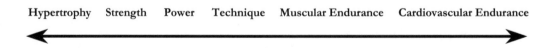

Hypertrophy   Strength   Power   Technique   Muscular Endurance   Cardiovascular Endurance

Figure 8-4. The continuum of adaptation persistence. Cardiovascular endurance is the least persistent, hypertrophy the most persistent. Significant loss of VO_2 max (cardiovascular endurance) can occur in a matter of days, whereas the significant decay of added muscle mass (hypertrophy) may take many weeks or months following cessation of training. Weight training using any range of reps maintains muscle mass. It is suggested here that structural changes that contribute to performance are more persistent than metabolic changes contributing to performance.

That the most persistent parameter should be included first, farthest away from the planned event, makes good sense when laying out the training cycle. And it is logical that the least persistent parameter should be included in close proximity to the planned event wherever possible. In this way a summation effect is achieved, with all training parameters included as phases in a sequence that leads to the most effective performance enhancement at the correct time.

The phases may differ according to the sport the program is designed for. An exception to the general concept of adaptation persistence might occur if the performance parameter most pertinent to the contest is not technique, as might be the case in a strongman competition. Powerlifting programs will differ markedly from weightlifting programs, which will be different from programs designed for throwers, strongman competitors, or Highland games athletes. For example, a sequence of phases may be designed without a hypertrophy component if it has little to do with performance or if the athlete is already carrying enough muscle mass; this is typically the case with advanced athletes, having developed most of their muscle mass during the novice and intermediate phases of training. Depending on the contested events, a strongman program might not include a lot of work heavily dependent on technique, since a five-event contest does not allow for a tremendous amount of specialization, and might instead focus on strength as a common component of several of the events. And to the extent that muscular endurance – especially grip strength and endurance – is developed using exercises that are typically found as contested events, sufficient technique training may be accomplished at the same time.

Several groups of four-week blocks may be assembled into a training cycle of many months' duration (fig. 8-5). The primary factor affecting the organization of such a cycle would be, of course, the competitive schedule. Remember, any athlete who needs programming at this degree of complexity is a competitor in a sport, and the requirements of the sport dictate the programming. Another important factor is the athlete's personal competitive history, which allows for the analysis of individual strengths and weaknesses that require focused attention in the programming. Form and technique problems are addressed in each workout, but an inadequate strength base would be addressed over a period of months, which requires that multiple training blocks be devoted to it.

We will use preparation for a strongman contest as an example for the building blocks model. Unlike the smooth transitions characteristic of TSFOSB programming, the building blocks method utilizes phases that may have relatively little in common, resulting in what may seem like abrupt transitions. The only requirement is that enough time be allotted in each block to allow for a complete overload event to occur before moving to the next block. The blocks are organized in a way that takes advantage of adaptation persistence so that each training parameter receives enough attention at the most useful point in the cycle, and the suddenness of transitions is irrelevant. Illustrated below are selected weeks from each of the blocks.

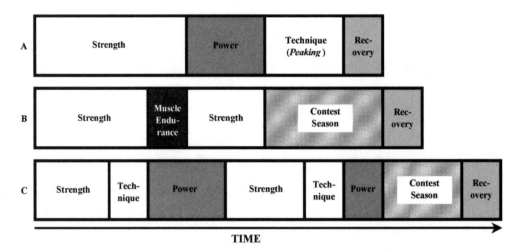

Figure 8-5. Three examples of sequencing the components of a longer-term training plan. A) A sample program for a weightlifter. B) A sample program for a strongman competitor. C) A sample program for a Highland games athlete. Each individual program should be arranged with the most persistent component block first and the least persistent last, with respect to the limitations and needs of the particular sport.

As the name suggests, the strength block is critical to strongman competition. Strength makes size more useful (there are lots of big weak men). Strength is the whole purpose of the sport, since all other aspects of it derive from strength: heavy implements must be carried a long way and handled through turns; heavy odd objects must be lifted; trucks must be pulled; heavy yokes must be carried. The strength blocks produce, ultimately, the most important training effect of the whole cycle, the one that directly contributes the most to success at the contest.

<u>Sample Week 1 - Strength Block</u>
Heavy loads and low reps

Exercise	Reps	Work Sets
Day 1		
Squat	3	8
Fat bar row	3	8
Fat bar clean and push press	3	5
Weighted dips	10	3

Day 2

Tire flip	5 flips	10
Farmer's walk	100' no turn	3
Farmer's deadlift	5	5
Stone series (3)	1	5

Day 3

Squat	5	5
Press	1	10
Deadlift	5	5

Day 4

Yoke walk	50'	4
Sled drag	100'	5
Keg carry	100' one turn	5

Because some strongman events require the execution of multiple repetitions, or the use of a prolonged muscular effort, local muscle endurance is nearly as important as strength and is very dependent on it. Training for local muscular endurance involves higher numbers of reps with lighter weights and shorter rest intervals. Prolonged isometric holds and gripping and carrying exercises are an important component, since many strongmen events are of precisely this nature. Glycolytic metabolism dominates this type of activity, which typically lasts for 60 to 90 seconds of work with heavy weights.

Sample Week 1 - Muscular Endurance Block
High reps, moderate/light loads, high speed, low rest

Exercise	Reps	Work Sets
Day 1		
Clean and press	5	8, 1 min. rest
Barbell row	10	5, 2 min. rest
Squat	3	10, 1 min. rest
Day 2		
Tire flips	10 flips	5
Farmer's walk	100', 1 turn	8
Farmer's hold	For max time	2
Day 3		
Fat bar push press	10	3
Deadlift	1	20, 30 sec. rest
Front squat	5	5
Dips, bodyweight	To failure	2
Day 4		
Log press	3	10, 1 min. rest
Sled drag	100'	4, 5 min. rest
Stone (or sandbag) carry	To failure	1

The final segment of training is a peaking block. Following the general contest preparation model, the peaking block will have the highest intensity training and the lowest volume of all four blocks, done with a high degree of contest specificity. Non-contest-specific work is limited to one day per week, and contest events are trained in a way that allows for maximum recovery while exposing the athlete to all the events scheduled for the show.

Sample Week 2 – Contest Season
Heavy loads and low reps

Exercise	Reps	Work Sets
Day 1		
Farmer's walk	50', 1 turn	5
Log press	To failure	3
Day 2		
Squat	5	5
Clean	5	5
Deadlift	3	3
Weighted dips	5	5
Day 3		
Yoke walk	50'	4
Stone series (5)	1	3
Day 4		
Tire flip	10	5

The week before the contest completes the taper period. Light non-specific work is done twice this week for the express purpose of preventing staleness before the event. The loads should be no heavier than 80% of 1RM, and for low reps, light enough that recovery from the previous weeks is not interrupted but the ranges of motion used in the contest are fresh and open.

Week 5 – Taper
Light loads and low reps

Exercise	Reps	Work Sets
Day 1		
Back squat	2	5
Barbell rows	3	5
Glute-ham raises	5	3
Day 2		
Clean	1	5
Press	1	5

The duration of the blocks used can vary but, in general, each block for a newly advanced trainee is four weeks in duration. Shorter blocks are not used since the advanced trainee cannot significantly improve a training parameter in less time. An exception might be a technique block for an experienced weightlifter whose form is very solid. There is no technique block allocated for a strongman cycle.

Technique is an interesting component of training. By this point in an athlete's career, many thousands of repetitions have been done. This athlete is a virtuoso of movement, having mastered the techniques of his sport. The motor pathways of good technique are firmly entrenched, and this allows short focused periods of neuromuscular refreshment to refine performance for competition. Riding a bike is analogous. The first few minutes back on the saddle are a little wobbly. But in short order all the synapses that form the cycling motor pathways have reconnected, and balance, steering, and pedaling stroke are back in excellent form after just a few minutes. Re-educating the body on a previously mastered technical task does not require long periods of focused repetition of the skill. It is regained with short periods of focused technical work or by including technical practice within other blocks of training.

Yet for sports extremely dependent on very precise technique, it must be refined and focused right before the competition. Technical mastery is more critical for sports that involve aimed implement throws and the Olympic lifts, where very small errors are amplified by the distance thrown or the difficulty of making a correction during a movement that takes less than a second to perform. Technical execution at this level decays rapidly, but for an advanced athlete it is recovered just as quickly.

For the strongman competitor, technique training is a problem because of both the huge number of possible events that may be contested (only five of which are usually included in a given competition), and the specificity of the competition apparatus to the event site. For this reason, strongman training emphasizes physical readiness for competition with no specific block of training geared toward technical refinement beyond practice on the actual events. Although there are technical issues to deal with, they are not of the magnitude experienced in the snatch or the javelin, and can be addressed during the strength and muscular endurance blocks as skills are practiced and equipment mastered. Strongman competition is designed to test the general capabilities of the contestant, and is not something for which a great deal of specific technique preparation is intended or necessary.

Because of the nature of strongman competition, some general exercises can be used very effectively to prepare for the more specific versions that might be encountered at the contest. Muscular endurance and glycolytic capacity for several events can be developed by using the farmer's walk at various distances and loads in the muscular endurance block. Various forms of sled dragging, stone lifting, tire flipping, and grip-dependent exercises such as fat bar deadlifts can be used to develop strength for many of the different events usually encountered at strongman contests. At the same time physical capacity is being trained, technical abilities that can be applied to competition events are being practiced. In this way, every block of training can be used to develop "technical" ability in the strongman athlete.

A key element in avoiding overtraining for advanced athletes in every sport is the recovery phase, which allows the body to fully recuperate, both physically and psychologically, after a long training cycle. This period incorporates activities collectively referred to as **active rest**. During this phase, both volume and the intensity levels are greatly reduced, and activities with an athletic movement component are pursued. Fairly strenuous recreational activities that do not involve the athlete's primary sports are suitable for the active rest phase, provided that the athlete is capable of participating in them without a high risk of injury. The purpose of an active rest phase is to allow for complete recovery and supercompensation, but in a way that does not cause detraining. If the athlete is responding well to training, the duration of this resting phase between training cycles should be no longer than two weeks.

Not infrequently, an athlete can perform a new PR following a week off. This occurs despite the fact that the meet performance was also a PR the previous week. If this occurs, the athlete has mistimed or misloaded training, the taper, or both, since additional supercompensation took place after it was anticipated. This indicates that the performance PR was not what it could have been had programming been more precise. These mistakes will happen to every athlete and coach, and they are opportunities to learn.

The Hormonal Fluctuation Model

The hormonal fluctuation model is another way to organize advanced training. It is designed specifically to manipulate the anabolic/catabolic hormone axis that controls much of the stage 2 response to heavy training, and to do so in a predictable, schedulable way. It utilizes longer blocks of training, up to eight weeks, during which intensity, volume, and technique are manipulated to culminate in peak performance on the date of a scheduled event.

HFM is different from the previously discussed models, which are derived from older versions of periodization. Remember Thing 2: *It becomes productive for more advanced athletes to organize periods of training into longer segments of time, the primary feature of which is a progression from higher volume and lower intensity toward lower volume and higher intensity.* However, here is **Thing 3**: Thing 2 does not always apply.

The hormone fluctuation model relies on a response to stress brought on by an increase in both volume *and* intensity. This runs contrary to the conventional wisdom governing advanced programs, but the fact is that both models work. HFM works as well as "Thing 2" models and in some cases may work much better, in that the homeostatic disruption it is capable of producing is much greater.

It is normal for coaches to divide training cycles into multiple shorter blocks containing variations in intensity and volume – periods of high-intensity or high-volume training followed by periods of lower-intensity or lower-volume training. The periods of lower workload are intended for regeneration and recuperation in order to prepare for the next period of increased workload, or for a competition. Several researchers have demonstrated that the testosterone-to-cortisol ratio decreases – that is, the level of testosterone drops relative to the cortisol level – during very high workloads and then increases during subsequent reduced workloads. In elite rowers, a few weeks of very intense rowing training caused the T/C ratio to drop significantly. After two weeks of dramatically reduced training load, T/C ratios recovered to normal levels or higher, while performance levels increased. A study of elite weightlifters demonstrated similar findings during a six-week training period immediately before a major competition. This study was designed to test the T/C ratio response to a high workload. T/C ratios dropped during weeks one and two, the period of most intense training. Recovery or supercompensation of T/C ratios occurred over the next four weeks, which consisted of two weeks of "normal" training – about 80% of maximal work tolerance – followed by two weeks of significantly reduced training. Again, performance improved and correlated well with testosterone-to-cortisol ratios. These studies demonstrate that, when an advanced athlete works very hard at maximal or near maximal levels for about two weeks, and then dramatically offloads for two to four weeks, the T/C ratio depresses with the highly elevated workload and then recovers to baseline or beyond upon offloading, and a performance increase correlates with this recovery. Peak performance should coincide with peak T/C ratio, and this performance peak probably occurs as a result of the recovery of the ratios to baseline or beyond.

Laboratory measures of the testosterone/cortisol ratio have been used to guide the training of advanced and elite athletes in the sport of weightlifting. Results from thesis research by Glenn Pendlay and Michael Hartman (2000, 2002) have demonstrated that adjusting training load to optimize T/C ratios leads to improved training and performance results. The intense work done in maximal effort weeks depresses testosterone levels and elevates cortisol. The ratio of the two should be depressed between 10% and 30% if the training is to be an effective adaptive stimulus. Depression of less than 10% does not produce a homeostatic disruption large enough to drive adaptation, and more than 30% is excessive for timely recovery and may well mark the beginning of the descent into overtraining. Maximal loading of greater than two weeks' duration generally produces excessive T/C ratio depression and is counterproductive. The end result of this laboratory experimentation is a series of training models that have consistently produced strength improvements in a group for whom gains are hard to produce: advanced and elite trainees.

This training organization deviates from the concept that intensity should increase as volume decreases. Here, as intensity increases or decreases, so does volume. It is the parallel manipulation of both volume and intensity that produces the overload event, providing both the stress and the opportunity for recovery. The model consists of a period of escalating workload over two weeks, a period of maximal workload for either one or two weeks, then a tapering of workload for two to four weeks. There are three basic variations, with cycles of different durations: 1) five weeks, 2) six weeks, and 3) eight weeks. Each of these cycles is intended to be used for different purposes or populations. The five-week cycle is appropriate for athletes just entering the advanced stage, or for connecting a series of longer HFM cycles. The six-week cycle can be used for populations with a high anabolic capacity (trained teens and young adults) to lead into a competition or as a connected series. The eight-week cycle is appropriate for very advanced or elite trainees as a lead-up to a competition or testing period.

Five-Week Model

Week	1	2	3	4	5
Load	Light	Medium	Maximal	Medium	Light

Six-Week Model

Week	1	2	3	4	5	6
Load	Light	Medium	Maximal	Maximal	Medium	Light

Eight-Week Model

Week	1	2	3	4
Load	Light	Medium	Maximal	Maximal

Week	5	6	7	8
Load	Medium	Medium	Light	Light

At this point in the athlete's career, the selection of exercises has narrowed to those that are specific to competitive goals, and to those exercises that specifically address what should be the well-defined weaknesses of the athlete.

The example we'll use for this model is that of a young advanced male weightlifter following a 6-week version of the model.

You can use the repetition continuum illustrated in figure 4-4 to select the appropriate repetition range needed to attain your program's specific goal. But as mentioned above, certain exercises preclude specific repetition schemes – competitive weightlifters do not use skill-dependent explosive exercises like the snatch and the clean and jerk for high reps; assistance exercises are not done for singles. Since strength is as important as appropriate technique for our hypothetical young weightlifter, the example here uses doubles and singles, with a heavy emphasis on the competitive lifts and their variants.

Since reps are low – singles and doubles – the volume is defined by the number of sets. Weeks one and two are low and moderate volume, intended to be build-up that prepares the trainee to tolerate the tremendous workloads to be encountered in the following two weeks. These weeks are also used as technical refinement periods. During weeks three and four, the intent is to stress the trainee maximally to disrupt homeostasis and drive adaptation. An average of 8 sets per exercise is used, although 10 to 12 sets could be used depending on the trainee's capacity. Finally, the last two weeks taper to an average of 4 sets. This limited volume of training allows recovery and supercompensation to occur by the end of week six, the scheduled meet or test period.

As volume increases, so does intensity. As with volume above, weeks one and two are light and moderate in intensity, and weeks three and four are very intense, with the trainee reaching a daily 1RM or 2RM for every exercise. Basically, the athlete is going as heavy as possible every session, and is encouraged to do so. This is a most critical time in the cycle, the application of a homeostatically disruptive stress that will significantly depress T/C ratio. Research has demonstrated that trainees will average about 94% of their 1RM during these two weeks. Hitting an absolute all-time best 1RM is not expected, just the best effort possible on that day – a "relative maximum" in the old Soviet parlance. As fatigue accumulates and bar speed drops due to decreasing neuromuscular efficiency, technical movements like the snatch will suffer more than absolute strength movements like the squat. Weeks five and six are taper weeks, with severe reductions in intensity as well as volume, intended to bring about hormonal recovery and supercompensation (and improved performance) on competition day. Load variation is especially important in weeks five and six. These weeks require lower average intensities, but very limited heavy work is necessary in order to ensure that the athlete stays sharp for the planned competition or testing. So the last day of week five includes a very limited amount of 90% work, as does the first day of week six.

This type of program is very stressful. Late in week three, during week four, and well into week five, the athlete will exhibit mood changes, unusual soreness, lack of "good sleep," and will exhibit numerous other symptoms that are often associated with overtraining. A certain amount of viciousness and irritability should be expected. While the athlete's psychological well-being is important, it is not the primary concern at this point in the cycle. For the competitive athlete, the performance goal must be the primary focus, not the enjoyment of a warm and fuzzy training experience. At this point, testosterone levels should be depressed and cortisol levels elevated, and the trainee is now ready to recover and supercompensate. This recovery of hormone ratios to normal levels – the increase in testosterone levels relative to cortisol – enables supercompensation, and the goal of the cycle is to set up precisely this situation so that recovery can and will proceed.

During week five, even though the workload is greatly reduced, the athlete will still be sore, moody, and "flat" (i.e., exercises will still seem tough, heavy, and slow). As week six approaches, things get much better. The athlete's perception may even be "I'm not doing any work" relative to the high workload of the previous weeks. Accompanying this feeling is usually the desire to do more sets and reps with more weight than programmed. Yielding to this temptation will flatten the recovery curve and blunt the now-climbing supercompensation response, and it will radically decrease the effects of the cycle as it comes to an end in week six. There will be a strong temptation in week six for the trainee to test the water a few days before the competition. Patience here will reward the hard work of weeks three and four; a lack of patience will waste it.

Within this training organization there is tremendous capacity for variability. Any goal can be achieved – mass, power, or strength. Rep schemes, exercise choice and variation, intensities, and even exercise modalities can be varied to provide the appropriate level of stress to reach an athlete's goals. As long as the workload follows the same general pattern (build-up followed by maximal work followed by taper) and allows sufficient time for both overload and recovery/supercompensation, any exercise modality could be programmed using this model. Every coach and athlete should experiment.

Six-Week Model

Week	1	2	3	4	5	6
Repetitions	2	2	2/1	2/1	1	1
Sets	3	4	8	8	4	4
Percent 1RM	75	85	90+	90+	85	80

Week 1 *Day 1*	Week 2 *Day 1*	Week 3 *Day 1-Session 1*	*Day 1- Session 2*
Power snatch	Snatch	Snatch	Back squat
Power clean	Power clean	Clean & jerk	Snatch pull
Push jerk	Jerk		Clean pull
Back squat	Back squat		
Day 2	*Day 2*	*Day 2*	
Hang power snatch	Power snatch	Snatch pull	
Hang power clean	Clean	Clean & jerk	
Deadlift	Press	Back squat	
	Front squat		
		Day 3	
		Snatch	
		Press	
Day 3	*Day 3*	Front squat	
Snatch	Snatch		
Power clean	Clean & jerk	*Day 4-Session 1*	*Day 4-Session 2*
Jerk	Front squat	Snatch	Back squat
Front squat		Clean & jerk	Snatch pull
	Day 4		Clean pull
	Snatch	*Day 5*	
	Push press	Snatch	
	Deadlift	Jerk	
		Back squat	

Week 4		Week 5	Week 6
Day 1-Session 1	*Day 1-Session 2*	*Day 1*	*Day 1*
Snatch	Back squat	Snatch	Snatch
Clean & jerk	Snatch pull	Clean & jerk	Clean & jerk
	Clean pull	Back squat	Back squat
Day 2			
Snatch pull		*Day 2*	*Day 2*
Clean & jerk		Snatch	Snatch
Back squat		Jerk	Clean & jerk
		Front squat	Front squat
Day 3			
Snatch		*Day 3*	
Press		Snatch	
Front squat		Power clean	
		Press	
Day 4-Session 1	*Day 4-Session 2*	Back squat	
Snatch	Back squat		
Clean & jerk	Snatch pull	*Day 4*	
	Clean pull	Snatch	
Day 5		Clean & jerk	
Snatch		Deadlift	
Jerk			
Back squat			

Peaking. Regardless of the type of cycle used to prepare for competition, the final two to four weeks prior to the event must include a reduction in both volume and intensity. Intensity is reduced by decreasing the percent of maximum load used in training. A limited number of near maximal attempts are retained in the program during this period but are carefully distributed and separated by one or two workouts (only one to three heavy lifts once or twice per week in taper weeks). These heavier attempts maintain neuromuscular readiness and prevent detraining. Volume is reduced by limiting the number of reps performed, using singles and doubles only, and by decreasing both the number of sets and number of exercises included in a workout. The intent of these last weeks of training is to allow the body to recuperate so that it can respond with maximum effort and efficiency when challenged to do so. While there is no conclusive data regarding the timing of the last workout prior to competition, and different sports have differing conventional wisdom on such things, a good rule of thumb is two days between the last workout and competition, with the last heavy workout occurring five to seven days previous. Individual differences play a huge part in this decision, and personal experience will ultimately be the deciding factor for the advanced athlete.

It is likely that the most advanced athletes in the world will not require programming beyond the complexity presented here. If they do, their experiences in having reached that point will have equipped them for this adventure. Athletics at the elite level is a highly individual thing, and all who have the ability to perform at this level have also acquired the ability to exercise judgment commensurate with the physical capacities they possess. Experiment, learn, and, above all, teach those of us who want to know.

"Today it is almost heresy to suggest that scientific knowledge is not the sum of all knowledge. But a little reflection will show that there is beyond question a body of very important but unorganized knowledge which cannot possibly be called scientific in the sense of knowledge of general rules: the knowledge of the particular circumstances of time and place."

—F.A. Hayek

9 - Special Populations
Does this stuff work for everyone?

We have argued that highly individualized training is necessary to reach close to full genetic potential, and that the closer the trainee gets to his or her genetic potential, the more important this specificity becomes. But this raises a question: Do the training models presented here, when applied at the appropriate level – novice, intermediate, and advanced – work for all populations? Do they work for women, children, older people, and injured people? And the answer is: Yes, they pretty much do.

Women

It is very important to understand the following true thing: women are not a special population. They are *half* (more, actually) of the population. With very, very few exceptions, they are trained in exactly the same way as men of the same age and level. By virtue of a different hormonal profile, the rate and the magnitude of change in strength and mass will differ, but the biological processes that bring about those changes are otherwise the same as those in men. Since the processes are the same, the methods used to affect progress are also the same. And the response to the method depends on the effectiveness of the method, not the sex of the individual using it. Many excuses have been made over the centuries that exercise has been practiced, sometimes by women, but usually *for* them. The bottom line is that everyone, regardless of sex, gets out of a correctly designed training program exactly what they put into it. Ineffective "firming and toning" routines have no basis in physiology, and the results obtained from them demonstrate this rather conclusively.

That said, there are several important differences between the performances of men and women, both in the weight room and on the field. As a general rule, women do not have the same level of neuromuscular efficiency as men. This is probably due to the differences in hormonal profile and the much lower levels of testosterone, and it is evident across the spectrum of performance. Women can use a higher percentage of their 1RM for more reps than men can, probably because their 1RM performance is not as efficient in demonstrating their true absolute strength. Their performances at max vertical jumps, throws, snatches, cleans, jerks, and other explosive movements that involve high levels of motor unit recruitment are performed at lower levels than those by men of the same size and level. And, while levels of absolute strength relative to muscle mass are essentially the same in the two sexes, women's upper-body movements suffer from the large relative difference in local muscle mass distribution.

As a practical matter, if daily, weekly, or monthly programming models are used to increase strength or power, some modifications are required for women since the intensities used are based on the individual 1RM, and women can work with a higher percentage of this 1RM for reps. For example, table 7-2 indicates that 70% for 10 reps would constitute a heavy set with a high adaptive stimulus, when, for women, this is only a medium set with a moderate adaptive stimulus. By the same token, if increased mass is the goal, a relatively larger amount of high-volume work over a longer time at a slightly higher intensity would be needed. Table 9-1 adapts the data in table 7-2 for female populations.

But if the hormonal fluctuation model (HFM; see chapter 8) is used, no modifications are absolutely required. Even though female testosterone levels are lower, a depression of the ratio of testosterone to cortisol is the important factor, and the hormonal fluctuation model has been effective in accomplishing this in both sexes. The menstrual cycle, however, may introduce another scheduling factor: there is a testosterone peak at 12 days before ovulation that may affect the way the HFM works for women. Scheduling maximal workloads to nearly coincide with this peak could possibly accelerate recovery and supercompensation. However, no data has yet to demonstrate that such timing would significantly improve performance. The variability of discomfort and associated effects of menses requires close cooperation between trainee and coach. For simplicity and comfort, for some women it may be appropriate to program an offload week during menses.

One other consideration: the average American female is both iron and calcium deficient. Both of these deficiencies may affect health and performance. Low iron stores can affect metabolism and oxygen transport, leading to a perception of chronic low energy or fatigue. Altering the diet to include more iron-rich foods, cooking with cast iron cookware, and considering iron supplementation is a good idea. Low calcium intakes predispose every age group to lower bone density and degeneration (osteopenia). Virtually every study examining weight training with osteoporotic women shows dramatic improvement in bone density. Calcium supplementation improves on that effect.

So, there are differences in the physical characteristics of the two sexes, but they still are trained the same way. The mechanisms of progress and development, while constrained at different levels by the hormonal milieu, operate the same way. Mammalian physiology is much older than the human species; with very few exceptions, the rules are the same for all of us. Tissues adapt to stress by getting stronger, and the response to the stress is a function of the stress, not the sex of the organism to which the tissue belongs.

		Relative Intensity		
		Light	*Medium*	*Heavy*
	100	---	---	1
	90	---	2	5
Intensity	**80**	5	8	10
(% of 1RM)	**70**	8	10	12
	60	10	12	15
	50	15	25	25+
		Low	*Moderate*	*High*
			Adaptive Stimulus	

Table 9-1. The women's version of Table 7-2, illustrating the difficulty of a rep scheme as it varies with volume and intensity. The numbers in the table represent reps.

Figure 9-1. Women are more likely to believe that weight training is unimportant to health and sports performance than men. There is also a social and media-driven misconception that all weight training produces big, masculine, muscle-bound physiques. This generally does not occur in women without anabolic steroids. The strongest women in the United States perform at their best and look healthy and athletic through the use of correctly designed weight training programs.

Youth

The long history of the human race demonstrates conclusively that the children and youth of our species are quite capable of handling loads while remaining uninjured, and indeed reach their physical potential despite (or perhaps because of) work that is often regarded as heavy by modern society. Every big, strong, healthy farm kid who grew up hauling hay attests to this obvious fact. The population-wide paucity of adults stunted or otherwise irreparably damaged by the handling of heavy loads – barbell or otherwise – attests to the ability of humans of all ages to successfully adapt to the stresses of work and growing up with vigorous physical interaction with their environments.

Although the most recent revision of the ACSM's standards of care and resource manual now considers youth weight training to be safe and healthy, there remains in the medical community a strong bias against using physically taxing methods of strength training on teenage and younger populations. One professional association of pediatricians recommends that only moderate weights with moderate repetitions be used. They strongly discourage high-volume work (enough sets and reps to increase muscle mass) and high-intensity work, the kind necessary to develop strength and power. They provide a variety of reasons for training youth using only machines with predetermined movement pathways, thus limiting the development of balance and coordination. This group of medical professionals actually recommends that all high-intensity and high-volume training be postponed until *full sexual maturity*. This would effectively remove the vast majority of high school athletes from weight rooms and compromise an athlete's safety and performance during full-contact sporting events (which, interestingly enough, are not discouraged).

When the scientific and medical literature is evaluated objectively, a different picture emerges. Training loads (relative to 1RM), frequencies, and durations similar to those commonly used in the training of competitive weightlifters are effective in increasing strength in children, and a significant body of scientific evidence and practical experience supports this fact. Strength increases in youth are closely related to the intensity of training; higher-intensity programs can and do increase strength in preadolescents in six weeks or less. This is because the mechanisms of adaptation are functioning the same way they do in adults, albeit without the benefit of the adult hormonal milieu.

The safety of this type of training for kids is well documented. Programs supervised by qualified coaches, and in which training loads are prescribed and monitored by professionals, have proven to be safer than typical physical education classes. Several studies since the 1970s have reported extremely low to zero rates of injury during training programs of from several weeks to a year in duration and have suggested that weight training prevents injury rather than causes it. Even the handling of maximal weights by children has been scrutinized for safety. Dr. Avery Faigenbaum showed that properly supervised maximal lifting in 6- to 12-year-olds resulted in no injuries, providing further evidence that even high-intensity training, properly supervised, can be a safe and healthy undertaking for children.

Properly conducted weight training programs are safe for children for the same reason they are safe for everyone else: they are normal human movements that are scalable. The loads used can be precisely adjusted to the ability of the child to use them with correct technique. Correct technical execution prevents injury, since by definition "correct" means controlled, even for explosive movements. The load on a 5-kg bar can be increased one kilogram at a time, allowing very fine control over the stress that a child experiences in the weight room. Contrast this with team sports that involve ballistic skills, a speeding ball, and other kids moving rapidly under varying degrees of control. Uncontrolled impact and rapid deceleration are inherent in such sports and the forces they apply to a child's body are unpredictable, completely unscalable, and therefore unsafe, as injury rates conclusively demonstrate. If you add pads to this scenario, which blunt the perception of the effects of impact between the players, you are bound to get the leverage-type injuries that occur when kids run into each other knowing it won't hurt very badly.

If a young athlete has a well established history of weight training and has access to a coach, simple progression, weekly programming, and even advanced periodization can be extremely effective training models. The hormonal fluctuation model would be most appropriate and effective for advanced, older youth athletes who have previously progressed through weekly or monthly periodization, due to its difficult nature and the lack of mature "hardness" in most younger athletes.

Recommendations. Based on the available medical and scientific data and the decades of experience of the authors, we strongly recommend the following guidelines for youth weight training:

1. Weight training programs for youth should be conducted by well-trained adults. In the current absence of educational opportunities at the collegiate level, adults become well-trained through personal experience, coaching experience, study, and association with other competent professionals. It is incumbent upon parents to evaluate the qualifications of those potentially charged with coaching their children.
2. To effectively and safely coach youth weight training in a group setting, a coach/trainee ratio of 1:12 or better is recommended. Every weight room is a teaching environment, not just a fitness facility where kids exercise. Any facility – private, commercial, or educational – that allows children and adolescents to train without instruction and active supervision at an adequate coach/kid ratio is inviting problems.
3. Weight training should take place in facilities properly equipped to support safe training practices.
4. Properly supervised skill-based weightlifting programs (and gymnastics, dance, soccer, martial arts, and all other physical programs) are appropriate for children and can commence as early as 6 years of age.
5. Total exercise training time *from all sources* should be counted when considering the cumulative effect of all of the child's physical activities.
6. The use of maximal training loads has been proposed to place the young athlete at risk of injury. No data currently exists that substantiates this claim. The use of maximal and near-maximal loads is encouraged, under the proper supervision using proper warm-up and proper technique. These loads should be used cautiously and applied only as part of a regimented training program for technically proficient trainees.

7. Training should be fun. Kids are motivated by fun. When training is no longer fun, kids will no longer train.

Figure 9-2. A huge amount of data shows that weight training does not diminish growth in children. In contrast, there is no data to show that it does. Millions of people who grew up hauling hay on farms disprove this preposterous nonsense. Carla and her daughter Samantha Nichols are pictured here, with Samantha at 13, 14, and 17 years old, 5' 51/2", 5' 8", and 5' 9" respectively. Samantha was a national junior champion weightlifter at age 9 and has been competitive in the sport since then. Weight training has apparently failed to stunt her growth.

Masters

Masters athletes, usually defined as individuals 35-40 years of age and over, depending on the sport, are a growing population. As the U.S. population ages, masters competitions are increasing in popularity across the spectrum of sports. Depending on the sport, it is not uncommon to see younger masters-age-group athletes do quite well in national and international events competing against much younger athletes. Powerlifting has a long tradition of masters athletes winning in open competition. Absolutely nothing prevents a middle-aged trainee from getting stronger, bigger, and more powerful but his own attitude about training and age.

As humans advance beyond middle-age, some significant changes generally occur. Sarcopenia (loss of muscle cells), increased body fat, performance loss, and reduced flexibility are common effects of aging. This is largely because the average adult has a greatly reduced activity level and becomes increasingly sedentary, which leads to a loss in muscle mass (atrophy); in the totally inactive older adult, this loss is compounded by sarcopenia. The loss of functional muscle causes a loss of performance. It has been demonstrated that about 15% of performance capacity can be lost per decade with inactivity, and even when activity is maintained at a relatively high level the loss of performance proceeds with age. The logical extension of this accumulating loss in performance is ultimately the loss of functional mobility.

The loss of muscle also means the loss of metabolic machinery; muscles account for most of the calories a healthy person burns daily, and smaller muscles burn fewer calories. Most people don't reduce the amount of food they consume as activity diminishes, and the result is an average increase in body fat of 2.5 to 3% per decade.

The loss of muscle mass has another insidious effect that becomes more perceptible at an advanced age: a loss of proprioception and balance. The ability to process information the body receives about its position in space is important to performance for an athlete, and in an older adult it is crucial for safety. It is developed and maintained with exercise that requires balance and coordination, and barbell training fits this description perfectly.

In fact, barbell training is the best prescription for the prevention of all of these age-related problems. Staying in (or getting into) the gym slows the decay in muscle mass and pushes the onset of atrophy back for decades. Even in the 60- to 90-year-old range, training reduces the loss of muscle mass to less than 5% per decade. Several studies have shown that 80-year-olds who were inactive but began training with weights actually gained muscle mass and improved their strength, proprioception, and balance. This effect was directly related to the amount of leg work included in the program and the resulting improvements in leg strength. Leg strength was also responsible for improving the ability to walk faster in older people. In one study, twelve weeks of strength training was shown to increase walking endurance by 38%, something walking by itself fails to do.

Less obvious to those unfamiliar with weight training is the fact that lifting weights alone will improve flexibility. Moving through a complete range of motion serves as a very effective dynamic stretch while at the same time serving as a strength stimulus. This is most useful for older trainees with marked loss of range of motion. Osteoarthritis is a clinical condition caused by degenerative changes in joints and a loss of joint function. Patients with arthritis typically reduce their activity level to eliminate discomfort, which actually exacerbates the condition.

Several studies have shown that increasing the strength of the musculature around an affected

Figure 9-3. Older adults are not necessarily weak adults. Regular training can lead to a lifetime of strength. This 402-pound deadlift by 72-year-old Darrell Gallenberger is the result of perseverance and good training habits.

joint decreases pain and improves function significantly. A number of these studies used squats to reduce knee pain.

A significant consideration for the masters athlete is the reduction in recovery capacity over the years. For serious masters competitors, periodization of training is particularly important, and periods of offloading should be longer and more pronounced than for younger athletes. When using monthly programming models, the week of recovery should have a larger percentage of intensity reduction than for younger age groups—as much as 10 to 15% rather than the 5% frequently used in TSFOSB (two steps forward, one step back) models. If using the hormonal fluctuation model with the older athlete, it should follow the 8-week cycle, with a smaller volume of training during the two weeks of maximal work. A volume reduction of 5% per decade past 30 years of age is recommended.

When novice masters trainees are started on a program, the process is the same for that of a younger novice; all the same rules apply, within the framework of reduced recovery ability and the initial physical condition of the trainee. Masters athletes may find that intermediate-level programming such as the Texas method works better when adopted sooner than a younger novice would need to; for a person with age-compromised recovery ability, a weekly increase in load is easier to adapt to than the workout-to workout progress required by linear progression and will provide for longer continued improvement. The principles of stress and adaptation still apply, and they always will as long as basic health remains intact.

The bottom line is that unless a person has significant pathology (is terribly sick) or is post-geriatric (no longer living), that person can benefit from a weight training program similar to those used with younger populations at the same level of training advancement.

Post-Rehabilitation Trainees

All athletes who train hard enough to compete will get injured. This is the sorry truth of the matter, and anyone dissuaded from competition by this fact would not have made a good competitor anyway. Progress involves hard training, and hard training eventually involves pushing past previous barriers to new levels of performance. To the extent that this can cause injury, successful competitive athletics is dangerous. It is a danger that can and must be managed, but it is important to recognize the fact that athletes get hurt. If they want to continue to be athletes afterwards, it is equally important to understand how to manage and rehabilitate injuries successfully so that they don't end a career. Also, accidents happen, both related and unrelated to training.

Severely damaged tissue cannot be repaired through rehabilitation. Rather, the surrounding healthy tissue is strengthened in order to take over the load once carried by the now non-functional tissue. If someone has a survivable heart attack, such as a myocardial infarction, part of the heart muscle dies (fig. 9-4). The dead tissue no longer contributes to the contraction of the heart, but the heart continues to beat and deliver blood. Immediately after the infarction, the efficiency with which the heart delivers blood is low, but without missing a beat, the remaining healthy, functional heart muscle begins to adapt because it continues to be loaded while you do not die. In order to adapt to the missing force generation capacity of the damaged tissue, the remaining muscle contracts more forcefully and rapidly increases in mass. The end result is the recovery of the heart's ability to generate contractile force even having lost some of its original muscle irrecoverably. The change in contractile geometry of the ventricle will not actually allow the return to 100% of normal function; instead of the geometry of a normal heart, the post-infarction heart is shaped like a Chinese teacup on its side, with the necrotic tissue forming a lid. This altered geometry, even with thicker walls after hypertrophy, is inherently less efficient than the original ventricle, but it functions well enough that normal activities can eventually be resumed.

Severe muscle damage in other parts of the body constitutes a similar but less dire situation. If a muscle is severely damaged to the point of necrosis, not only will the remaining tissue adapt to the loss of function of the damaged tissue by increasing its functional capacity, but the surrounding muscles that normally aid the damaged muscle in its biomechanical role will assume part of the workload. This is classically illustrated in the scientific and medical literature in "ablation" experiments, where the gastrocnemius muscle (major calf muscle) is removed and the underlying soleus and plantaris muscles rapidly adapt and assume the load once carried by the gastrocnemius (fig. 9-5). It is well documented that these newly stressed muscles change dramatically, both chemically and structurally, after ablation in order to return the whole mechanical system to "normal" function. The recovered structures are not as good as the original equipment, but they function at a high percentage of the original capacity.

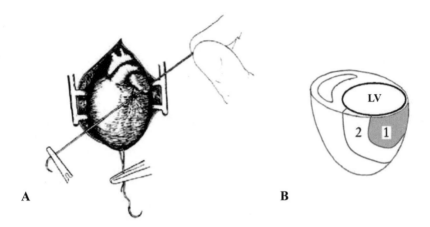

Figure 9-4. If a coronary artery is blocked through atherosclerosis or, as in the case above, experimentally blocked by tying off the left main coronary artery in the rat (A), the muscle tissue that loses its circulatory supply (B1) will be irreversibly damaged. The tissue immediately surrounding the injured tissue (B2) and any other undamaged tissue will immediately become overloaded and assume the pressure generation load once uniformly distributed over the entire ventricular mass (Selye's stage 1). Although the heart's function is reduced and a period of recovery is needed, the surviving healthy tissues continue to carry an overload during convalescence that results in an increase in the strength and mass of the surviving muscle (Selye's stage 2). LV = Left ventricle.

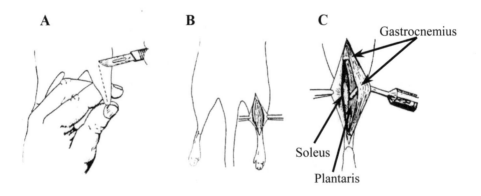

Figure 9-5. In ablation experiments, a muscle is surgically removed (A, B, and C). In most hypertrophy experiments, the ablated muscle of choice is the gastrocnemius (C, both heads), leaving the underlying plantaris and soleus to carry the walking load once carried by the gastrocnemius. In this case, the surgical removal of the gastrocnemius places the rat, and specifically the rat's leg, in Selye's stage 1. Rats undergoing this procedure begin walking on the operated leg within 24 hours, and within one to two weeks their activity level and gait are the same as those of normal rats. The overloaded soleus and plantaris have adapted (Selye's stage 2). It is normal to see about a 75% increase in soleus and plantaris mass with this type of overload.

In both the previous scenarios, recovery of function occurred after only a short period of reduced loading, essentially the duration of time needed for the resolution of inflammation and any other blatant pathology. A rapid return to an increasing functional load is required to induce adaptation and recovery. Even in the infarcted heart, a return to normal load represents a functional *overload* of the remaining tissue: the same amount of force must initially be generated by a smaller muscle mass, so it is a higher relative load. The adaptation that facilitates the return to normal function is a response to the stress to the system produced by the injured area's decrease in function. The injury that necessitates the compensation is the source of the stress to the surrounding tissues, and they respond by adapting to the new demands placed on them. *Without the injury, the adaptation would not occur, just as no adaptation ever occurs in the absence of stress.* While caution is necessary to avoid further injury, the belief that rehabilitation can occur in the absence of overload represents a failure to comprehend the basic tenets of the physiology and mechanics of the living human body.

Most injuries experienced in the weight room, on the field, and in daily life do not rise to the severity of necrosis of any tissue. They are inconvenient, painful, aggravating, and potentially expensive to deal with, but they do not alter the quality of life for a significant period of time. But the same principles apply to healing them that apply to more severe injuries, because the mechanisms that cause them to heal are the same. The concept of "letting" an injury heal beyond an initial few days reflects a lack of understanding of the actual processes that cause the return to function. A less severe injury that does not involve tissue necrosis nonetheless involves an overload of the immediate ability of the compromised tissue, thus stimulating the processes that cause repair. In this particular instance, care must be taken to ensure that the structure that is healing receives its normal proportion of the load, because the object is to return this particular structure to full function, not to allow the adjacent structures to assume the load and thus preventing the injury from healing fully. This is accomplished by the enforcement of very strict technique during exercise of the injured area. It hurts more this way, but the long-term return to full function depends on the correct amount of stress to the injured area.

During supervised rehabilitation, the workloads used should be light enough to allow recovery of function locally, within the injured tissue, but this load will not be stressful enough systemically to maintain advanced fitness levels. When the athlete is released to unrestricted activity, enough detraining has occurred that a change in programming will be required. Six to eight weeks in rehabilitation can result in the loss of enough overall performance to warrant return to a program of simple progression, even for an elite athlete. Once pre-injury or pre-disease performance levels have been regained, a return to normal training at that level can follow. As discussed earlier, strength is a resilient quality, and strength lost through detraining can be recovered much more rapidly than it was initially gained.

"It has become almost a cliché to remark that nobody boasts of ignorance of literature, but it is socially acceptable to boast ignorance of science."

—Richard Dawkins

Novice Example Program

Novice
Example

Young Angus McSnort

Mon 8/2/04	Wed 8/4/04	Fri 8/6	Mon 8/9	Wed 8/11	Fri 8/13 (Be careful)
Squat	Squat	Squat	Squat	Squat	Squat
45×5×3	45×5×2	45×5×2	45×5×2	45×5×2	45×5×2
65×5	65×5	75×5	75×5	75×5	75×5
85×5	85×5	95×5	95×5	105×5	105×5
105×5×3	105×5	115×5	115×2	125×2	135×2
	120×5×3	125×5×3	135×5×3	145×5×3	155×5×3
Press	Bench	Press	Bench	Press	Bench
45×5×2	45×5×2	45×5×2	45×5×2	45×5×2	45×5
55×5×3	65×5	55×5	65×5	55×5	65×5
Deadlift	85×5	60×5×3	85×2	65×5×3	85×2
88×5×3	95×5×3	Deadlift	95×1	Power Clean	105×5×3
	Deadlift	88×5	100×5×3	Bar×3 x many reps	Deadlift
Age: 17	88×5×2	110×5	Deadlift	55×3×2	88×5
Bodyweight: 158	110×5	132×5	88×5	65×3	110×5
	132×5	154×2	110×5	75×3	132×5
	154×5×2	165×5	132×2	88×3×3	154×1
		(back rounding)	154×1		176×5
			165×5×2 better		

Y. A. McS.

Mon 8/16	Wed 8/18	Fri 8/20	Mon 8/23	Wed 8/25	Fri 8/27
Squat	**Squat**	**Squat**	**Squat**	**Squat**	**Squat**
45x5x2	45x5x2	45x5x2	45x5x2	45x5x2	45x5x2
75x5	85x5	85x5	95x5	95x5	95x5
105x2	115x3	125x5	135x5	135x5	135x5
135x1	145x2	155x2	165x2	175x2	185x2
165x5x3	175x5x3	185x5x3	195x5x3	205x5x3	215x5x3

Mon 8/16

Press
45x5x2
55x5
65x2
70x5x3

Power Clean
55x3x3
75x3+2
88x3 (40k)
42.5k x 3x3

Bodyweight: 165

Wed 8/18

Bench
45x5x2
75x5
95x3
110x5x3
115x5
120x5

Back Ext.
BWx10x3

Chins
BWx6
BWx5
BWx3

Fri 8/20

Press
45x5x2
55x5
65x5
70x2
75x1
78.5x5x3

Deadlift
88x5
132x5
154x2
176x1
198x5

Mon 8/23

Bench
45x5x2
75x5
95x5
110x2
120x5x3

Back Ext.
BWx10x3

Chins
BWx7
BWx5x2

Bodyweight: 169

Wed 8/25

Press
45x5x2
60x5
70x2
80x5x3

Power Clean
55x3x2
75x3
40kx3
45x3x5

Fri 8/27

Bench
45x5x2
75x5
105x2
125x5x3

Back Ext.
BWx10x3

Chins
BWx7
BWx6
BWx5

"We are the recipients of scientific method. We can each be a creative and active part of it if we so desire."

—Kary Mullis

Intermediate Example Programs

Texas Method
Example

Jesus Quintana   Age: 28
                  Bwt: 225

M

(Week 1)

Squat
/5x5 across

Bench
5x5 across

Deadlift
5RM

W

Squat
2x5x 80%
of Monday

Press
3x5 across

Glute/Ham
5x10

Chins

F

Squat
5RM

Bench
5RM

Power Clean
5x3 across

(Week 2)

Squat
5x5 across

Press
5x5 across

Deadlift
5RM

Squat
2x5x80%

Bench
3x5x90%
of last Monday

Glute/Ham
5x10

Chins

Squat
5RM

Press
5RM

Power Clean
5x3

J. Q.

Mon 5/2/05	Wed 5/4	Fri 5/6	Mon 5/9	Wed 5/11	Fri 5/13 (Be careful)

Mon 5/2/05

Squat
45×5×2
135×5
185×5
225×2
275×1
305×5×5

Bench
45×5×2
95×5
135×5
185×5
220×5×5

Deadlift
135×5
225×5
275×2
315×1
370×5 ☆

Wed 5/4

Squat
45×5×3
135×5×2
185×2
225×1
245×5×2

Press
45×5×2
95×5
115×2
135×2
155×5×3

Glute/Ham
BW×10×2
20×10×3

Chins
BW×15
BW×14
BW×13
BW×11×2

Fri 5/6

Squat
45×5
135×5×2
225×5
275×2
315×1
340×5 ☆

Bench
45×5×2
95×5
135×5
185×2
215×1
235×5 ☆

P.Clean
40K×3×2
60×2
70×1
80×1
90×1
100×1
110×3×5

Mon 5/9

Squat
45×5×2
135×5
185×5
225×2
275×1
310×5×5

Press
45×5×2
95×5
115×2
135×1
155×5×5

Deadlift
135×5
225×5
275×2
325×1
375×5 ☆

Wed 5/11

Squat
45×5×2
135×5×2
185×2
225×1
245×5×2

Bench
45×5×2
95×5
135×3
185×1
200×5×3

Glute/Ham
BW×10×2
20×10
25×10

Chins
BW + 10lbs
×10×3

Fri 5/13 (Be careful)

Squat
45×5×2
135×5×2
225×3
275×1
315×1
345×5 ☆

Press
45×5×2
95×5
115×2
135×1
155×1
168.5×5 ☆

P.Clean
40×3×2
60×2
70×1
80×1
90×1
100×1
112.5×3×5

181

Split Routine
Example

Woojus Geeshman

M	T	Th	F
Bench Press 5×5 across	Squat 5×5 across	Press 5×5 across	Squat 10×2 DE
Press 10×3 DE	Power Cleans 6×3 across	Bench Press 10×3 DE	Rack Pull 1×5
Weighted Chins 3× failure	Back Ext. 5×10	Pullops	Halting DL 1×8
	Reverse Hypers 3×15		

Age: 23
Bwt: 187

10/9/06 Mon	10/10 Tues	10/12 Thur	10/13 Fri (be careful!!)	10/16 Mon	10/17 Tues
Bench	Squat	Press	Squat	Bench	Squat
45x5x2	45x5x2	45x5x2	45x5x3	45x5x2	45x5x2
135x5x2	135x5x2	95x5	135x3x3	135x5x2	135x5x2
185x3	225x3	135x5	225x3	185x3	225x3
225x2	275x1	165x2	225x3 fast	225x2	275x1
255x1	315x1	180x1	255x1 fast	260x1	315x1
272x5x5	365x1	192x5x5	285x2x10	273.5x5x5	365x1
	410x5x5		fast paused	rest	395x1
15 min rest		Bench	= on box		415x5x5
		45x5x2	(1 min)	Press	
Press	P.Clean	135x5x2		45x5	P.Clean
45x5	60x3x2	185x3		95x5	60x3x2
95x5	80x2	185x3x2	Rack	95x3	80x2x2
95x3x2	90x1	fast	Pull #3pin	fast	90x1
fast	100x1	215x2 fast		115x1x2	100x1
115x2	110x1	230x3x10	135x5	fast	110x1
135x1	115x3x6	(1min fast)	225x5	135x1	115x1
145x3x10	(2 min)		315x3	145x3x10	117.5x3x6
(1 min, fast)			405x1	(1 min fast)	(2 min)
	Glute/Ham	Rollups	455x1		Glute/Ham
Chins	BWx10	BWx18	515x5	Chins	BWx10
BWx3x3	45x10x4	BWx16x2	straps	BWx3x3	45x10x3
		slight kip		30x10	50x10x2
25x12	Reverse	(5 min)		30x9x2	
25x10	Hypers				Rev.
25x9	50x15x3			(5 min)	Hyp.
(5 min)					50x15x3

10/19 Thur	10/20 Fri	10/23 Mon	10/24 Tues	10/26 Thur	10/27 Fri
Press	Squat	Bench	Squat	Press	Squat
45x5x2	45x5x2	45x5x2	45x5x2	45x5x2	45x5x2
95x5x2	135x5x2	135x5x2	135x5x2	95x5x2	135x5x3
135x3	185x2	185x5	225x3	135x3	185x2
165x2	225x2 fast	225x3	275x2	155x1	225x2
185x1	265x1 fast	255x1	315x2	175x1	225x2 fast
193.5x5x5	280x2x10	275x5x5	365x1	185x1	255x1 fast
	1 min fast		405x1	195x5x5	280x2x10
Bench	paused on box	Rest	420x5x5		1 min fast
45x5x2		Press		Bench	
135x5x2	Halting DL	45x5	Power Clean	45x5x2	Rack Pull #3 jan
185x3	135x5x2	95x5	60x3x2	135x5	135x5x2
185x2 fast	225x3	95x3 fast	80x2	185x3	225x5
215x1	315x2	115x2 fast	90x1	185x2 fast	315x2
230x3x10	405x1	135x1	100x1	215x1 fast	405x2
1 min fast	475x8 Straps	145x3x10	110x1	230x3x10	455x1
		1 min fast	115x1	1 min fast	495x1
Pullups		Chins	120x3x6		520x5 Straps
BWx18		BWx3x2	2min		
BWx17		30x11	fast 2 sets	Pullups	
BWx16		30x9x2	2.5 min	BWx19	
slight kip		5min		BWx17x2	
5min				slight kip	
				5min	

184

Starr Model
example

(Week 1)	**M**	

M

Squat
light

Bench
light

Press
light

Back Ext.
Chinups

(Week 2)

Squat
light

Press
light

Bench
light

Back Ext.
Pullups

Seamus Queeze

W

Squat
Heavy

Press
Heavy

Deadlift

W

Squat
Heavy

Bench
Heavy

Deadlift

F

Squat
med.

Bench
Medium

Push Press

Power Snatch

F

Squat
med.

Press
med.

DB bench

Power Clean

Age : 25
Bwt : 253

9/15/03 Mon	9/17 Wed	9/19 Fri	9/22 Mon	9/24 Wed	9/26 Fri
Squat	Squat	Squat	Squat	Squat	Squat
45×5×2	45×5×2	45×5×2	45×5×2	45×5×2	45×5×2
135×5×2	135×5×2	135×5	135×5×2	135×5×2	135×5×2
225×3	225×3	225×3	225×3	225×3	225×3×2
275×1	315×2	315×2	275×1	225×2	275×1
315×5×3	365×1	365×1	315×5×3	315×1	315×1
	405×1	405×5×3		365×1	365×1
	445×5×2		Press	415×1	410×5×2
Bench		Bench	45×5×2	450×5×2	
45×5×2	Press	45×5×2	95×5×2		Press
135×5×2	45×5×2	135×5×2	125×2	Bench	45×5×2
185×3	95×5×2	185×3	145×1	45×5×2	95×5
225×5×3	135×3	225×2	165×5×3	135×5	125×2
	165×2	265×1		135×3	155×1
Press	195×1	285×5×3	Bench	185×2	175×1
45×5	227×5×2		45×5×2	225×2	195×5×2
95×5		Push Press	135×5	275×1×2	
135×2	Deadlift	95×5×2	185×3	305×1	DB bench
155×5×3	135×5	135×3	225×5×3	322×5×2	50s × 10
	225×3	175×2			70s × 5
Glute/Ham	315×2	205×1	Glute/Ham	Deadlift	90s × 3
BW×10	405×1	225×5×3	BW×10	135×5	100s × 2
45×5	455×1		45×10	225×2×2	110s × 11
85×10×3	490×5	P. Snatch	85×10×3	315×2	110s × 9
		40k × 3×3		405×1	110s × 8
Chinups		50 × 3×2	Pullups	455×1	Power Clean
BW×5×2		60×1	BW×5	495×5	60k × 3 × 2
25×5		70×1	25×2		80 × 2
55×10×3		75×1	75×11		100 × 2
		80×2×5	75×10		115 × 1
			75×8		125 × 3
					130 × 3 × 3

9/29 Mon	10/1 Wed	10/3 Fri	10/6 Mon	10/8 Wed	10/10 Fri
Squat	**Squat**	**Squat**	**Squat**	**Squat**	**Squat**
45x5x2	45x5x2	45x5x2	45x5x2	45x5x2	45x5x2
135x5x2	135x3x2	135x5	135x5x2	135x5x2	135x5x2
225x3	225x3	225x3x2	225x3	225x3	225x3
275x1	275x1	275x1	275x1x2	315x2	315x2
315x5x3	315x1	315x1	315x5x3	365x2	365x1
	365x1	365x1		405x1	405x5
Bench	415x1	415x5x2	**Press**	435x1	
45x5x2	455x5x2		45x5x2	460x5	**Press**
135x5x2		**Bench**	95x3x2	460x<u>4</u>	45x5x2
185x3	**Press**	45x5x2	125x2		95x5
225x5x3	45x3x2	135x5x2	145x1	**Bench**	125x3
	95x5x2	185x3	165x5x3	45x5x2	155x1
Press	135x2	225x3		135x5x2	175x1
45x5x2	165x1	255x1	**Bench**	185x5	195x5x2
95x3	185x1	275x1	45x5	225x2	
125x1	205x1	290x5x2	135x5	275x1x2	**DB Bench**
145x1	215x1		185x3	305x1	50s x10
155x5x3	228.5x5x2	**Push Press**	205x1	323.5x5x2	70s x5
		95x5	225x5x3		90s x3
Glute/Ham	**Deadlift**	135x5		**Deadlift**	100s x2
BWx10	135x5	175x3	**Glute/Ham**	135x5	110s x13
45x5	225x5	205x1	BWx10	225x2	
85x10x2	315x3	227x5x3	45x5	315x1	**Power Clean**
95x10	405x2		85x10	405x1	60x3x2
	455x1	**P. Snatch**	95x10x2	455x1	80x2
Chinups	500x5	40kx3x2		505x<u>3</u>	100x1
BWx5x2		50x2	**Pullups**		110x3
25x3		60x2	BWx5	tired	120x3
57x10x3		70x2	25x2		130x3
		75x2	50x1		
		80x2x4	75x12		
			75x10x2		

"And above all things, never think that you're not good enough yourself. A man should never think that. My belief is that in life people will take you at your own reckoning."

—Isaac Asimov

Credits

We would like to acknowledge the following individuals for their contribution of images to this book:

Photograph of Bud Charniga by Jim Kilgore

Photographs of Carrie Klumpar by Torin Halsey

Micrography courtesy of Dr. David Saunders, Northern Iowa University

EMG and force tracing courtesy of Dr. Alexander Ng and Jacqueline Limberg, Marquette University

Photograph of Darrell Gallenberger courtesy of Darrell Gallenberger

All other graphics by Lon Kilgore and Mark Rippetoe

We would like to acknowledge the contributions of the following individuals for their input to various sections of this text:

Dr. Michael Stone for providing some of the elusive details on the history of periodization.

Dr. Michael Hartman for his thesis perspective on Hormonal Fluctuation.

Becky Kudrna for her section comments on exercise variation, hormonal responses to exercise, and women's training.

Glenn Pendlay for our many discussions regarding Two-Factor Models, Hormonal Fluctuation, and practical applications.

Dr. Chad Touchberry for his reading and commentary on Classical Periodization.

Dr. Scott Mazzetti for his sharing of data regarding energy costs of slow vs. fast repetition speeds.

Tom Mitchell, NASA Florida State Chairman for his perspectives on Strongman training.

"Human beings, who are almost unique in having the ability to learn from the experience of others, are also remarkable for their apparent disinclination to do so."

—Douglas Adams

Index

Note: Bold print page numbers indicate major discussions; t = Table

200

" Hard, intense work of the body … is the most conclusive evidence of our own being that we could possibly have."

—James Dickey

Author Information

Mark Rippetoe is the author of *Starting Strength: Basic Barbell Training*, *Strong Enough?*, numerous magazine and journal articles, and the co-author of *Practical Programming for Strength Training*. He has worked in the fitness industry since 1978, and has owned the Wichita Falls Athletic Club since 1984. He graduated from Midwestern State University in 1983 with a Bachelor of Science in geology and a minor in anthropology. He was in the first group certified by the National Strength and Conditioning Association as CSCS in 1985, and is a USA Weightlifting Senior Coach, CrossFit Coach, and USA Track and Field Level I Coach. He was a competitive powerlifter for ten years, and has coached many lifters and athletes, and thousands of people interested in improving their strength and performance.

Lon Kilgore is a professor at Midwestern State University where he teaches applied physiology and anatomy. He has also held faculty appointments at Kansas State University and Warnborough University (IE). He graduated from Lincoln University with a Bachelor of Science in biology and earned a Ph.D. in anatomy and physiology from Kansas State University. He has competed in weightlifting to the national level since 1972 and coached his first athletes to national championship event medals in 1974. He has worked in-the-trenches, as a coach or scientific consultant, with athletes from rank novices to professionals and the Olympic elite, and as a collegiate strength coach. He has been a certifying instructor for USA Weightlifting for more than a decade and a frequent lecturer at events at the US Olympic Training Center. His illustration and authorship efforts include books, magazine columns, and research journal publications.

Stef Bradford, Ph.D. is the operations manager of The Aasgaard Company. She received her doctorate in pharmacology from Duke University in 2004. She has been strength training for most of her life and a competitive Olympic weightlifter for several years. She teaches barbell training in seminars throughout the country.

"It matters if you just don't give up."

—Stephen Hawking